State Governors in the Mexican Revolution, 1910–1952

LATIN AMERICAN SILHOUETTES

Series Editors: William H. Beezley and Judith Ewell

Recent Titles in the Series

For a complete listing of titles, visit www.rowmanlittlefield.com/series.

State Governors in the Mexican Revolution, 1910–1952

Portraits in Conflict, Courage, and Corruption

Edited by Jürgen Buchenau
and William H. Beezley

ROWMAN & LITTLEFIELD PUBLISHERS, INC.
Lanham • Boulder • New York • Toronto • Plymouth, UK

ROWMAN & LITTLEFIELD PUBLISHERS, INC.

Published in the United States of America
by Rowman & Littlefield Publishers, Inc.
A wholly owned subsidiary of The Rowman & Littlefield Publishing Group, Inc.
4501 Forbes Boulevard, Suite 200, Lanham, Maryland 20706
www.rowmanlittlefield.com

Estover Road, Plymouth PL6 7PY, United Kingdom

Copyright © 2009 by Rowman & Littlefield Publishers, Inc.

British Library Cataloguing in Publication Information Available

Library of Congress Cataloging-in-Publication Data
State governors in the Mexican Revolution, 1910–1952 : portraits in conflict, courage, and corruption / edited by Jürgen Buchenau and William H. Beezley.
   p. cm. — (Latin American silhouettes)
Includes bibliographical references and index.
ISBN-13: 978-0-7425-5769-7 (cloth : alk. paper)
ISBN-10: 0-7425-5769-3 (cloth : alk. paper)
ISBN-13: 978-0-7425-5770-3 (pbk. : alk. paper)
ISBN-10: 0-7425-5770-7 (pbk. : alk. paper)
[etc.]
   1. Governors—Mexico—Biography. 2. Mexican states—History—20th century.
3. Mexican states—Politics and government—20th century. 4. Mexico—History—
1910–1946—Biography. 5. Mexico—History—Revolution, 1910–1920—
Influence. 6. Mexico—History, Local—20th century. I. Buchenau, Jürgen, 1964–
II. Beezley, William H.
   F1234.S764 2009
   320.4720922—dc22
   [B]

                                                             2008048414

Printed in the United States of America

♾™ The paper used in this publication meets the minimum requirements of American National Standard for Information Sciences—Permanence of Paper for Printed Library Materials, ANSI/NISO Z39.48-1992.

To Anabel and Blue

Contents

Preface

On June 14, 2006, Governor Ulises Ruiz of Oaxaca ordered local police to remove the protesters that had occupied most of the historic center of the state capital of the same name since May 22 of that year. The protesters were teachers who demanded better pay as well as a series of reforms designed to help poor students by providing free meals, uniforms, books, and medical care. In the ensuing melee, at least four people died, and the protest turned radical, with a newly formed opposition group vainly demanding the governor's resignation. Ruiz was a member of the Partido Revolucionario Institucional (PRI, or Institutional Revolutionary Party), Mexico's long-ruling party that had lost a presidential election for the first time in seventy-one years just six years before. Amidst a hotly contested campaign to elect a successor to the man who had ousted the PRI, president Vicente Fox, Ruiz's crackdown on the teachers assumed national significance. Both the PRI and Fox's party, the conservative Partido Acción Nacional (PAN, or National Action Party) came to stand for the neoliberal status quo defended by these parties' two presidential nominees, particularly PAN candidate Felipe Calderón. The opposition, on the other hand, came to represent the neopopulist critique of globalization, and through that critique, the left-leaning presidential candidacy of Andrés Manuel López Obrador of the Partido Revolucionario Democrático (PRD, or Democratic Revolutionary Party). Just as Ruiz's crackdown exacerbated the electoral conflict on the national level, so the election made the political conflict in Oaxaca worse. In July 2006, two weeks after federal elections authorities indicated that Calderón had probably won the election by a hair's breadth, members of the anti-Ruiz coalition blocked access to the coliseum in which thousands of people had hoped to witness the Guelaguetza, Oaxaca's premier dance festival and a major tourist attraction.

The case of Ulises Ruiz demonstrates the significance of state governors in the history of modern Mexico. Three years before the Oaxacan imbroglio inflamed political passions both at the national and the state level, the authors of the chapters of this book joined efforts to write a collaborative volume on state governors and the institution of the governorship during the Mexican Revolution. In 2004, we organized two panels dedicated to this subject at the annual meeting of the Rocky Mountain Conference on Latin American Studies in Santa Fe, New Mexico, and the congress of the Latin American Studies Association in Las Vegas.

The authors who joined us in this collaborative undertaking have written diverse and intriguing contributions. Separately and collectively, they confirmed our hypothesis about the significance, variety, and colorful nature of this group of revolutionaries. As governors, they took both the ideals and the legal statements of the revolution and, each in their own way, tried to make them into daily practices of the people in their state. This volume responds to two historiographical trends. First, a general inspiration resulted from the outstanding volumes by Douglas F. Southall Freeman, *Lee's Lieutenants* (1970), in which the author explored the nature of the U.S. Civil War to demonstrate that Robert E. Lee, the commander of the southern armies, could neither win nor lose the war alone. Despite the political science emphasis on the presidents of the revolutionary government, we believe that they could not and did not carry out revolutionary campaigns alone. In a more direct way, we have drawn on the important work by a succession of historians who have examined the course of the revolution in states such as Chihuahua, Yucatán, Veracruz, Tlaxcala, Oaxaca, and San Luis Potosí. These historians, such as Héctor Aguilar Camín, Francisco Almada, Raymond Buve, Romana Falcón, Heather Fowler Salamini, Paul Garner, Gilbert Joseph and Allen Wells, and Carlos Martínez Assad, among many others, did not specifically examine the governors of these states. Instead, they investigated the broader revolutionary experience that, of course, included the policies, politics, and projects that gave a unique character to the revolution in each state and represented what the revolution meant to local people. This book builds on this important work about the revolution at the state or regional level. It is an effort to move beyond the emphasis on presidential programs to see how they actually worked out at the state level, and explore the relationships between national bureaucrats—of the ministry of public education and representatives of the agrarian reform institute—and state governors.

We thank all those involved in these presentations and discussions, and particularly five colleagues who share our interest in revolutionary governors: Anna Ribera Carbó, Víctor Macías, Carlos Silva, Yves Solís, and Lawrence Taylor. We also acknowledge the encouragement we received from Susan McEachern and Jessica Gribble of Rowman & Littlefield. Finally, we appreciate the financial assistance of the Graduate School at UNC Charlotte.

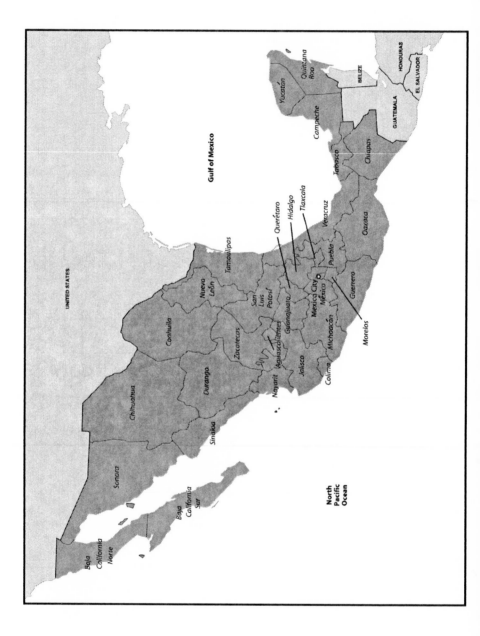

1

The Role of State Governors in the Mexican Revolution

William H. Beezley

[He was] a senator, and might suddenly, when least expected, rise to the dizzy heights of state governor.[1]

During the years from 1910 to 1952, Mexican revolutionaries destroyed the old regime, re-created a new national government, built an official political party, and then discarded in practice the essence of their revolution. Until the emergence of a new, powerful central state in the 1940s, the weakness of the national administration during the military phase of the revolution (1910–1920) and the period of reconstruction (1920–1940) allowed for the appearance of powerful state governors who promoted revolutionary programs that featured their personal stamp. The governors provided the revolution with useful versatility, as these individuals initiated programs to address what they considered the most glaring needs—whether the issue was land, labor, housing, or health care—at the local and regional levels. The flexibility of state governors also offered test cases for the implementation of national revolutionary laws and campaigns. This experience was even more significant in the cases where a former governor became president, a typical path to power between 1924 and 1940 in particular. Thus Plutarco Elías Calles, a former governor of Sonora, was president from 1924 to 1928; Emilio Portes Gil held the governorship of Tamaulipas on two occasions before serving as interim president from 1928 to 1930; Abelardo L. Rodríguez served as military governor of Baja California, then as substitute president from 1932 to 1934; and Lázaro Cárdenas, a former governor of Michoacán, was president from 1934 to 1940. The regimes of all of these former governors strongly reflected their political experience at the state level. The national needs for land redistribution, labor reform, educational campaigns, and poverty relief had regional characteristics that often required programs sensitive to traditions of land tenure, working patterns, indigenous languages, and rural to urban migration. Until well into the 1920s and in some locations even later, governors remained the principal intermediaries between the revolutionary programs of the national government and the people for whom they were designed. Along with recognition of local and regional needs, familiarity with local political rivalries, and flexibility in responding to state conditions, the powerful governor fulfilled one of the ideological goals of the early revolutionaries. As the central government consolidated its power during World War II, this powerful governor disappeared, swept aside by a new, civilian generation of presidents starting with Miguel Alemán (1946–1952).

Francisco I. Madero initiated the revolution on November 20, 1910, to install liberal democracy in a nation under the sway of dictator Porfirio Díaz. In spite of the Constitution of 1857, which guaranteed basic civil rights, democratic government, and the autonomy of state and local administration, Díaz had ruled with an iron fist for decades. In July, he had won another term in a farcical election that featured Madero, Díaz's opponent, in jail on trumped-up charges. To bring about the fall of the dictatorship known widely as the Porfiriato, Madero declared the annulment of the July elections and articulated two interrelated goals. First, he countered the Porfirians' principal weakness, the tendency to centralize authority to achieve modernization, by promising to restore honest democratic elections and to limit officeholders to one term. This campaign received expression in the slogan "Effective Suffrage, No Reelection"—a slogan that Díaz had himself used during his successful 1876 coup d'état against recently reelected president Sebastián Lerdo de Tejada. Díaz had ruled for thirty out of the past thirty-four years, and he had won reelection only after jailing Madero in the 1910 presidential race. Second, Madero and his followers took up arms to demand the restoration of the rights of the *municipio libre*, or free municipality. Under Díaz's dictatorship, state governors as well as *jefes políticos*, the president-appointed prefects who managed local administration, depended on the dictator for their political survival. Madero and his followers attacked the president's centralized political authority and the technocratic elites of the capital city with this campaign for the autonomy of municipal governments. They therefore intended to create a federal system that would renew the autonomy, within constitutional limits, of state and municipal governments. The Maderistas, the followers of Madero, were especially intent on reviving the authority of governors. This meant in practice the elimination of the jefes políticos and the restoration of democratic elections for governors, who would serve only one term. In Madero's view, these state executives became the keystone to the forging of a new regime.

Yet Madero could not have foreseen that his campaign would mark only the beginning of a decade of warfare. Although the rebels triumphed within six months, paving the way for Madero's election to the presidency, political stability would not return until the 1930s. Madero's government faltered under the onslaught of several revolts, and the president fell victim to a bloody coup d'état in February 1913. During the following eighteen months, a new coalition of rebels emerged whose members pursued a broad and often contradictory array of campaigns ranging from land reform to better conditions for urban workers, limits on the power of foreign investors, and the Maderistas' goals of true democracy. The ensuing warfare led to the complete disintegration of central political authority and widespread death and destruction, as the rebels first triumphed and then turned against each other. It was not until mid-1915 that one faction had vanquished its enemies and created a new national government. The process of rebuilding the central government proved to be long and arduous in the face of assaults from rival military officers, the Roman Catholic Church, intransigent Porfirian survivors, especially the owners of large estates, and foreign entrepreneurs. Violence, including assassination, characterized the politics of the era.

In many cases, the weakness of the national government did not extend to the state regimes. Amidst the fighting, various governors established strong, enduring state governments that undertook radical reform programs. These programs were often more radical than First Chief Carranza—the leader of the Constitutionalists—or other national leaders would have countenanced if they had found themselves in effective control of the nation's territory. Moreover, some of the revolutionaries who served as state governors used their office to experiment with programs that they later brought to the presidency. The later emergence of the corporate, authoritarian national regime after World War II, in which an official revolutionary party occupied the presidency until the year 2000, has led many historians to exaggerate the strength of the national government in the 1920s and 1930s.

As a result of their focus on the supposed power of the national state—a focus that historian Alan Knight has labeled "statolatry"—these scholars have overlooked the critical significance of regional authorities in the revolution.[2]

REVOLUTIONARY GOVERNORS IN OFFICE

Once the revolutionaries claimed victory at Ciudad Juárez in May 1911, Madero believed that he had the opportunity to put his political views into practice. As Díaz resigned and went into exile, the resultant treaties between the Maderistas and the federal government called for an interim president, Francisco León de la Barra, to manage elections, and the appointment of interim state governors, especially in the north, to provide a peaceful transition. Madero hoped to name interim governors who were energetic and eager to reform Porfirian political structures at the state level, and who would prepare the states for free elections. However, the old order proved more resilient than Madero had hoped, and in many states, veteran Porfirians assumed the office of interim governor. In addition, Porfirian officers remained in charge of the federal army, and many army units remained in the field under their command. It was not surprising that many governors disappointed Madero's hopes for initiating political change. The Maderistas then focused their attention on the general elections, which would sweep them into power at the federal and state levels. For the position of governor, Madero favored men who would take the initiative to establish democratic politics and initiate programs that addressed the needs of the local population. The transition to Maderista state administration has not been systematically examined, but several historians have studied the governors who came to power in the October 1911 elections.[3]

Some of these case studies of state government under Madero reveal instances in which the new governors were overwhelmed by their task. In the northwestern border state of Sonora, for example, José María Maytorena, the scion of a powerful hacienda family, won election as the first revolutionary governor of the state. He initiated election reforms and expanded educational programs, but did nothing to resolve smoldering labor issues in the state's copper mines and Yaqui demands for the return of their ancestral farmlands. He was ultimately eclipsed by military leaders, among them Alvaro Obregón and his ally, Plutarco Elías Calles.[4] Manuel Mestre Ghigliazza, elected as the governor of the southeastern state of Tabasco, found even less success. Described as a romantic and worldly intellectual, he proved to be a dilettante with revolutionary convictions who lacked courage. Thus his governorship turned from "rule to misrule." He eventually found his niche some years later as director of the national library.[5]

The Maderista governors of the northern border states of Chihuahua and Coahuila were more successful. In Chihuahua, Abraham González had been closely allied with Madero from the time the latter had initiated his first presidential campaign. González served a crucial role in recruiting both Pascual Orozco, Jr., and Pancho Villa, the revolution's first successful military commanders. He also raised money and purchased and shipped arms and ammunition to both Orozco and Villa during the fighting. During the first months of 1911, González established a provisional state government in sections of Chihuahua held by the rebels, and he had begun to provide safe passage papers to civilians and to collect taxes in the region. As an important reform, he implemented Madero's directive to end all head taxes in the region. He also organized both the city and district governments following the decisive battle for Ciudad Juárez. Once in the governor's chair, he attempted to implement the anti-reelectionist goals that had been spelled out in the party's presidential platform of 1910. The statement called for modest reforms, including the expansion of education, freedom of the press, legislation favorable to factory workers, small farmers, and indigenous peoples, and laws for the equal access to natural resources. Moreover, the governor addressed what would become a major revolutionary issue: the continued presence of armed rebels who had not laid down their arms after the Maderista victory. He arranged the mustering out of troops, providing veterans with fifty pesos and a railroad pass each, and his agents paid a bonus of twenty-five pesos for each weapon submitted to authorities.[6]

Less socially committed than González, Venustiano Carranza, a onetime Porfirian and staunch Madero ally, was elected governor of Coahuila, Madero's home state. He moved forward slowly with political reforms. He planned the replacement of Porfirian authorities throughout Coahuila and the creation of a new revolutionary bureaucracy. He quickly acted to establish control over natural resources, especially water rights of both the Nazas River and the Rio Grande, and mineral rights in the coal mining zone. Carranza identified three major threats to his projects: the Díaz bureaucracy, the federal army, and the foreign proprietors and investors who had operated under favored conditions for three decades. However, the governor had no intention of introducing social reforms that would further divide the state's peoples or disrupt its economy. *Peones* (poor rural laborers) soon learned that the governor did not plan to do anything by decree; instead, Carranza waited for the legislature to take legal action to improve their social conditions. Nevertheless, the governor did move to ensure that state citizens all had the right to vote, protection before the law, access to education, and fair taxation. He even took tentative steps toward labor organization and arbitration with employers.[7]

Leaders like González and Carranza may well have registered an even greater impact as governors if Madero's administration had remained stable. However, that was not to be. From the outset, a series of rebellions challenged the Maderistas for authority in the north and in the southern state of Morelos—conditions that limited the radius of action of both the president and the state governors. In response, Madero placed his trust in the Porfirian military officer Victoriano Huerta, who helped quash the most serious of the rebellions, the Pascual Orozco revolt of 1912. Over time, Huerta became convinced that Madero was not fit to be president. In February 1913, yet another rebellion—one led by unrequited Porfirians—prompted Huerta to conspire with the rebels and the U.S. ambassador Henry L. Wilson in a plot to overthrow Madero. On February 18, Huerta had Madero and vice president José María Pino Suárez arrested and forced them to resign. Several hours later, Congress swore him in as the new president. As one of his first acts in office, Huerta demanded that the state governors swear loyalty to his government. A few days later, Madero and Pino Suárez were assassinated on their way to prison, most likely on the orders of Huerta or one of his allies. Afraid of further reprisals, all but three governors recognized the new state of affairs. These holdouts were Carranza, González, and Maytorena, Madero's most important allies at the gubernatorial level. Within weeks, military officers in Chihuahua arrested and murdered González, and Maytorena went into exile without declaring himself either for or against Huerta.

By early March, Carranza stood alone as the only elected governor to openly challenge the unconstitutional seizure of the presidency, the unpunished killings of Madero and Pino Suárez, and the implementation of a new dictatorship. In his Plan de Guadalupe of March 23, 1913, the Coahuilan called on other governors to challenge the unconstitutional seizure of the presidency, the murder of Madero and his vice president, and the implementation of a military dictatorship. Under the plan, Carranza took the title "First Chief of the Constitutionalist Army," so that he would subsequently be free to seek presidential election as a civilian. He benefited from the rise of three other major regional centers of opposition to Huerta: Chihuahua, under the leadership of Pancho Villa; the Sonoran revolutionaries under Obregón, and Emiliano Zapata's peasant army in Morelos. In July 1914, this coalition defeated Huerta and drove him into exile. Whether known as Villistas, Obregonistas, Carrancistas, or Zapatistas, the rebels understood themselves as revolutionaries, but they diverged greatly in their political goals. Thus, soon after their victory, the revolutionaries turned on each other in a civil war that pitted Villa's Division of the North and the Zapatistas against Obregón's and Carranza's armies. As a pragmatic politician, Carranza sought to gain the upper hand in the conflict by appealing to the poor majority, both urban and rural, that did the bulk of the fighting. In February 1915, early on in the conflict with Villa, he decreed the nation's first land restitution law to assist in the mobilization of followers. Upon Obregón's victory later that year, he spearheaded the effort to write a new revolutionary constitution, approved in the city of Querétaro in February 1917. This constitution embodied many of the ideals that the revolutionaries had fought for, combining Madero's political program with economic nationalism, anticlericalism, and social reform. It not only followed Madero's precepts in outlawing reelection in the executive branch, but it was also the first constitution in the world that contained a number of social guarantees, including the national patrimony over land and the subsoil, an eight-hour day for workers, and provisions to allow a sweeping land reform. Elected president by the same convention that approved the constitution, Carranza turned to governors to consolidate political authority and implement the new order at the state and local levels. However, both Carranza and a powerful array of counterrevolutionary groups, including foreign investors and conservative governors, opposed many of the social and anticlerical articles of the constitution, and these provisions found only piecemeal implementation. For example, it was not until the Cárdenas presidency (1934–1940) that the federal government carried out a far-reaching land reform totaling forty-nine million acres and expropriated the foreign-owned oil industry. Throughout this period—under Madero, under Carranza, and thereafter—state governors played a crucial role in either accelerating or slowing the implementation of revolutionary reforms.

How this was done, within a spectrum of different campaigns, forms the subject of this book. This is neither a prosopography of all the governors from 1910 to 1946, nor a statistical compilation comparing their actions. Rather, the book relies on the presentation of representative examples of governorships that offer case studies of the diverse state executives from different eras of the revolution. The authors have also examined governors of states from different regions of the nation to demonstrate the extreme regional differences at the time—one of the difficulties that kept the national government weak.

For the first decade of the revolution, 1910–1920, we include studies of three governors who ruled during the most intense violence. This decade witnessed a population decline of over one million due to casualties, emigration to the United States, and the Spanish flu epidemic of 1918. It also twice featured U.S. troops on Mexican soil: in 1914, the U.S. occupation of the ports of Tampico and Veracruz, and in 1916–1917, John J. Pershing's Punitive Expedition, which chased Villa through the state of Chihuahua after his attack on the town of Columbus, New Mexico. It also saw social confusion as thousands of people moved to the cities, fleeing the destruction of homes, villages, and families in the countryside. These governors had to reestablish order, satisfy revolutionary veterans, confront vestiges of the old regime, and, perhaps most difficult, exude confidence that the regime would survive.

Three governors, Benito Juárez Maza in Oaxaca, Salvador Alvarado in Yucatán, and Plutarco Elías Calles of Sonora, offer telling portraits of the regional nature of the revolution during this violent decade. The son of the famous Benito Juárez who distinguished himself as a protagonist of the Liberal Reforma of the 1850s, the hero of the effort to reclaim Mexico from a French occupation army in the 1860s, and the country's only indigenous president since the achievement of independence in 1821, Juárez Maza took office under Madero. Unlike González and Carranza, who ruled in states where the revolution had succeeded, Juárez faced an entrenched Porfirian state administration. The new governor never escaped his father's shadow. His death from a heart attack cut short his administration and leaves author Francie Chassen-López to wonder if he can even be called a revolutionary governor.

Yucatán, another state far from the early fighting of the revolution, nevertheless featured insurrectionary uprisings against the Porfirian society. The details of the gubernatorial regimes under Madero can be found in the state archives and in a careful, persuasive monograph by Allen Wells and Gilbert Joseph.[8] During the war between the factions, Yucatán remained an outpost of the Old Regime, controlled by allies of Huerta closely associated with the state's henequen planter class. After the Constitutionalist victory over Villa and Zapata, first chief Venustiano Carranza planned to centralize control under this authority, and he confronted ongoing unrest from his old enemies. Consequently, he imposed governors where he did not have close allies. He appointed the native Sinaloan Salvador Alvarado to lead a Constitutionalist army to Yucatán and establish himself as governor. From 1915 to 1918, Alvarado carried out one of the most radical state programs in the nation. Professor Stephanie Smith explains that in additional to aiding rural workers, Alvarado was the first governor to give particular attention to women. He sponsored the nation's first feminist congress and attempted to identify and develop policy to benefit the majority Maya population

Meanwhile, one of the revolutionaries from the emerging region of the North, Plutarco Elías Calles of Sonora, combined a commitment to social reform with an abiding hostility to organized religion. As a result, his biographer, Jürgen Buchenau, refers to Calles as a Mexican Jacobin. Indeed, from 1915 to 1919, Calles implemented policies that would have been recognized by the original French Jacobins. Buchenau argues that Calles used his governorship as a dress rehearsal for presidential ambitions, testing social reform programs and populist politics, the most successful of which were used during his eventual presidential administration. Thus Calles launched a failed attempt to outlaw the consumption of alcohol in Sonora,[9] expelled all Catholic priests from the state, and with his ally Adolfo de la Huerta crafted ambitious legislation protecting workers from abuses by their employers and provided the legal base for land reform.

These three governors therefore constitute three diverse examples of the governorship in the turbulent 1910s. One was a local individual promoted to office by the president in his native state; another, an outsider thrust on the state population by the president to ensure compliance with revolutionary programs; and the third, a revolutionary veteran who took the governorship as a platform to work out policies that he envisioned for national reforms. The latter two had revolutionary troops at their disposal to ensure the success of their regime, while the first had to move carefully because he was not a veteran of the revolution and did not have a military force of his own. Obviously, the conclusion is that among the governors during this decade, generals with personal armies proved most successful. This pattern poses interesting questions about how presidents eventually reined in the revolutionary generals, so that Mexico later on avoided the experience of the military regimes of South America.

Once the Sonoran Triangle (the three Sonoran politicians de la Huerta, Obregón, and Calles) assumed power after Carranza's overthrow in 1920, these men confronted a bloated revolutionary army. They discharged soldiers and retired officers as a general policy, and in 1923 and 1929, two failed military revolts against Obregón and Calles greatly reduced the number of *divisionarios*, the powerful divisionary generals. After Obregón's assassination in July 1928, only weeks after winning election to a second term as president, Calles exerted powerful influence from behind the scenes as the *jefe máximo*, or supreme chief, of the Mexican Revolution. In that capacity, he helped engineer the creation of a ruling party that would eventually negotiate and broker political power at the national, state, and local level. The initial structure of the official party, created by Calles in 1929 as the National Revolutionary Party (PNR), recognized the powerful role of governors and other *caciques*, or local strongmen.[10] Under the guise of affiliating the regional parties that served as springboards for their political ambitions, the PNR brought these powerful caciques under the same umbrella. The party also incorporated significant military figures as well as representatives of the middle class, urban workers, and the rural poor. However, this party needed many years to centralize its authority, and the regional parties initially remained intact in their affiliation with the PNR. Thus it is not surprising that the jefe máximo saw it necessary to depose twenty-one state governors between 1928 and 1934.

While they centralized authority, the Sonoran presidents relied on the governors to help implement the new revolutionary Constitution of 1917. Because the constitutional provisions required enabling legislation to initiate national policies, several governors issued state decrees or legislation to carry forward the social programs without waiting for the national regime to act. In this way, the most radical of programs reached the people in an uneven patchwork of state programs. Adalberto Tejeda in Veracruz, Tomás Garrido Canabal in Tabasco, and José Guadalupe Zuno Hernández in Jalisco—three governors of the era—provide a fascinating selection, representative of the willingness of state administrators to undertake their own programs with or without the backing of the president. Their experimental character led historian Carlos Martínez Assad to call these state regimes "laboratories of the revolution."[11]

Tejeda, as Andrew Grant Wood demonstrates, carried out what was at the time the most radical land reform program in the nation. In the course of two governorships during the years 1920–1924 and 1928–1932, Tejeda's policies provoked major responses from landowners, but more important than creating resistance, his land reform program demonstrated the social and economic potential of these land redistribution policies as well as the economic consequences following a change from commercial to subsistence programs. Above all, Professor Wood captures the insecurity, tension, and fear of society caught up in significant social changes.

Less economically radical than those of Tejeda but far more anticlerical were the programs of Governor Garrido Canabal of Tabasco. Garrido has been immortalized as a nameless police lieutenant in Graham Greene's novel of revolutionary anticlericalism, *The Power and the Glory*.[12] His efforts to eliminate the Roman Catholic Church reached vicious proportions and have shaped his legacy. He clearly pushed the limits of anticlericalism during his long governorship (1922–1935) and ultimately, President Cárdenas removed him from office. While many have focused on his anticlerical programs, he was representative of several governors who used their office to build a personal regime with a state power base. Although holding the formal title of governor, they in fact became regional strongmen whom presidents approached with circumspection, until they decided that they did or did not need their support. If the former, the president ignored their programs; if the latter, the president forced them from office. In the case of Tabasco, Kristin Harper demonstrates that Garrido went about constructing his state regime by initiating an extensive road building program that gave residents their first reliable overland transportation system, including connections to markets and the port. The roads also allowed the governor to respond quickly to any challenge to his authority. Roads lacked the dramatic quality of the railroads which had newly arrived in other states. Sanctioned and supported by Calles's road building program at the national level, however, they had a much more widespread effect upon the state.

Another one of the laboratories of the revolution directed by a state governor was in Jalisco, where Governor Zuno demonstrated that his strongest commitment was to *tapatío* regionalism and traditions. Moreover, although Zuno and other men held all the political positions in the state, public programs required the support of women, who had their own networks as powerful in many ways as those of men. As María Teresa Fernández Aceves demonstrates, the survival of Zuno's regime, a governorship in conflict with President Calles, only makes sense by examining the activities of these women in Jalisco. Beneath the obvious level of politics, gender relationships and enduring regional traditions and loyalties endorsed revolutionary programs at the same time that they resisted national policies. In an era when President Calles routinely ousted state governors, his inability to remove Zuno and his allies was perhaps his most spectacular failure at the state political level.

President Lázaro Cárdenas pushed revolutionary reform programs to their apogee at the same time that he firmly adopted revolutionary institutions, especially by entrenching the corporate nature of the revolutionary party (with a new name, the Mexican Revolutionary Party, or PRM). After

Cárdenas had dispatched Jefe Máximo Calles and labor leader Luis Morones to exile in the United States in April 1936, his national government achieved greater strength with its reorganized party, powerful cabinet members, and the nation's slow economic recovery from the Great Depression. The restructured PRM eliminated the regional parties and restricted the actions of governors, some of whom resisted to maintain their independence. Moreover, the strength of the national government increased along with a burgeoning bureaucracy, the members of which represented national authority and limited the radius of action of governors. Representatives of federal influence in the states included teachers, agrarian reform officials, and agents of other federal ministries.[13] Three governors who represent the spectrum of state administration and relations with Cárdenas are Marte R. Gómez of Tamaulipas (1937–1940), Efraín Gutiérrez of Chiapas (1936–1940), and Maximino Avila Camacho of Puebla (1937–1941).

The Cardenista governors came with a variety of experiences beyond fighting in the revolution. An agronomist by training, Marte R. Gómez governed the northeastern state of Tamaulipas from 1937 to 1940, where he attempted to balance the critical social and economic issues of the revolutionary promises of land redistribution and the need for higher agricultural production. As Michael Ervin demonstrates in his chapter, Gómez tried to promote cooperativism as he attempted to redeem the revolution's commitment to agrarians. He later served as the national minister of agriculture, oddly a ministry not written about by historians, where he applied his experience as governor to national programs.

The isolation of the southernmost state of Chiapas on the Guatemalan border kept that state out of much of the revolutionary violence from 1910 to 1940. The governors of the state, for the most part ranchers and planters, remained hostile to the revolution's agrarian programs.[14] In late 1936, president Lázaro Cárdenas leveraged his friend Efraín Gutiérrez—the subject of Steven Lewis's contribution—into the governor's office to enforce revolutionary programs. During his first two years, Gutiérrez dictated a flurry of land and labor reforms, and he introduced Cardenista *indigenismo* that struck fear in the hearts of highland Ladino (mestizo) elites. As the national regime turned to crucial questions of oil nationalization and the international politics that resulted in World War II, however, Gutiérrez became a weak, absentee governor, and local politicians overturned most of his agrarian initiatives.

Even with the growth of the national government's authority and Cárdenas's commitment to break regional and state strongmen, some governors remained independent powers. Perhaps the most powerful and certainly the most colorful of these governors was Maximino Avila Camacho, brother of Manuel, who served as president from 1940 to 1946. Even when he was not the governor of Puebla in name, Maximino still dominated the state. A revolutionary veteran, he astutely manipulated politics and economics in Puebla with the connivance of Cárdenas and help of his brother Manuel. Although Maximino was well known for his inept, corrupt, and authoritarian behavior, the chapter by Timothy Henderson and David LaFrance shows that at times, revolutionary presidents made deals with such individuals to maintain order as they tackled other reform programs. Avila Camacho's governorship from 1937 to 1941 serves as a case study of presidential-gubernatorial relations, the key to the political system. This powerful cacique and governor has never received a full monographic study. Until the publication of a biography, the most complete source remains Ángeles Mastretta's novel, *Arráncame la vida*.[15] This example demonstrates Cárdenas's pragmatism in his selection of governors. Some Cardenista governors like Avila Camacho and his Sonoran counterpart, Román Yocupicio, were far more conservative than the national administration, but they served a useful purpose as loyal allies against Callistas in those states.[16]

The book closes with an examination of Baltasar Leyva Mancilla of Guerrero (1945–1951). This governor straddles the revolutionary era and the years of the economic miracle guided by a new generation of administrators who replaced the revolutionary veterans and illustrates the decline of the revolution at the state level. Governor Leyva Mancilla thus presided over the state of Guerrero during the transition from the revolutionary to the PRI national regime. During his governorship, Acapulco's golden age as a preeminent resort began. This focus on tourism and development marked a strong contrast to the preceding decades of revolution. The people of Guerrero constituted an armed society and had been close to ungovernable since the beginning of the revolution because of the ongoing violence between landed elites and frustrated land reformers. Neither side had suffered enough losses to prevent enduring conflict after 1920. The next twenty-five years were marked by a struggle for land and power between *agraristas* and shifting coalitions of landowners, *licenciados* (college graduates; often lawyers), violent entrepreneurs, and the (generally despised) "professional politicians," men who rose through unions, the bureaucracy, elected office, and federal contacts. As Paul Gillingham demonstrates, Leyva Mancilla ended this cycle of violence in concert with the national government (and with far less autonomy than the preceding governors) and imposed the government's vision of development on his state.

WORLD OF REVOLUTIONARY GOVERNORS

These governors, whose careers are described and analyzed in the chapters that follow, represent only a glimpse at the powerful revolutionary veterans and committed politicians who held office from 1911 to 1952. Some governors became celebrities, others notorious, and others synonyms for social programs, revolutionary policies, indiscriminate violence, and brigand-like corruption. A few governors slipped into obscurity, where they have remained. Two who became nearly household names were both from San Luis Potosí: Saturino Cedillo and Gonzálo N. Santos.

Cedillo's revolutionary career ran parallel to those of many others of his generation. He and other family members from Ciudad de Maíz, San Luis Potosí, answered Madero's call for revolution in late 1910. He proved more adept than other revolutionaries by choosing the wrong side twice and still surviving. Disappointed by Madero's modest political reforms and neglect of revolutionary veterans, he joined the Orozco revolt in 1912. A year later, he joined the Constitutionalist campaign against Huerta and then fought with the Villistas until they lost to Obregón. During the 1920s, he battled against the de la Huerta revolt of 1923 and against the Cristero Rebellion (1926–1929). He dominated his home state as governor from 1927 to 1931, where he developed great influence over the agrarians in the region. He used his efforts in favor of land reform as a stepping-stone to national politics. In 1933, he was one of the founders of the National Confederation of the Campesinos (the CNC), and he mobilized its members in support of Cárdenas at the official party congress that same year. There, he cast a deciding ballot for the nomination of Cárdenas for president. Only four years later, he raised a rebellion against the pro-Cárdenas governor of San Luis Potosí, dying in the struggle in 1939.[17]

Santos, governor from 1943 to 1949, became famous for his outrageous and often vulgar declarations. For example, he claimed that as governor he imposed the law of the three *ierros* against his opponents: *encierro, destierro y entierro*, that is, prison, exile, and burial. Therefore, he had no need for bureaucrats, but only gravediggers. The accusations and evidence of political self-interest and corruption resulted in his nickname, "El Alazán Tostado," the tan sorrel. Nevertheless, he became an early member of the official party and worked closely with Presidents Calles, Cárdenas, and Avila Camacho. He always traveled with an armed bodyguard that included his personal security agent, known as la Mano Negra (the black hand), a notorious murderer. During the 1940 presidential elections, he was accused of taking a group of three hundred pistoleros around the capital city, breaking up rallies in support of the rival to the official candidate and using violence and intimidation to win the vote for Avila Camacho.

When he became state governor of San Luis Potosí in 1943, Santos focused his administration on public policies distinct from the land reform policies of Cedillo. His programs focused on the city and stressed public works that garnered support from the railway union (such as completing the new railroad station). Additional construction projects included a new central hospital that also served as a teaching center for the medical school of the Autonomous University, a state teachers' college, a new dam, and two new markets in the capital city. The capstone of this program came with the construction of a water and drainage system in the city, requiring an investment of twelve million pesos, largely provided by the federal government. His administrative style rested on the promotion of the cult of personality in the manner of nineteenth-century caudillos. At the end of his first year in office, he had a celebration organized that included local and national political guests. It featured the state band as well as other union and school bands and various mariachi groups who all joined together to perform "las mañanitas" for him. After a special session of the state legislature, the evening of the anniversary concluded with a dance and spectacular fireworks display. After leaving office, he retired to his 87,000 hectare hacienda with his family and bodyguards. In retirement, he wrote his revealing, and often vulgar, memoirs.[18]

Most other governors did not achieve the independence of these two famous governors of San Luis Potosí. Some did not even have authority over their own states, such as in Sonora during 1914 and 1915, where pro-Villa governor Maytorena battled with the Obregón supporter Calles. Others found themselves overwhelmed by the revolutionary armies, especially from 1911 to 1916. In Aguascalientes, after the military dictator Victoriano Huerta fled into exile, Pancho Villa called for a convention to decide the nation's future. Venustiano Carranza objected, and Villa's convention mobilized opposition to Carranza that resulted in a two-year civil war. During the convention, the governor of Aguascalientes, Víctor Elizondo, got crossways with Villa, who had him executed. The new governor of the state, Benito Díaz, was appointed by Villa and initiated no policies or programs not suggested by the general. Less than six months later, Carranza's armies conquered the state, and Alvaro Obregón appointed Roque Estrada as the new governor. This kaleidoscope of governors in Aguascalientes made it impossible for any of them to accomplish anything.

Other governors experienced the same relationship with powerful generals who dominated other states. Thus, Cedillo only served as governor for four years, but for more than a decade, his shadow obscured other men who held the office. In Chihuahua, Villa ruled as governor although his title remained General of the División del Norte. No one doubted that Villa, and not the governor, was the ultimate authority. In Puebla, General Maximino Avila Camacho dominated the state whether or not he sat in the governor's chair with his personality, his business and bureaucratic partners, and his gunmen. It is this pattern that lately has led to insightful studies of revolutionary caciques.

Besides the examples already mentioned, a few other powerful governors used their office to get to the presidency. Men such as Abelardo L. Rodríguez of Baja California del Norte built a strong political and financial base through state administration.[19] He brought to the presidency his experience in dealing with the businessmen on both sides of the border, in regulating and profiting from the vice trade, and in recognizing the needs and ambitions of Mexicans far from the nation's capital. Other governors attempted to do the same and failed, such as Francisco J. Mújica, onetime governor of Michoacán before Cárdenas, whom he mentored politically in his rise to the governorship.[20] Mújica followed a common path, serving as state governor and in several administratively prominent and highly visible offices. Unfortunately for his ambitions, the national economy, international politics, and domestic social realities pushed Cárdenas to select another nominee for the office in 1940. Those governors who attempted to become president and failed would make an interesting group study.

Revolutionary governors had much greater freedom of action than the members of the presidential cabinet, even when they headed major federal bureaucracies, such as the land reform agency or the ministry of public education. Especially during the 1920s and 1930s, governors had to confront continuing local violence, advance reform programs, battle rural revolts, and mobilize local people in support of the weak national regime. The governor remained a powerful political figure even during the first years of the official party.

Organized in 1929, the PNR was initially little more than a group of the most powerful leaders in the nation, including numerous governors: a "confederation of caciques," as political scientist Luis Garrido has labeled it.[21] In 1938, Cárdenas reorganized this party, gave it a corporatist structure, and used it to begin bringing independent leaders under his authority, both generals and governors. The renamed Partido Revolucionario Mexicano (PRM, or Mexican Revolutionary Party) moved away from the traditional federalism (representation by states) to constituent representatives based on occupation (peasant, worker, soldier, or public servant). The party would be restructured once again in 1946 as the Partido Revolucionario Institucional (PRI, or Institutional Revolutionary Party). Shorn of its military sector, this newly organized party diminished the autonomy of governors even further. Beginning with Cárdenas's changes, the party took precedence over most governors and played an essential role in their selection as candidates. Party membership, loyalty, and service became increasingly important as the bona fides for office, and the governors' degree of autonomy vis-à-vis the central government greatly decreased.

Thus concluded a process of political centralization that had steadily gained momentum during the eras of Carranza, Obregón, Calles, and Cárdenas. By the 1930s, a number of national and state revolutionary leaders had recognized that many issues could not be resolved by state executives. In some cases, national officials and organizations had already moved into action. Labor, for example, required national solutions, especially when confronting international corporations. President Cárdenas had acted decisively when he nationalized the petroleum industry in 1938. Moreover, issues of natural resources, especially water rights that involved several states, international boundaries, or both, could not be managed by state governments. The official party had taken up the need for national management of natural resources in its 1934 six-year plan.[22] Moreover, the need for national administration of indigenous programs had also been recognized.

NATIONAL BUREAUCRATS REPLACE STATE GOVERNORS

The era of the independent, freewheeling governor was coming to an end in 1946 as the national regime passed into the hands of a new generation that was more impressed by university training, technical skills, and party loyalty than by revolutionary service. Bureaucratic chiefs replaced state governors as the decision makers who affected the lives of ordinary citizens. By the end of the century, the president stood well beyond the governors as the national executive, dominating politics, administration, and financial decisions. Second to the president in authority and prestige was not a governor or general, but the mayor of Mexico City. Technocrats, often with master's or doctoral degrees from prominent foreign universities, began to dominate the PRI and to serve as president in the second half of the twentieth century. PRI governors served more as party bureaucrats than politicians.

Nevertheless, during the 1990s, the governorship once again recovered its crucial role as the PRI began to lose control to the conservative National Action Party (or PAN) in several states in central and northern Mexico. Thus, serving as governor of one of these states did provide important political experience to fuel presidential ambitions of those outside the official party. Certainly that was the case with Vicente Fox, onetime governor of Guanajuato, when he campaigned against the PRI in 2000. As the opposition party candidate, he won the presidency. Since his victory, political observers have been scrambling to understand what the demise of the PRI means for established patterns of politics and administration. The victories of Fox and, in 2006, of fellow PAN member Felipe Calderón, a man who had once unsuccessfully run for the governorship of Michoacán, revitalized national politics and paralleled the resurgence of the governors as political actors. Even the national congress has become a vibrant center of political debate and decision making that had been lacking since the 1920s.

As state governors reemerge as more independent and powerful politicians, the time seems especially propitious for a reevaluation of the governors who played an essential role in the creation of the revolution, the nation's social, economic, and political changes brought by a generation of revolutionaries who dominated the nation from 1911 until 1946. The essays that follow offer the reader an introduction to the personalities, ambitions, politics, and peccadillos of an array of these governors. The essays provide, if not a representative sample, a varied selection from the spectrum of individuals who represented the revolution to the residents of the different states.

NOTES

1. Fernando del Paso, *Palinuro of Mexico*, trans. Elisabeth Plaister (Normal, IL: Dalkey Archive Press, 1996), 8.
2. Alan Knight, "The Mexican Revolution: Bourgeois? Nationalist? Or Just a 'Great Rebellion'?" *Bulletin of Latin American Research* 4, no. 2 (1985): 1–37.
3. William H. Beezley, "Research Possibilities in the Mexican Revolution: The Governorship," *Americas* 29, no. 3 (Jan. 1973): 308–13.
4. Susan M. Deeds, "José María Maytorena and the Mexican Revolution in Sonora (Part 1)," *Arizona and the West* 18, no. 1 (1976): 21–40, and "José María Maytorena and the Mexican Revolution in Sonora (Part 2)," *Arizona and the West* 18, no. 2 (1976): 125–48.
5. Andrés Iduarte, *Niño: Child of the Mexican Revolution*, trans. James F. Schearer (New York: Praeger Publishers, 1971), 145–46.
6. William H. Beezley, *Insurgent Governor: Abraham González and the Mexican Revolution in Chihuahua* (Lincoln: University of Nebraska Press, 1973).
7. William H. Beezley, "Governor Carranza and the Revolution in Coahuila," *Americas* 33, no. 1 (July 1976): 50–61.
8. Yucatán. Archivo general del estado. Libro de decretos, vol. 25bis, expediente 1, números 407 to 506, for June 5 to Aug. 7, 1911; Allen Wells and Gilbert M. Joseph, *Summer of Discontent, Seasons of Upheaval: Elite Politics and Rural Insurgency in Yucatán* (Stanford, CA: Stanford University Press, 1996).
9. See also Gretchen Pierce, "Sober Revolutionaries: Ethnicity, Class, and Gender in the Anti-Alcohol Campaigns in Jalisco, Oaxaca, and Sonora, Mexico, 1910–1940" (Ph.D. diss., University of Arizona, 2008).
10. Alan Knight and Wil Pansters, eds., *Caciquismo in Twentieth-Century Mexico* (London: Institute for the Study of the Americas, 2005).
11. Carlos Martínez Assad, *El laboratorio de la Revolución: El Tabasco garridista* (Mexico: Siglo XXI, 1979; 2nd ed. 2007).
12. Graham Greene, *The Power and the Glory* (London: William Heineman, 1940).
13. Michael A. Ervin, "The Art of the Possible: Agronomists, Agrarian Reform, and the Middle Politics of the Mexican Revolution, 1908–34" (Ph.D. diss., University of Pittsburgh, 2002); Mary Kay Vaughan, *Cultural Politics in Revolution: Teachers, Peasants, and Schools in Mexico, 1930–1940* (Tucson: University of Arizona Press, 1997); Guillermo Palacios, *La pluma y el arado. Los intelectuales pedagogos y la construcción socio-cultural del 'problema campesino' en México, 1930–1934* (Mexico: El Colegio de México/Centro de Investigación y Docencia Económicas, 1999) and "Postrevolutionary Intellectuals, Rural Readings and the Shaping of the 'Peasant

Problem' in Mexico: El Maestro Rural, 1932–1934," *Journal of Latin American Studies* 30, no. 2 (May 1998): 309–99.

14. See also Thomas Benjamin, *A Rich Land, a Poor People: Politics and Society in Modern Chiapas* (Albuquerque: University of New Mexico Press, 1996); and Steven E. Lewis, *The Ambivalent Revolution: Forging State and Nation in Chiapas, 1910–1945* (Albuquerque: University of New Mexico Press, 2005).

15. Ángeles Mastretta, *Arráncame la vida* (Mexico: Ediciones Océano, 1988).

16. Jürgen Buchenau, *Plutarco Elías Calles and the Mexican Revolution* (Lanham, MD: Rowman and Littlefield, 2007), 181.

17. Romana Falcón, *Revolución y caciquismo: San Luis Potosí, 1910–1938* (Mexico: El Colegio de México, 1984).

18. Enrique Krauze, *Biography of Power: A History of Modern Mexico, 1810–1996,* 2nd ed. (New York: Harper Perennial, 1998), 610–12; Gonzálo N. Santos, *Memorias* (Mexico: Grijalbo, 1984).

19. Jürgen Buchenau, "El general Abelardo L. Rodríguez y la Revolución Mexicana," in *Caudillos e instituciones: Crisis y soluciones. Ciclos en la historia de México,* ed. Norma Mereles de Ogarrio (Mexico City: Fideicomiso Archivos Plutarco Elías Calles y Fernando Torreblanca, forthcoming); and José Alfredo Gómez Estrada, *Gobierno y casinos: El origen de la riqueza de Abelardo L. Rodríguez,* 2nd ed. (Mexico City: Instituto Mora, 2007). Professor Buchenau is currently working on a larger study of Rodríguez's career.

20. Anna Ribera Carbó, "Francisco J. Múgica, gobernador de Michoacán: 1920–1922," ms. under consideration by the *Latin Americanist*.

21. Luis Javier Garrido, *El Partido de la Revolución Institucionalizada: La formación del nuevo estado en México (1928–1945)* (Mexico City: Siglo Veintiuno Editores, 1982), 103.

22. Emily M. Wakild, "Resources, Communities, and Conservation: The Creation of National Parks in Revolutionary Mexico under President Lázaro Cárdenas" (Ph.D. diss., University of Arizona, 2007).

2

Benito Juárez Maza of Oaxaca

A Revolutionary Governor?

Francie R. Chassen-López

On June 10, 1910, Benito Juárez Maza boarded the train in Mexico City en route to Oaxaca to begin his first campaign for governor and to follow in the footsteps of his illustrious father.[1] Juarista liberalism had already become the standard of the burgeoning opposition to the dictatorship of Porfirio Díaz (1876–1911), which accused the president of betraying Benito Juárez García, the hero of the Liberal Reform. Francisco I. Madero, too, asserted his right to unfurl this banner as he campaigned for the presidency in 1910. In the city of Oaxaca, the Normal School students, campaigning for both Madero and Juárez Maza, entitled their newspaper *La sombra de Juárez* (the shadow of Juárez). While this shadow now hung ominously over the dictatorship, it also loomed over the son. In order to become a political player in his own right, Benito Juárez Maza would have to emerge from this shadow. He never did.

After his death in 1872, the Liberal intelligentsia consciously encouraged the cult of Benito Juárez. They hoped to achieve a social consensus through reconciliation and thus cultivated, in Charles Hale's apt phrase, a "unifying liberal myth." Throughout Mexico, streets, parks, plazas, towns, and cities took on the names of the symbols and heroes of the Independence movement and the Liberal Reform as a more secular and nationalist political culture took shape. In 1883, the city of Oaxaca changed many older religious street names to reflect this historical trend. Public celebrations, such as those on the anniversary of Juárez's death (July 18) attended by the president, successfully instilled this culture in the hearts and minds of Mexicans and legitimized Díaz as the "indispensable perpetuator" of national unity and the grand Juarista liberal tradition.[2]

Although clearly not endowed with the intelligence and political acumen of his father, Benito Juárez Maza was the heir, the living Juárez. Diverse societies bearing his father's name invited him to become an honorary member or even president: the Sociedad Benito Juárez of San Antonio, Texas, the Sociedad Benito Juárez of Morelia, the Sociedad Mutualista Hijas de Juárez of Monterrey, and, of course, the Asociación Juárez of Oaxaca. From the start, the political career of the son was overshadowed by the cult of his father, who had become the patron saint of Mexican liberalism.[3]

CHILDHOOD AND DIPLOMATIC CAREER

Benito Juárez Maza was born on October 29, 1852, in the city of Oaxaca, where he entered primary school. During the War of the Reform, in 1859, the family moved to Veracruz to join then president Benito Juárez, who had established the Liberal capital there in opposition to Conservative-held Mexico City. After the victory of the Liberals in 1861, the Juárez family moved to Mexico City, but the French Intervention forced them to escape to the north, arriving in Monterrey in 1863. As the French and the Conservatives installed Austrian-born Emperor Maximilian in Mexico City, President Juárez sent his wife and children to New York City, where they lived in a humble house on East Thirteenth Street. Juárez Maza finally finished his elementary education there.[4]

In 1867, once again in the nation's capital with his father installed in the presidency, Juárez Maza entered the newly inaugurated National Preparatory School under the positivist leadership of Gabino Barreda. Although he stopped attending law school after the death of his father, he later worked as an apprentice in the law firm of Modesto Martínez in Mexico City. President Porfirio Díaz assumed a protective attitude toward Juárez Maza. At the time, Díaz was eager to make Mexicans forget his rebellion against President Juárez in 1871 to protest the president's decision to seek reelection to a second term. As part of his campaign to unify the Liberal party, Díaz had begun promoting a personality cult of the elder Juárez, and he portrayed himself, a decorated hero of the war against the French, as following firmly in his footsteps. Thus, in 1877, Díaz appointed Juárez Maza private secretary to the minister of foreign relations, Matías Romero, and the following year, he sent him as secretary of the legation in Washington. Juárez Maza later held similar diplomatic posts in Europe, first in Germany and later in France. Such a diplomatic career was a good way to keep Juárez Maza out of Mexican politics while Díaz established his role as sole perpetuator of his father's legacy. While serving as first secretary of the legation in Paris, Benito Juárez Maza married Maria Klerian Picoys (daughter of a French colonel) in 1888.[5]

That same year, the newlyweds returned to Mexico, where "Don Beno," as he was fondly called, became a federal deputy, first representing the territory of Tepic, and later, districts in the states of Mexico and Oaxaca. His colleagues in Congress considered him a dedicated Juarista liberal who opposed Díaz's conciliation with the church. He later served as municipal president of Texcoco near Mexico City, where he focused on advancing primary education. In 1905, he was again sent to the United States as first secretary of the Mexican embassy, and in 1907, he returned to Mexican political life.[6]

POLITICAL CAREER

Like his father, Benito Juárez Maza was a dedicated mason. Freemasonry had brought the ideas of the Enlightenment including the liberal critique of Catholicism and monarchical regimes to Mexico. Its *logias* (lodges) were secret organizations with elaborate ritual, based on equality and fraternity of all men (no women). Juárez Maza had begun his Masonic career on January 8, 1875, at age twenty-three, in the logia "Toltecas" where he obtained the high grade of maestro. By 1904, when the Rito Nacional Mexicano was initiated in honor of his father, Juárez Maza was elected its *gran luminar* (great luminary).[7] Behind the different logias were the *camarillas* (rival political factions); thus, masonry forged a vital link in the patron-client networks of nineteenth-century liberals.

At the dawn of the twentieth century, liberals (many of them masons) throughout Mexico organized in response to the growing power of the Catholic Church and sought to revive the liberal party. On June 28, 1901, the "Ponciano Arriaga Liberal Club" of San Luis Potosí addressed various members of Congress on the subject. To Benito Juárez Maza they wrote: "You, Mr. Juárez carry the illustrious name, the name of the most illustrious genius of América, who put the clergy in their place." They implored him to support the rebirth of liberalism, but to no avail.[8]

Benito Juárez Maza finally joined the opposition in December 1908 when he attended a meeting which resulted in the formation of the Partido Democrático, or Democratic Party (January 22, 1909), the first party organized to test the political waters after president Porfirio Díaz declared in the Creelman interview that he did not plan to run for reelection in 1910. It aspired to assure a "free and popular government," which would act in "compliance with the Laws of the Reform, respect for liberty and life, [and] the moralization of the judicial system." Guided by a number of Mexico's middle-class intelligentsia who opposed the influence of the Científicos (a group of wealthy advisers to Díaz led by Treasury secretary José Limantour), the Partido Democrático elected Benito Juárez Maza as its first president. Another founding member, Ricardo García Granados, noted that he "was an honorable gentleman, but with scarce political skill who owed his prestige to the name inherited from his illustrious father, thus it should be understood that he was neither the principal organizer nor the director of that organization."[9] Científico sympathizers immediately attacked this party as an instrument of General Bernardo Reyes's presidential (later vice-presidential) ambitions. For moderate liberals, Juárez Maza's assumption of the presidency of the Partido Democrático reinforced the relationship between Juarismo and the democratization of Mexico.

THE RUN FOR GOVERNOR IN 1910

In mid-1909, local dissidents published an open letter to the president that severely criticized the elitist and arbitrary Científico governor of Oaxaca, Emilio Pimentel. In response, the oligarchy of the Central Valleys of Oaxaca (the Vallistocracia) published a "Vote of Gratitude and Confidence from Oaxacan Society to the Governor of the State, Lic. Emilio Pimentel" on July 14, 1909. The opposition counterattacked in an extensive critique entitled *Trial of the Administration of Lic. D. Emilio Pimentel*, published in late January 1910. Although Pimentel didn't announce his decision to seek reelection until late March 1910, the elite political machine had already begun organizing Pimentelista political clubs in the state capital and various towns.[10]

Although they had split over the reelection of Pimentel in 1906, these anti-Científico moderate and radical liberals in Oaxaca reunited and mobilized to find an alternative candidate in 1910. They sent a commission to the nation's capital to speak with their ideal candidate, Benito Juárez Maza, who accepted the challenge. Moderate lawyers of the Asociación Juárez, Heliodoro Díaz Quintas, Constantino Chapital, and Miguel de la Llave, worked tirelessly alongside the radicals Juan Sánchez and Arnulfo San Germán (whose *El Ideal* emerged as a Juarista newspaper) for his candidacy. The campaign rapidly gained momentum among Oaxacans. As Sierra Juárez caudillos Fidencio Hernández and Guillermo Meixueiro explained to Porfirio Díaz later that year, "it is understood that they are in love with the sacred name of Juárez."[11]

The Vallistocrat press of the city of Oaxaca attacked Don Beno viciously. *El Correo del Sur* alleged that he could not "possibly be any competition for Sr. Pimentel" since his "meager political significance to be able to figure in the upcoming elections" was "public and notorious." *El Voto Público* reprinted a scathing article from Mexico City's pro-Científico *El Debate* that condemned his ingratitude to Díaz. It also repeated *El Tiempo*'s insult on the formation of the Partido Democrático in 1909: "Sr. Juárez, who is an honorable man, . . . has done nothing, nor performed any act that would make him stand out in national politics. . . . There is only the name, that of Juárez; but if there is a name, there is no man behind it."[12] Such demeaning attacks on Juárez Maza intensified precisely because his surname posed the strongest threat imaginable to the status quo in Oaxaca.

But while working jointly with the radicals[13] for this new Juarismo, moderate oppositionists had still not thrown their support to Madero and the Antireeleccionista party nationwide. In contrast, the city of Oaxaca's radical pro-Maderista artisans had formed the "Club Central Antirreleccionista de Oaxaca" and postulated Juárez Maza for governor on April 10. They received the congratulations of the National Antirreleccionista Convention in Mexico City on their choice of a "democrat of the highest standing." The Normal School students' Club Estudiantil "Lic. Verdad" (including women such as Juana Ruiz) worked with them to disseminate Maderista and Juarista propaganda. Victoriano D. Báez joined them and Leopoldo García's paper *La Sombra de Juárez* became the voice of the pro-Maderista students. Even students from the traditionally more conservative Institute of Science and Art, such as Manuel Herrera and Celestino Pérez, collaborated with the Maderistas of the Normal.[14]

The 1910 Juárez Maza candidacy excited considerable enthusiasm in the Sierra Norte, the family's *patria chica* (the locality from which the family came). Although Juarismo and Porfirismo were at odds throughout the nation, in the highlands, Serranos failed to see a contradiction between supporting Porfirio Díaz for president and Benito Juárez Maza for governor.[15] Seriously alarmed by these developments, caudillos Guillermo Meixueiro and Fidencio Hernández addressed an open letter to Serranos:

> Oaxaca de Juárez, Oaxaca. June 4, 1910. To municipal presidents, agents, and principals of the Sierra Juárez. My dear friends and countrymen: We are aware that motivated by the upcoming gubernatorial election, some people have tried to provoke disturbances in the district, availing themselves of the respectable name of our dear friend, don Benito Juárez, junior. They who do this are not sincere friends of the serrano towns, because without a doubt they would like us to appear to the Republic and go down in History as disloyal ingrates. You and the rest of our brothers know that since the revolution of 1876, the Sierra Juárez, by the unanimous vote of its citizens, proclaimed as Supreme Military chief our present president, General don Porfirio Díaz, to whom we protested solemn fidelity and adhesion. At the same time the Sierra solemnly offered that as long as he lived the serranos would never oppose General Díaz's instructions or programs and at all moments second him with effectiveness and good will. . . . As we are always consistent with our commitments, we must vote in favor of Lic. Pimentel.[16]

Still General Díaz did not take Juárez Maza's campaign any more seriously than he was taking Madero's challenge nationwide. He was, however, annoyed by the personal ingratitude of Juárez Maza. Pimentel had informed Díaz that Don Beno was abusing the name of Díaz "to the ignorant . . . making them believe that you had sent Benito. I don't think he will find any echo." The president responded: "It's over a year since Benito has shown his face around here, since he joined his first [political] club. Therefore whatever he says about me is not true. I believe he is a man who is so lacking in seriousness that he is really not dangerous."[17]

Don Beno arrived in Etla on June 11, 1910. The enthusiastic welcome he received contrasted with the lackluster reception for Madero six months before. But when the Juaristas tried to meet on Fortín Hill, under the statue of the candidate's father overlooking the city of Oaxaca, the authorities foiled their plans, just as they had done to Madero the previous December.[18] The Pimentel regime was not about to enable Juárez Maza's followers to lay claim to the great reformer or help them further splinter the unifying liberal myth.

On June 14, Juárez Maza left for Mexico City. From Tehuacán, he issued a manifesto "to the democratic sons of Oaxaca" and promised Oaxaca's "patriotic and democratic people" that if elected "he would follow to the best of his abilities the example of his VENERABLE FATHER when he was governor of Oaxaca."[19] Never shy about employing his father's name to garner support, his whole campaign tour of Oaxaca had lasted a paltry three days. Díaz had, perhaps, assessed Juárez Maza's reliability correctly.

The native-son slate supported by the moderate opposition for the 1910 elections—Porfirio Díaz for president, Félix Díaz for vice president, and Benito Juárez Maza for governor—revealed the intrinsic contradictions of what I have called Oaxaca's dual legacy.[20] Oaxacans' primary loyalties were tied to Juárez and Díaz, a formula that had ensured southern ascendancy for over fifty years, and that dual legacy was inseparable in many minds. Yet elsewhere in Mexico (and among Oaxacan radicals), the opposition was reinventing Juarismo as a weapon to be used against the dictatorship. Don Beno's brief campaign reflected his own ambivalence, insecurity, and doubt. As heir apparent, he was particularly well situated to knock Oaxaca off the fence, but unfortunately he lacked the political acumen and will to captain the opposition.

Two days before the election, a manifesto "to the artisans and to the people" appeared, signed by 260 members of the "Josefa Ortiz de Domínguez Feminist Group." These "wives and daughters of artisans and of humble wage laborers" spoke out "to alert all citizens to vote and elect C. Benito Juárez[,] father of the people[,] who knows how to treat us with tenderness and affection." They declared that "women should encourage men to struggle in an orderly and peaceful manner for the people's causes and if there are still men who are cowardly and effeminate who for fear or for convenience are not resolved to take active part in the campaign of the people's only candidate Benito Juárez, then we will encourage and inspire them with the civil valor that they lack." This manifesto turned the tables on the affronts to Don Beno's virility, by insisting that the only manly thing to do was to support this paternal figure. And if the men hesitated, female Juarista courage would rouse them to action.[21]

Official returns from the June 26 elections indicated an easy victory for Pimentel, who received 149,808 votes, while 11,468 voted for Juárez Maza (there were 353 votes for various other candidates). The latter did, however, carry the district of Ixtlán of the Sierra Juárez, despite the caudillos' warnings. Don Beno's showing was also strong in the Centro and Zimatlán districts.[22] Given the workings of the Porfirista political machine, the true vote count will probably never be known.

El Ideal denounced Pimentel's victory as a "shameful triumph" imposed "by brute force." The Juaristas challenged the election results and carried their protest and demand for nullification to the local legislature, the National Congress, and the Supreme Court (which dismissed the case). Veracruz's governor Teodoro Dehesa advised Díaz to accede to a Juárez Maza victory in order to calm tensions while a commission of Serranos from Ixtlán brought him a similar petition. As usual he rejected any perceived imposition. But dissident political activity had ignited Mexico as opposition gubernatorial candidates challenged the Porfirista political machine. No sooner had the celebrations of the centennial of Mexican independence ended, then the Chamber of Deputies declared Porfirio Díaz president for the eighth time and rejected the Maderista demand for nullification, setting the stage for revolution.[23]

THE REVOLUTION IN OAXACA

Contrary to popular belief, an active opposition existed in the patria chica of Porfirio Díaz. In January 1911, Sebastián Ortiz rose up in Ojitlán in the district of Tuxtepec. In February, a revolutionary conspiracy was uncovered in the city of Oaxaca and those implicated were thrown in jail. For example, Luis Jiménez Figueroa and his father, José Ruiz Jiménez, both longtime dissidents, were picked up on February 2, along with Partido Democrático propaganda and numerous letters from Juárez Maza and Díaz Quintas. Other dissidents had missives from those who would soon lead the revolution in the Cañada and the Mixteca, as well as from Sebastián Ortiz.[24]

In March 1911, Díaz eliminated the Científicos from his cabinet and governorships in an effort to shore up his government. Pimentel solicited a leave of absence in Oaxaca. In the next six weeks, Oaxaca had six different regimes, a crisis dubbed the "Dance of the Governors" by historian Francisco José Ruiz Cervantes. But despite revolutionary uprisings throughout the nation and in various regions of Oaxaca, the Vallistocracia still controlled the local congress. They elected none other than Brigadier General Félix Díaz—don Porfirio's nephew—as provisional governor, provoking a furious popular reaction. Oaxacans gathered spontaneously in the streets in demonstrations and loudly rejected the dictator's nephew while they proclaimed Benito Juárez Maza as the people's candidate for governor.[25] While Maderista armies converged on the state capital from the Mixteca and the Cañada, the election of Félix Díaz by the elite-controlled local legislature polarized and destabilized the situation further.

The moderate Juaristas in the state capital saw this conjuncture as the ideal opportunity for Juárez Maza to come to power. During the Ciudad Juárez negotiations, the Maderistas had suggested the appointment of friendly governors and cabinet members to ensure the return to order: José María Maytorena for Sonora, Abraham González for Chihuahua, and Benito Juárez Maza for Oaxaca. Of those three Maderistas, however, only González became interim governor. Porfiristas still made the decisions in the state capital of Oaxaca, and Félix Díaz, en route to the city, was still the legal governor of the state. When Porfirio Díaz submitted his resignation to Congress on May 25, only two deputies voted against this resignation, one of whom was Benito Juárez Maza. This last gesture of loyalty to the dual legacy was useless, since the vote was a foregone conclusion.[26]

Finally, on June 8, 1911, the local congress elected Heliodoro Díaz Quintas provisional governor. Moderate liberal, founder of the Asociación Juárez, longtime supporter of Juárez Maza, and eleventh-hour Maderista, Díaz Quintas represented the symbolic victory of the revolution in Oaxaca. His main task was to oversee the elections for governor in July in which Félix Díaz faced off against Juárez Maza. Juarista and Felicista Clubs immediately appeared in Oaxacan cities and towns, despite the fact that neither of these candidates fulfilled the residency requirement of having lived in the state for the previous three years. On July 7, a pitched battle between Juaristas and Felicistas left five dead and many wounded in Ocotlán. As the provisional government prepared the nation for general elections in October, Oaxacan politics seemed dangerously trapped in the dual legacy.[27]

Once again "feminist" clubs mobilized for the Juárez Maza campaign in the city of Oaxaca, and in Ocotlán, Ejutla, Tlacolula, and Teposcolula. Other feminista clubs formed to further the candidacy of Díaz, for example, in Ocotlán, and this led to a public debate in the Oaxaca city press. The Juarista *El Avance* supported women's right to political participation (although not to vote) and published feminist manifestos. The Felicista *Regeneración* ridiculed women's groups and impugned the morality of those who participated while *Sufragio Libre* encouraged women to get involved if they supported Félix Díaz. Although neither side suggested it, *El*

Correo del Sur asserted that to give women the vote would be "immoral, absurd and impolitic."[28]

By this time, Madero was seriously unhappy with both candidates, who had previously supported his rival, General Bernardo Reyes. Clearly opposed to Félix Díaz, he also questioned the competence of Juárez Maza. Madero wrote provisional president Francisco León de la Barra that he never "believed that Juárez Maza had the ability to be governor." Madero wondered if state authorities could not delay the election until they could find a more suitable candidate. De la Barra asked Díaz Quintas if this were possible, to which Juárez Maza's closest associate replied that it would only increase tensions in the state. Both Madero and de la Barra had to agree. Oaxacan anti-reelectionists would soon annoy Madero further when they rejected his new running mate for the vice presidency, José María Pino Suárez, and insisted on voting for Francisco Vázquez Gómez.[29]

JUÁREZ MAZA, REVOLUTIONARY GOVERNOR?

Benito Juárez Maza was elected governor of Oaxaca on July 30, 1911, with 169,854 votes against his opponent Félix Díaz, who received 4,562 votes. He was inaugurated on September 23 and two weeks later, he appointed Díaz Quintas secretary of government (whom many believed to be the power behind the throne). Although this was the governorship that many Oaxacans had long anticipated, his regime lasted a mere seven months since he died of a heart attack on April 20, 1912.[30] Put into power by the revolution, one wonders what reform projects he might have undertaken had he had more time. In a mere seven months, his accomplishments were few.

In fairness to Juárez Maza, he was faced with almost constant political upheaval, uprisings, invasions of forces from neighboring states, and outright rebellions. In September, Zapatista incursions in the districts of Silacayoapan and Huajuapan in the Mixteca demanded his attention. In October, there were disturbances in Tehuantepec and Nochixtlán, and then separate rebellions in the Cañada and the Papaloapan regions. An ongoing confrontation with José F. Gómez boiled over in November and led to the major rebellion of his period in Juchitán. In December, a confrontation in Tlalixtac in the Central Valleys would lead to another serious uprising, the Ixtepejana Rebellion.[31]

A look at the list of laws and decrees emitted during his regime shows practically no policy initiatives, although Juárez Maza did take some liberal stances. In a letter to Oaxacan lawyer Manuel Brioso y Candiani, he asserted that "rudimentary schools" should be set up in the most isolated areas, for example, the Chinantla and Mixes, "where there is no sign of culture at all."

Discounting the customs and traditions of these indigenous peoples as culture, he declared that his government was dedicated to "work in the most efficient way" toward the "improvement of the indigenous race and the development of our progress."[32]

As a Juarista liberal, Juárez Maza believed fervently in the power of education. He advocated before the local congress for the establishment of new schools, such as in San Blas Guichixu in Tehuantepec. He inaugurated various schools in the city of Oaxaca, such as the "Enrique Rebsamen" (January 1912). In December 1911, deputy Faustino G. Olivera, a radical teacher jailed by Pimentel, recommended to the state congress that the governor's salary be reduced so that the difference would go to support two or three more schools. Juárez Maza ignored this suggestion as well as Olivera's impassioned plea to increase teachers' salaries.[33]

In March 1912, the construction workers of the city of Oaxaca appealed to Juárez Maza to establish a minimum salary and maximum hours of the workday. While the governor recognized the laboring class as "one of the bases of any democratic regime" and deserving of protection, he believed that the state government should "not involve itself in affairs that are outside its purview." As a laissez-faire liberal, he envisioned the government as a "regulating power" that should "not intervene in everything." Thus, "any improvements should not attack the law or established social order," "trample on private interests," or "limit individual initiative." Dodging the ball, he recommended further study of the question and his untimely death cut off the possibility of a solution.[34]

Throughout his short seven months in office, Juárez Maza faced a radical faction in the state legislature led by Faustino G. Olivera and Rafael Odriozola, leaders of the revolution in Oaxaca. On November 7, Olivera demanded that the government "rectify" its appointments of unpopular officials in the districts, alluding directly to the crisis in Juchitán. On November 23 he attacked the proposed budget and demanded that the *capitación*, the hated regressive head tax, be reduced. As noted above, he also advocated for educational causes. None of these initiatives were successful, nor did they receive the governor's support. Although Juárez Maza had declared the abolition of the *jefaturas políticas* as one of his goals, this was not accomplished either.[35]

In a highly symbolic decision, the governor refused to grant permission for the traditional celebration of the Battle of April 2, commemorating the victory of Porfirio Díaz over the French. When a young woman placed a bouquet of flowers at the monument to the battle on the Calzada Porfirio Díaz on April 2, the police chief ordered them to be removed. A few hours later, groups of Porfiristas came to her aid and then marched (sans permission) shouting "mueras" (death) to Madero, Díaz Quintas, and *jefe político* Chapital. Cornered by the police, they congregated at the house of

Guillermo Meixueiro, where they were well received. They continued to roam the streets that night, throwing rocks, breaking windows, and causing general alarm. The governor later explained to Meixueiro that he had prohibited the demonstration fearing that it would be used to excite the "multitudes" against the state and national government and even lead to bloodshed. In a frank letter to Juan Chapital, he accused the organizers of being Felicistas, clericals, and Pimentelistas, yet he did not connect his decision to a defense of the revolution.[36]

Both Díaz Quintas and Juárez Maza considered private property sacrosanct when Oaxaca's haciendas came under threat. In August 1911, twenty-five Maderistas invaded the estates of Esteban Maqueo Castellanos, who feared they intended to divide up his land. Although Díaz Quintas admitted that this well-known Científico "managed his haciendas as if he were a viceroy," he provided the needed protection and guarantees when so ordered by President de la Barra. In March 1912, the *terrazgueros* (sharecroppers) of the Hacienda Valdeflores, property of the wealthy Spaniard Wenceslao García, appealed to Governor Juárez Maza because local authorities in Zimatlán refused to deal with their complaints of harsh and demeaning treatment by overseers. Juárez Maza arranged an audience between the workers and García to air their differences but the hacendado failed to appear or send a representative. Highly irritated, the governor reached an agreement with the sharecroppers reaffirming their right to freely cut wood in the hacienda's forests and pasture their animals on the hacienda's lands, and promising that no *faenas* (Sunday work) should be imposed, which he communicated to Wenceslao García by letter. He also ordered the jefe político to ensure that the sharecroppers were treated "prudently" and given "guarantees," and again wrote to García requesting that he correct the behavior of his employees.[37] Thus, in this case, the governor backed the terrazgueros of the Central Valleys in defense of their customs and traditions.

Unrest plagued Juárez Maza throughout his governorship. On September 18 and 19, Zapatista incursions in the northwest corner of the state, some led by Zapata himself, attacked border towns in the district of Silacayoapan looking for recruits and supplies. In October, the Zapatistas occupied the district capital and sacked local commercial establishments. These incursions continued sporadically in Silacayoapan, Huajuapan, and Coixtlahuaca for the entire period. In the south, in October, a violent confrontation between two barrios of Tehuantepec resulted in six dead and ten wounded, including the assassination of Porfirista lawyer Carlos Woolrich. The supporters of the arbitrary jefe político Alfonso Santibáñez and his brothers, who supposedly represented the revolutionary forces, were responsible. With the powerful Woolrich family demanding justice, the governor sent in Constantino Chapital to calm the situation. Santibáñez was relieved of his post and sent to prison.[38]

In the district of Nochixtlán, residents had been complaining to the minister of the Interior on the lack of "guarantees" and "security." Resentment of Spanish merchants, a constant of the revolution throughout Mexico, reared up in Nochixtlán on the night of October 8, when fifteen intoxicated locals shouting "death to Gachupines" attempted to sack the store of Gregorio Pardo. He armed his employees and servants, who forced the attackers to flee. But the local municipal authorities refused to help, given their sympathies for the perpetrators, the Avendaño clan, who were influential Maderistas. By October 11, the governor had sent in forces but conflict continued between local political factions.[39] Trying to steer a neutral course, Juárez Maza did not always take a clear stand for those allied with the Revolution.

THE CHEGOMISTA REBELLION IN JUCHITÁN

The governor faced his most serious challenge on November 2, 1911, when the Juchitecos rebelled against the imposition of an unpopular jefe político. This conflict, and *istmeño* separatism in general, had its roots in the region's longstanding resentment over the Vallistocracia's dominance of state politics. The Isthmus of Tehuantepec (Oaxacan and Veracruzana portions) had briefly existed as a distinct province on two occasions (1823–1824 and 1852–1855). As governor, Benito Juárez García had faced a drawn out battle with the Juchitecos over communal rights to salt flats and grazing lands in the isthmian rebellions of the 1840s and 1850s, which turned into his greatest defeat. The issue for Juárez senior as well as Juárez junior was the defense of state sovereignty between a rebellious region and the intervention of the federal government.[40]

José F. Gómez ("Che"), of a comfortable ranching family of Juchitán, had studied law at Oaxaca's Institute of Science and Art. Elected municipal president of Juchitán in 1893, Che Gómez's popularity emanated from his role as intermediary for the indigenous pueblos vis-à-vis the state and his defense of communal customs and traditions, which gave villages rights to pasture their livestock on private lands and to use the region's salt flats. The powerful Juchiteco congressman, Rosendo Pineda (a Científico), who represented private interests affected by those rights, convinced Porfirio Díaz to remove Gómez from Juchitán for many years to bureaucratic posts outside the state, even as far away as Baja California.[41]

Che Gómez returned to Juchitán in 1910. Although he was on a first-name basis with Porfirio Díaz, in 1911 he considered himself representative of the revolution and was elected municipal president of the town, taking over on May 28. He clearly intended to utilize his great popularity and that of the Verdes (green party) now that they had defeated the Rojos (red

Porfirista party). But his means were not democratic when, according to Henderson, he attempted to suppress rival newspapers (*El Demócrata*) or imprison his enemies. As municipal president, he ran for deputy to the state congress from Juchitán and won, but in truth, the post he most desired was jefe político of his district. This brought him into direct confrontation with authorities in the city of Oaxaca who saw him as a threat to their authority on the isthmus.[42]

Although he labeled his enemies "Científicos and Porfiristas," they actually were the most avid supporters of Benito Juárez Maza in Juchitán and maintained close ties with the Juaristas in the city of Oaxaca. In June 1911, when the state government was considering the appointment of Francisco León as jefe político, Gómez reacted vigorously since this army colonel had brutally quashed a rebellion in Juchitán in 1882. He warned Governor Díaz Quintas that if the state government attempted to make "impositions from the past," it would find itself in "serious difficulties."[43]

The government gave in and instead named Gómez's brother-in-law, Julio González, on a provisional basis. But when his period concluded, Che Gómez took over as jefe politico, leaving his cousin Félix O. Gómez as municipal president. This growing family dominance was intolerable to Díaz Quintas and Juárez Maza, who named Enrique León to the post on October 25. Always the astute politician, Gómez advised León that he was agreeable to stepping down, but given the "unassailable will of the people" and their "threatening attitude," he could not yet hand over the jefatura política lest it result in a "conflict of grave consequences." He telegraphed president de la Barra on October 27 that the state government was provoking a revolution by this imposition, this "felony," and that Juchitecos as "free people" needed to sustain a government "attuned to its temperament and exigencies." A group of Juchiteco merchants assured the president that Gómez should continue as jefe político because he protected private property and enjoyed the "full confidence of the people." In contrast, Juárez Maza reported to de la Barra that Che Gómez intended to "establish caciquismo and absolute domination in that region, including its separation from the state of Oaxaca."[44] The governor's authority was being challenged by Oaxaca's historically most rebellious region.

Having arrived in Juchitán on October 30, Enrique León immediately requested the handover of the jefatura política. On November 2 when he reiterated his demand, some two thousand Juchitecos rebelled and assaulted the local barracks where he was located (federal forces numbering only two hundred soldiers). The battle lasted four hours and attacks continued for the next three days until reinforcements arrived, leaving hundreds of casualties on both sides. The rebellion quickly spread to Santiago Guevea, Chihuitán, Laollaga, and Guichivere. In Oaxaca, *El Avance* accused Gómez of an alliance with Emilio Vázquez Gómez, who had broken with the Madero government, and particularly with Angel Barrios and Manuel Oseguera, who had seconded the Vazquezgomista movement (but continued to support Juárez Maza) from the Cañada region of Oaxaca on November 6. In November, Félix Castrejón, an engineer, and his followers rebelled, thereby seconding the Vazquista Plan of Tacubaya in Valle Nacional in the northern district of Tuxtepec.[45]

Francisco Madero was inaugurated on November 6, 1911. Four days later, Juárez Maza asked him for federal support for the Oaxacan state government in this conflict. The governor warned that "the treasonous hand of Emilio Pimentel and the Científico Party" were anxious to "engineer an estrangement" between them. Juárez Maza also accused Che Gómez of wanting to "form a little republic similar to those of Central America or even negotiate control of the Isthmus with the North Americans." Facing various uprisings and seeking a quick solution to unrest in a geographically strategic region, Madero directly intervened in the internal affairs of Oaxaca, exceeding his powers as president. In mid-November and without consulting Juárez Maza, he sent in General Gabriel Gavira, accompanied by Cándido Aguilar, to negotiate a peace. Gavira convinced Gómez to agree to travel to Mexico City with a guarantee of safe conduct to discuss the charges of rebellion pending against him. Aguilar would act as provisional jefe político until a popular plebiscite would elect a new jefe político. This intervention infuriated Juárez Maza, who reiterated to Enrique León that he was only to obey orders from the state government and not to hand over the jefatura política.[46]

On November 24, the Oaxacan state legislature petitioned the national congress to comply with Article 116 of the Constitution: to protect the state and send in federal forces to repress the rebellion. General Telésforo Merodio in the army's headquarters on the Isthmus in San Gerónimo found himself in the middle of a head-on collision between the state and federal governments. When he informed León that he was waiting for orders from the secretary of war, Juárez Maza sent him a telegram: "I understand that you are trying to resolve affairs related to Juchitán that only this government can decide. I inform you that I am prepared to sustain the sovereignty of this state and any act that may perturb it will incur the consequences."[47]

Nonetheless, Madero had previously communicated to governors that the revolution signified respect for the popular will and that they should refrain from impositions of unpopular officials. In a heated session on November 24, secretary of foreign relations Manuel Calero informed the Chamber of Deputies that Madero had privately suggested to the governor of Oaxaca that he "sacrifice a little of his official pride" and withdraw León if it would assure peace. The president had supposedly told Juárez Maza, "I won't lend you even one more soldier or Mauser if it is to sustain an unpopular jefe político." With this information, the Chamber of Deputies voted 106 to 16 against sending federal troops to Juchitán. Having failed to get federal aid, Juárez Maza decided to personally travel to Juchitán to "reestablish the constitutional regime" on the Isthmus.[48]

He arrived in San Gerónimo Ixtepec on December 4 to find that Che Gómez (en route to Mexico City) was at the same station and desired to speak with him. Juárez Maza absolutely refused and demanded that General Merodio immediately apprehend Gómez and hand him over to the local authorities. The General declined since Gómez carried a safe conduct pass signed by Madero. The governor, then, sent telegrams to local Oaxacan and Veracruz authorities on the Isthmus to arrest Gómez, emphasizing that his life be protected. The municipal president of Rincón Antonio (today Matías Romero) obeyed and imprisoned the Juchiteco and his escort.[49]

According to Rómulo Espinosa, who had gone to Rincón Antonio that day to sell coffee, the town was buzzing with the rumor that Che Gómez and his followers were to be murdered. At midnight on December 5, local police let Tomás Carballo, alias "Matanche," and his men take the prisoners from the jail to a nearby ranch where they executed eight of them, including Gómez (who had fifty-two bullet wounds). They later claimed that unknown bandits had assaulted the escort. The general consensus in Oaxaca was that Juárez Maza had given the orders. In his report to the local congress on December 21, Díaz Quintas recounted the numerous precautions taken to assure protection to Gómez, citing various telegrams sent to authorities. Nevertheless, in her testimony at the 1915 trial of "Matanche," Rosaura Bustamante, Gómez's widow, alleged that Juárez Maza's motivation for the murder was that her husband carried a letter from Juárez Maza, in which he proposed to forgive the Juchitecan rebellion if Gómez agreed to enlist in the cause of General Bernardo Reyes against the Madero government.[50]

With Gómez out of the way, Juárez Maza went to Juchitán on December 6 and offered an amnesty to Juchitecos who would put down their arms. By December 13, 2,474 locals had done so, although various bands continued to threaten the countryside. In January 1912, these guerrillas caused great alarm as they roamed the Isthmus. The main contingent of Chegomistas commanded by Felipe López did not lay down their arms until July 1912.[51]

THE BATALLÓN SIERRA JUÁREZ AND FURTHER UNREST

When Che Gómez rebelled, the governor had turned to his father's *paisanos*, who organized three distinct companies of Serranos, or mountain peoples, (in order to keep volunteers from feuding villages separate) in mid-November to safeguard the Central Valleys. The state government footed the bill for their equipment and training. When Juárez Maza returned to the city of Oaxaca in mid-December, the Sierra Juárez Battalion received him warmly. The second and third companies were disbanded on December 18; only the first, composed of volunteers from Nexicho and Ixtepeji, remained in service until his death.[52]

On December 7, the acting governor, Constantino Chapital, had sent a commission of Rurales to capture Manuel Carrasco, a local cacique responsible for various murders, in the town of Tlalixtac in the Central Valleys. They were unsuccessful and forced to flee, leaving one dead and various wounded. On December 28, Juárez Maza sent the remaining Sierra Juárez Batallion and a squad of Rurales after Carrasco, who was hiding out in Cuajimoloyas. On their way back to the capital with their captives, they also had to battle locals in Tlalixtac, where eight people died. Given the warlike reputation of these Serranos and their longstanding conflict over boundaries with Tlalixtac, this caused great alarm not only in Tlalixtac but also in the city of Oaxaca lest the intervillage feuding of these towns spill over into open conflict. In effect, with the death of their sponsor, the surviving battalion fled to the Sierra Juárez on April 24, 1912. A few weeks later their leader, Pedro León, was executed in a wave of repression unleashed by the new governor Alberto Montiel. This spark set off the bloody Ixtepejana Rebellion, which culminated in the razing of that town.[53]

In effect, unrest continued to plague Juárez Maza's governorship. In early January, combat between federal forces and those of Oseguera was reported in the Cañada. There were riots over a municipal election on the Costa Chica, near the border with Guerrero, and Zapatistas continued their incursions into the Mixteca. In early February, the governor strongly defended his secretary of government when workers demonstrated publicly against Heliodoro Díaz Quintas's arbitrary manner of governing. On February 14, the Vazquistas attacked Etla in the Central Valleys to forage for supplies, shouting *vivas* for Vázquez Gómez and Juárez Maza and *mueras* to Madero, even as they engaged federal forces.

The town of Chalcatongo was attacked by a force of over a thousand men from neighboring rival villages that murdered, sacked, and burned much of the town. In March, two hundred men at the command of Guadalupe Gómez terrorized the area around Tamazulapan. Longtime dissident Luis Jiménez Figueroa had also joined the rebellion in the Mixteca. In early April in Huajuapan, other groups seconded the Vazquezgomistas. Another group of foragers attacked the hacienda of San José Lagarzona in Ocotlán in the Central Valleys and was pushed back by the sharecroppers.[54]

CONCLUSION: DEATH AND LEGACY

Juárez Maza died suddenly on April 20, 1912, in the city of Oaxaca. His body was transported to Mexico City, where it was honored in the halls of

Congress. Although the doctors agreed that he had succumbed to a heart attack, rumors of poisoning circulated among the populace because the evening before he had dined with Lt. Rubén Morales, a Madero aide sent to negotiate with him. Already extremely resentful of Madero for his meddling in the internal affairs of the state, Oaxacans were quick to blame him for the death of their governor.[55]

Benito Juárez Maza had never been a revolutionary, so we could hardly expect him to be a revolutionary governor. Although his campaigns for governor had united moderates and radicals and were waged in the context of the revolution, his public speeches and announcements rarely referred to this epic. When challenged by the radicals in the state legislature to support their proposals of progressive legislation, he refused. In regional conflicts, he often failed to support the local revolutionaries. He defended private property as well as the traditions and customs of the indigenous peoples. While he took a paternalistic attitude to the working classes, he stopped short of regulating working conditions, one of the revolution's major goals. Although championed by women, he did not institute any progressive policies in their favor either. At each conjuncture, he failed to build a base among the middle and working classes that had supported his election. In contrast, he got on very well with the Vallistocracia—*El Avance* chronicled various soirées held in his honor attended by the city of Oaxaca's high society.[56] Perhaps only when irked, as in the case of Wenceslao García, did he act against them. Given this ambivalence and lack of revolutionary purpose, he set the stage for the reassertion of political dominance of the Vallistocracia and the ensuing repression of revolutionary forces that followed his death.

Although he was a mason and Juarista liberal, the similarities with his father stop there, as demonstrated by their different handling of the Juchitecos, the major thorn in the Juárez family side. Juárez senior, who understood that politics was about compromise and transaction, could be flexible and accept defeat. Juárez junior was rigid, tactless, and single-minded. When faced with Juchiteco defiance, Juárez senior first tried to compromise, then tried to defeat them, and finally had to accede to their customs and traditions (although he did quash their separatist state). Juárez junior, when confronted with that same resolution and lacking federal support, became even more stubborn in defense of state sovereignty.

Oaxaca has a history of defending state sovereignty over federal intervention and on two previous occasions (and again in 1915), it had reassumed its sovereignty vis-à-vis the federal government. But at no time did Juárez Maza threaten to withdraw recognition from the Madero government; on the contrary, his objective was to reaffirm states' rights in relation to federal powers. Nevertheless, he tactlessly threatened General Merodio. Was he thinking of pitting the Batallón Sierra Juárez against the federal army? And, did he actually order the elimination of his nemesis? It is difficult to believe him guilty of such a colossal error, when he was actually in the vicinity. But if he was not the intellectual author of Gómez's execution, he must be held responsible for the failure to protect the life of this popular leader. Che Gómez's murder created a martyr to Istmeño separatism and destroyed the credibility of Juárez Maza's government, if not in the state capital, certainly in the rest of Mexico.

Although he had not lived in Oaxaca since the age of seven, Juárez Maza suffered from the same myopic localism prevalent among the state's moderates, who were impervious to the significance of the revolution taking place around them. Stubbornly defending the sovereignty of the state government in its internal affairs against the intromission of the federal government, he failed to see the context of this conflict or understand Madero's desire to bring peace to a highly strategic area.

Most scholars writing about Juárez Maza have judged him to be inept, if not a "dolt," following the opinions of Madero and de la Barra. In his day, his opponents questioned his masculinity, making both gubernatorial campaigns so much a question of virility that the women of Oaxaca defended him. Peter Henderson reminds us that enlightened kings are often followed by mediocre offspring. Nevertheless, perhaps this is an unfair judgment. Had he not been the son of the Liberal Reformer, he might have had a distinguished career as a diplomat. The Ministry of Foreign Relations thought enough of his diplomatic skills that they sent him to inspect Mexico's consular offices in Germany, France, and Belgium in 1901.[57]

Juárez Maza was clearly not cut out for a life in the political spotlight. Sadly, he found himself in the middle of a twentieth-century revolution, where contending groups were vying to appropriate the legacy of his father and use his name for their own purposes. But clearly enjoying the attention his surname brought him and never loathe to play upon it, he could not resist the lure of Mexican politics. Unfortunately, in contrast to other revolutionaries, he never learned how to use the shadow of his father to make the revolution his own.

NOTES

1. I am grateful to María Isabel Grañen Porrúa, Francisco Toledo, and Francisco José Ruiz Cervantes for help accessing archival material for this study.

2. Charles A. Hale, *The Transformation of Liberalism in Late Nineteenth-Century Mexico* (Princeton, NJ: Princeton University Press, 1989), 9, 59, 256; Richard N. Sinkin, *The Mexican Reform, 1855–1876: A Study in Liberal Nation Building* (Austin: Institute for Latin American Studies, University of Texas, 1979), 77–79, 169; Andrés Portillo et al., *Oaxaca en el centenario de independencia. Noticias históricas y estadísticas de la ciudad de Oaxaca y algunas leyendas tradicionales* (Oaxaca: Imprenta del Estado, 1910), 7–9; Mark Overmyer Velásquez, "Leyendo la ciudad: Modernidades alterna-

tivas en la Oaxaca porfirista," *Todo es Historia* (July–Dec. 2001): 27–28. On civic celebrations, see William H. Beezley, Cheryl English Martin, and William E. French, eds. *Rituals of Rule, Rituals of Resistance: Public Celebrations and Popular Culture in Mexico* (Wilmington, DE: Scholarly Resources, 1994).

3. See Eugenio Klerian, D. *Benito Juárez. Biografía histórica* (Mexico City: Editorial Orion, 1966), 91–93. On the Asociación Juárez of Oaxaca, see Francie R. Chassen-López, "Los orígenes de la revolución en Oaxaca: Juarismo y porfirismo contra precursores y revolucionarios," *Eslabones* 5 (1993): 118–37, and *From Liberal to Revolutionary Oaxaca: The View from the South; México, 1867–1911* (University Park: Pennsylvania State University Press, 2004), ch. 10. On the Juárez cult, see Charles Weeks, *The Juárez Myth in Mexico* (Tuscaloosa: University of Alabama Press, 1987).

4. Klerian, *Juárez*, 37–39.

5. Klerian, *Juárez*, 39–42; Alejandro Morales, "Benito Juárez Maza," *Oaxaca Gráfico*, Apr. 25, 1955. In Europe, he became friends with Giuseppe Garibaldi, Victor Hugo, and Leon Gambetta.

6. Klerian, *Juárez*, 37–45; *Diario del Hogar*, Nov. 30, 1909.

7. In 1888, he headed the Gran Logia de Libres y Aceptados Masones of Mexico City and opposed other logia, especially the Gran Dieta that represented the political ambitions of Porfirio Díaz. Being a mason emerged as critical to advancement in liberal ranks during the nineteenth century and continued on well into the twentieth. Brian Hamnett, *Juárez* (London: Longmans, 1994), 29, 86; Francois-Xavier Guerra, *México: Del antiguo régimen a la revolución* (Mexico City: Fondo de Cultura Económica, 1988), 1:170; Klerian, *Juárez*, 77–80; Jorge Fernando Iturribarría, *Historia de Oaxaca*, vol. 4, *La Restauración de la Repúblicas y las Revueltas de la Noria y Tuxtepec 1867–1877* (Oaxaca: Publicaciones del Gobierno del Estado de Oaxaca, 1956), 194; José C. Valadés, *El Porfirismo: Historia de un régimen. El Crecimiento* (Mexico City: Universidad Nacional Autónoma de México, 1977), 2:292; Francisco Bulnes, *El verdadero Díaz y la revolución* (Mexico City: Ediciones Coma, 1982 [1920]), 142, 181; Jean-Pierre Bastián, "Jacobinismo y ruptura revolucionaria durante el Porfiriato," *Mexican Studies* 7, no. 1 (1991): 33.

8. Flyer, Copiadores Benito Juárez Maza, located in caja 6 1815–1912, Burgoa Library, Universidad Autónoma Benito Juárez de Oaxaca [hereafter CBJM]; see also Chassen-López, *From Liberal to Revolutionary Oaxaca*, 454–60. An earlier attempt to revive the liberal party took place in 1895, see Jean-Pierre Bastián, "Las sociedades protestantes y la oposición a Porfirio Díaz, 1877–1911," *Historia Mexicana* 37, no. 3 (1988): 490–92.

9. José López Portillo y Rojas, *Elevación y caída de Porfirio Díaz*, 2nd ed. (Mexico City: Editorial Porrúa, 1975), 387–92; Ricardo García Granados, *Historia de México desde la restauración de la República en 1867 hasta la caída de Huerta* (México City: Editorial Jus, 1956), 2:45–50; Klerian, *Juárez*, 81. Klerian says he was the Partido Liberal Rojo's candidate for vice president in 1904.

10. "Carta abierta dirigida al Señor General D. Porfirio Díaz, Presidente de los Estados Unidos Mexicanos," June 1909, in *Bibliografía política y civismo*, Colocación 3, Fondo Manuel Brioso y Candiani, Burgoa Library, University of Oaxaca; "Voto de gratitud y confianza de la Sociedad Oaxaqueña al Sr. Gobernador del Estado, Lic. Emilio Pimentel," Flyer Oaxaca, Oaxaca, July 14, 1909, 1. See *Proceso de la administración del Señor Lic. D. Emilio Pimentel* (Oaxaca: 1910), which was most likely written by

Heliodoro Díaz Quintas although it was signed by a list of fictitious names. On Juárez Maza's 1910 campaign, see Martínez Medina, "La campaña electoral para gobernador del estado de Oaxaca en 1910" in *Lecturas históricas del estado de Oaxaca*, vol. 4, 1877–1930, ed. María de los Angeles Romero Frizzi (Mexico City: Instituto Nacional de Antropología e Historia, 1990), 172 ff.; *El Correo del Sur*, Apr. 5, 1910.

11. Jorge Tamayo, *Oaxaca en el siglo XX* (Mexico City: 1956), 20; Martínez Medina, "La campaña electoral," 178; Iturribarría, *Oaxaca en la historia: De la época precolumbina a los tiempos actuales* (Mexico City: Editorial Stylo, 1955), 263; Alfonso Francisco Ramírez, *Historia de la Revolución Mexicana en Oaxaca* (Mexico City: Instituto Nacional de Estudios Históricos de la Revolución Mexicana, 1970), 19. See also "Siete meses de gobierno de Benito Juárez Maza: Del 23 de septiembre de 1911 al 20 de abril de 1912," *Oaxaca en México*, Apr. 1939, 9–10; Interview with Basilio Rojas, Dec. 8, 1982, Valle de Santiago, Guanajuato. The final quote is cited by Patrick J. McNamara, "Sons of the Sierra: Memory, Patriarchy, and Rural Political Culture in Mexico, 1855–1911" (Ph.D. diss., University of Wisconsin, 1999), 319.

12. *El Correo del Sur*, Apr. 15, 1910; *El Voto Publico*, May 22, 1910; Martínez Medina, "Génesis y desarrollo del maderismo en Oaxaca (1909–1912)," in *La revolución en Oaxaca 1900–1930* (Mexico City: Instituto de Administración Pública de Oaxaca, 1985), 104; Ramón Prida, *De la dictadura a la anarquía* (Mexico City: Ediciones Botas, 1958), 159, 201–5.

13. The main radical leaders, among them Angel Barrios, Plutarco Gallegos, and Miguel Maraver Aguilar, were in jail at this time, either in Mexico City or San Juan de Ulúa, having participated in a failed attempt at rebellion in 1906. See Chassen-López, *From Liberal to Revolutionary Oaxaca*, ch. 10.

14. Báez and García's participation demonstrates the relationship between dissidence and Protestantism in revolutionary Mexico posited by Jean-Pierre Bastián, who cited Juárez Maza as a "frank sympathizer and particular friend" of Protestantism. See Bastián, *Las disidentes: Sociedades protestantes y revolución en México, 1872–1911* (Mexico City: El Colegio de México and Fondo de Cultura Económica, 1991), 134, 224 ff. Celestino Pérez represented Oaxaca at the 1916 Constitutional Convention.

15. See Patrick J. McNamara on the highland enthusiasm for Juárez Maza, *Sons of the Sierra: Juárez, Díaz, and the People of Ixtlán, Oaxaca, 1855–1920* (Chapel Hill: University of North Carolina Press, 2007), 184–85.

16. Cited in Rosendo Pérez García, "Los primeros doce años del siglo XX en la Sierra Juárez, Oaxaca y una revolución de ocho meses," 1958, unpublished manuscript, 19, 30–34. The call to principals refers to the elders and respected senior members of the villages.

17. Eulogio Gillow y Zavalza, *Reminiscencias* (Puebla: Escuela Linotipográfica Salesiana, 1921), 379; Colección Porfirio Díaz [hereafter CPD], Universidad Iberoamericana, Mexico City, Telegrams, leg. 69, caja 4. The code transcription in this telegram is difficult to read and a few words may be incorrect. I am grateful to the Universidad Iberoamericana for permission to cite from this collection.

18. *El Correo del Sur*, June 15, 1910; "Siete meses," 10; see also Héctor Gerardo Martínez Medina and Francie R. Chassen, "El maderismo en Oaxaca," in *Memorias la revolución en las regiones* (Guadalajara: Universidad de Guadalajara, 1986), 1:208 ff.

19. *El Correo del Sur*, June 15, 1910; manifesto in Francisco José Ruiz Cervantes, ed. *Manifestos, planes y documentos políticos del Oaxaca revolucionario 1910–1920* (Oaxaca: Casa de la Cultura, 1987), 13–14.

20. Slate reported to the president by Juarista Ricardo Luna, CPD, Telegrams, leg. 69, caja 4. On the dual legacy, see Chassen-López, *From Liberal to Revolutionary Oaxaca*, ch. 8, 351 ff.

21. "Manifesto of the Agrupación Feminista Josefa Ortiz de Domínguez," in Ruiz Cervantes, *Manifestos, planes*, 15. Although they called themselves "feministas," they still accepted a subordinate role vis-à-vis men.

22. Statistics on this election are unreliable since they were submitted to the Congress by the jefes políticos who manipulated votes. Archivo General del Poder Ejecutivo de Oaxaca [hereafter AGEPEO], 1910, Congreso.

23. Martinez Medina, "Genesis," 97, 107 and "La Campaña electoral," 192–93; "Siete meses," 10; Jorge Vera Estañol, *Historia de la Revolución Mexicana: Orígenes y resultados*, 4th ed. (Mexico City: Porrúa, 1983), 95.

24. AGEPEO, February 1911, Gobierno, Centro, Relativo al movimiento sedicioso en esta capital.

25. *El Avance* was the major newspaper at the time but no institution in Oaxaca has a complete collection. Basilio Rojas summarized each day's news by year in his *Efemérides*, which will be cited here often. *Efemérides Oaxaqueñas 1911* (Mexico City: 1962), 45 ff.; Iturribarría, *Oaxaca*, 269; Francisco José Ruiz Cervantes, *La revolución de Oaxaca: El movimiento de la Soberanía (1915–1920)* (Mexico City: Fondo de Cultura Económica, 1986), 23.

26. Veracruz governor Teodoro Dehesa had advised Díaz to appoint Juárez Maza as governor instead of Félix Díaz when Pimentel took the leave of absence. See Peter V. N. Henderson, *Félix Díaz, the Porfirians, and the Mexican Revolution* (Lincoln: University of Nebraska Press, 1981), 30–31; Francisco Vázquez Gómez, *Memorias políticas 1909–1913* (Mexico City: Universidad Iberamericana and Ediciones "El Caballito," 1982), 191. On May 18, *El Avance* jumped the gun, rushing out a special one-page bulletin announcing "Benito Juárez, Governor of the State of Oaxaca," Boletín, *El Avance*, May 18, 1911. Peter Henderson, *In the Absence of Don Porfirio: Francisco León de la Barra and the Mexican Revolution* (Wilmington, DE: Scholarly Resources, 2000), 47–48. The Vallistocrat state legislature sent this telegram to Díaz on May 27 as he embarked from Veracruz: "The Congress of Oaxaca sends you its most affectionate regards on your departure, protesting to you its gratitude, loyalty and adhesion. History in its final justice will remember your name as one of the greatest benefactors of the fatherland," cited in Ramírez, *Historia*, 23.

27. See Chassen-López, *From Liberal to Revolutionary Oaxaca*, ch. 11; *Efemérides 1911*, 64–65; *El Avance*, June–July 1911. Félix Díaz called for elections and then resigned as governor so as to be eligible to run for the office.

28. See *El Avance*, July 1911, and *El Correo del Sur* cited in *El Avance*, July 26, 1911; *Regeneración*, July 16, 1911; *Sufragio Libre*, July 26, 1911.

29. Juárez Maza had commented to various Oaxacans that Madero would make sure he was elected, which annoyed the latter further. Peter V. N. Henderson, "Un gobernador maderista: Benito Juárez Maza y la revolución en Oaxaca," *Historia Mexicana* 24, no. 3 (1975): 379–80. According to Henderson, de la Barra did not consider Madero's argument to be "persuasive, even though he probably agreed Juárez Maza was a dolt," *In the Absence of Don Porfirio*, 123–24; Madero quoted by Héctor Zarauz López, "El Porfiriato y la Revolución Mexicana (1911–1912) en el Istmo de Tehuantepec" (licenciatura thesis, UNAM, 1993), 164–65; *Efemérides 1911*, 75–85.

30. *Efemérides 1911*, 77. This victory was so overwhelming that the Felicistas accused Díaz Quintas of fraud. See Henderson, *Félix Díaz*, 38–39. One sympathetic journalist affirmed that Governor Juárez Maza intended to represent the state's people, not just the elites. As an example, the governor fired a jefe politico who had unjustly fined two Indians and a police inspector who had stolen two wagonloads of stone, "Siete meses," 9.

31. On the Ixtepeji rebellion, see McNamara, *Sons of the Sierra*, 193–95.

32. See *Colección de leyes, decretos, circulares y demás disposiciones de los poderes legislativo y ejecutivo del estado de Oaxaca*, vols. 27 and 28 (Oaxaca: Imprenta del Estado, 1914); CBJM, April 18, 1912.

33. *Efemérides 1911*, 106–7; Basilio Rojas, comp., *Efemérides Oaxaqueñas 1912* (Mexico City: 1962), 10.

34. CBJM, March 26, 1912; *Efemérides 1912*, 20–21.

35. In January 1912, Olivera attacked the inclusion of Porfiristas Herminio Acevedo and Manuel Rueda Magro as local deputies while defending the seating of revolutionary but property-less Plutarco Gallegos, who had been questioned by the more conservative members of the state legislature. *Efemérides 1911*, 92–96, 106–7; *Efemérides 1912*, 7–8.

36. *Efemérides 1912*, 21–22; CBJM, Apr. 10 and 13, 1912.

37. Cited in Henderson, "Un gobernador maderista," 382–83, and *In the Absence of Don Porfirio*, 178. In July, a hacienda had been destroyed in Tehuantepec. Emilio Vázquez Gómez then had ordered the governor to have the property returned and to assure him of protection. CBJM, Apr. 9, 19, and 20, 1912.

38. *Efemérides 1911*, 77 ff.; Henderson, "Un gobernador maderista," 384–85; Martínez Medina, "La gestión," 268–69.

39. Martínez Medina, "La gestión," 269–70. On Benito Juárez García and the Juchitecos, see Francie R. Chassen, "¿Una derrota juarista? Benito Juárez García vs. los Juchitecos," in *Los pueblos indígenas en los tiempos de Juárez*, ed. Antonio Escobar Ohmstede (Mexico City: Universidad Autónoma Metropolitana and Universidad Autónoma Benito Juárez de Oaxaca, 2007), 37–68.

40. See Chassen-López, *From Liberal to Revolutionary Oaxaca*, ch. 7, on Juárez García in Juchitán and Víctor de la Cruz, "Rebeliones indígenas en el Istmo de Tehuantepec," *Cuadernos Políticos* 38 (1983): 64 ff.

41. Víctor de la Cruz, "La rebelión de los juchitecos y uno de sus líderes: Che Gómez," *Historias* 17 (1987): 57–61. See Zarauz López, "El Porfiriato," 153 ff.; Martínez Medina, "La gestión," 271–74.

42. This conflict is extremely complicated and what follows is a brief summary. See de la Cruz, "La rebelión," 62–69; Henderson, "Un gobernador maderista," 385–86; Angel Bustillos Bernal, *La revolución en el Istmo de Tehuantepec* (Mexico City: 1968); Ruiz Cervantes, "Promesas y saldos de un proyecto hecho realidad," in *Economía contra sociedad: El Istmo de Tehuantepec 1907–1986*, comp. Leticia Reina (Mexico City: Centro de Estudios del Agrarismo et al., 1994), 27 ff.; Howard Campbell, *Zapotec Renaissance: Ethnic Politics and Cultural Revivalism in Southern Mexico* (Albuquerque: University of New Mexico Press, 1994), 32 ff.

43. See communications from June 1911 in *Cartas y telegramas del Archivo de José F. Gómez* (Mexico City: Ayuntamiento Popular de Juchitán, 1982), 6–14. From the start, Juárez Maza distrusted Che Gómez. Gómez complained to Díaz Quintas that

he had sent a congratulatory message to don Beno when he returned to Oaxaca but that he had never received a response.

44. Official document, Nov. 1, 1911, in *Cartas y telegramas*, 15–17; *Efemérides 1911*, 88; Henderson, "Un gobernador maderista," 386–87. Enrique León was believed by Juchitecos to be a relative of the hated elder León, although this has not been substantiated. The last quote is from Martínez Medina, "La gestión," 277–78.

45. Letter from León to Díaz Quintas, Nov. 5, 1911, in *Cartas y telegramas*, 18–19; *Efemérides 1911*, 90–98. The rebel Juchitecos burned government archives at this point. Zarauz López reported that the Chegomista forces numbered 6,000 and that casualties reached 1,000; he could find no direct connection between Gómez and Vázquez Gómez. He also cites *El Imparcial's* correspondent, who interviewed some of the Chegomista soldiers and related that they were fighting because Gómez had promised them land, water, and control of the salt flats. "El Porfiriato," 169–204.

46. See Charles Cumberland, *Mexican Revolution, Genesis under Madero* (Austin: University of Texas Press, 1952), 185–86; Zarauz López, "El Porfiriato," 172. See communications in *Cartas y telegramas*, 23–35; "Informes al Departamento de Estado norteamericano sobre la rebelión de los juchitecos en 1911," in *Guchachi' Reza* 16 (1983): 13–19.

47. Zarauz López, "El Porfiriato," 178.

48. See Ismael Brachetti and Abraham Muñoz, *Monografía histórica: Tres intentos pro-soberanía del estado de Oaxaca 1857, 1871, 1915* (Oaxaca: Gobierno Constitucional del Estado, 1980); Ruiz Cervantes, *La revolución*, 71 ff.; Paul Garner, *La revolución en la provincia: Soberanía estatal y caudillismo en las montañas de Oaxaca (1910–1920)* (Mexico City: Fondo de Cultura Económica, 1988), 111 ff.; Díaz Quintas's report in *Efemérides 1911*, 114.

49. Ricardo Lopez Gurrión, *Efemérides istmeñas*, 2nd ed. (San Luis Potosí: 1982), 130–32; *Cartas y telegramas*, 50–59; Martínez Medina, "La gestión," 290–92.

50. Two men were able to escape this attack. Faustino Olivera questioned Díaz Quintas in Congress whether the detention of a deputy, who had immunity, was legal. But Gómez actually had a leave of absence as deputy at the time and his substitute was serving, which left his immunity open to question. *Efemérides 1911*, 102–25; see Tomás Carballo (A) "Matanche" Trial Testimonies (Juchitán: Casa de Cultura, 1980), 22–23. Since the trial took place after the death of Reyes, this was too suspicious and convenient an accusation. According to López Gurrión, Carballo held Gómez responsible for the death of his friend, Leonardo Arguello, in the November uprising. This author is the only source that alleges that Juárez Maza actually met with Carballo before the abduction and murders. *Efemérides istmeñas*, 132.

51. López Gurrión, *Efemérides istmeñas*, 133; *Efemérides 1912*, 10; Carlos Sánchez Silva, *Crisis política y contrarrevolución en Oaxaca (1912–1915)* (Mexico City: Instituto Nacional de Estudios Históricos de la Revolución Mexicana, 1991), 65–66.

52. *Efemérides 1911*, 94, 110; Arellanes, et al., *Diccionario histórico de la revolución en Oaxaca* (Mexico City: Instituto Nacional de Estudios Históricos de la Revolución Mexicana, 2000), 39–40; Francisco José Ruiz Cervantes, "El Batallón Sierra Juárez," *Guchachi' Reza* 9 (1981): 16–18.

53. *Efemérides 1911*, 104–5, 127; *Efemérides 1912*, 27 ff.; Pérez García, "Los primeros doce años," 41; Ruiz Cervantes, *La revolución*, 33–43. As might have been expected, Díaz Quintas was not elected by the state legislature to fill in as provi-

sional governor on the death of his friend. Instead, Alberto Montiel was chosen, which marked the direct return to power of the Vallistocracia.

54. *Efemérides 1912*, 8–20.

55. Tamayo, *Oaxaca*, 27; Sánchez Silva, *Crisis política*, 68. His body was provisionally interred in the Panteón Francés, but in 1953 it was moved to Guelatao, Oaxaca, his father's birthplace, as per his will. Klerian, *Juárez*, 47–48.

56. For example, see *El Avance*, Dec. 21, 1911; *Efemérides* 1911, 111–20.

57. Henderson, "Un gobernador maderista," 372; Klerian, *Juárez*, 45.

3

Salvador Alvarado of Yucatán

Revolutionary Reforms, Revolutionary Women

Stephanie J. Smith

In 1915 señora Maria Rosa Guillermo appeared before the military commander in Valladolid, Yucatán. This was a serious matter, and her father came with her for support and to add his testimony. In fact, Rosa was asking that the local revolutionary military tribunal do no less than "save her honor" by helping her to get married. Rosa told the military commander who presided over the court that in June 1912, she and her fiancée, the *profesor* Fulgencio Alcocer, went to the Civil Registry Office in Valladolid to register their intent to marry. This ceremony was crucial to Rosa since she was five months pregnant. Yet before their marriage took place, Fulgencio disappeared. He remained absent many months, during which time their child was born. Even when Fulgencio returned, however, he ignored Rosa. Furious, Rosa demanded that Fulgencio marry her and pay the dowry for his newborn daughter in the amount of 5,000 pesos.

The next day, Fulgencio told the commander his side of the story. Not surprisingly, he argued that Rosa's complaints against him were false. Although he did not deny having illicit loving relations with Rosa while he was a student from 1907 until 1909, this had been several years in the past. Since that time, Fulgencio insisted that he only occupied himself with carrying out the tasks of his profession, at least until he was thrown in jail for these recent charges. While Fulgencio may not have been seeing Rosa himself, the teacher revealed to the court that he had heard that Rosa was involved with three other young men, all of whom recently had engaged in loving relations with Rosa. And to further prove his point, Fulgencio presented the commander with five supporting documents, including a postcard and some pictures.

Upon hearing this testimony, Rosa's father flew into a rage, arguing that he vigilantly protected his daughter. Fulgencio countered this statement by saying that Rosa was known to sneak out behind her father's back, especially on trips to visit her mother on the family's finca. Most importantly, Rosa's rowdy behavior meant that the identity of the baby's father forever would remain a mystery. Evidently the presiding military commander failed to believe Fulgencio's damaging testimony, though, and in response he demanded that the couple marry. Contending that his marriage to Rosa was the only way to free himself from a certain prison sentence, Fulgencio reluctantly agreed. After signing the civil marriage certificate, Fulgencio stormed out of the court, complaining that everything that had occurred was not fair. Even worse, it was only at the judge's insistence that the new husband paid for the accompanying costs.[1]

The case of Rosa and Fulgencio reflects the remarkable changes that took place during the era of General Salvador Alvarado and Yucatán's revolutionary government from 1915 to 1918. During these few short years, Yucatán became the site of many of Mexico's most radical and far-reaching revolutionary measures that involved the emancipation of women, including the creation of the military tribunals where Rosa argued her case. Almost immediately upon his arrival in Yucatán, Alvarado established the revolutionary courts, administered by his hand-picked military commanders. In this manner, he acknowledged equal access to the judicial system and allowed women like Rosa to bring forward their cases and win restitution. And while the success of Rosa's marriage remains unknown, the revolutionary climate during the Alvarado era nonetheless allowed Rosa the opportunity to avenge her lost honor.

That Rosa appeared in court during Alvarado's governorship was no coincidence. As this chapter will explore, the tribunals were only one of many revolutionary edicts that directly concerned women. Overall, women played crucial roles in Alvarado's revolutionary plan for Yucatán's future, including symbolically in the governor's revolutionary discourse, and also as the focal point of many of his reforms. Alvarado thus targeted Maya and non-Maya women alike for revolutionary improvements, and to this end he issued a series of radical decrees.[2] With its feminist groups, emphasis on women's education and health, and laws directed toward women's advancement, the state of Yucatán thus served as an example to the rest of Mexico. Women, however, were not simply the passive recipients of Alvarado's edicts. To the contrary, they wrote letters to newspapers and organized during the feminist congresses; more conservative groups fought against the closing of local churches, and others demanded restitution for past wrongs through the military tribunals. That was the case with Rosa, as she insisted that revolutionary justice better her life and ensure her daughter's future.

The notion that women played a crucial role in the building of a nation provided the basis for Alvarado's gendered revolutionary reforms. Vowing to promote the emancipation of women, Alvarado contended that the time had arrived for women's freedom and that the days of female slavery belonged to the past.[3] He further argued that women could not enter the struggle for liberation, however, without first being properly prepared. According to the new governor, women required education in order to comply with their revolutionary responsibilities to build a new society, to rise to the moral and intellectual level of men, and to reject the "superstitious" ideas of the church.[4] Consequently, Alvarado asserted that not only was education the principal remedy for the majority of women's problems, but it also would provide the foundation upon which women could work to enhance their own lives.

Even as Alvarado stressed the need for improvements in women's lives, he nonetheless argued that a woman's place was within the home as a proper wife and mother. As a result, the governor contended that it was ". . . natural that marriage will be the preferred objective in the life of a woman, placing her job in the home as her highest social function."[5] In the end, while certain aspects of women's lives improved during the revolutionary years, Alvarado still defined their position within the nation-building process.[6] What this meant for women was that while they created spaces within the revolutionary environment to change their lives on an everyday level, revolutionary officials restricted women from more formal and explicitly political aspects of participation, such as the voting process.

ALVARADO AND THE REVOLUTION ENTER YUCATÁN

Born on July 20, 1879, in Culiacán, the capital of the northern state of Sinaloa, Alvarado moved to the small town of Pótam in neighboring Sonora as a child. Even as a young man, he was passionately involved in political issues. Alvarado claimed that by the early age of seven he had begun to understand that the organization of society needed to change.[7] When he grew older, he relocated to Guaymas to work in a pharmacy, among other places. In 1906, Alvarado moved to Cananea, headquarters of the U.S.-owned Cananea Consolidated Copper Company (CCCC). It was here that he began his political career by joining the Partido Liberal Mexicano and by becoming involved in a workers' strike against the CCCC—a strike which military forces brutally suppressed. By 1909, Alvarado decided that the path to Mexico's social and political change was through revolutionary struggle rather than peaceful elections, and after a short exile in Arizona, he joined the anti-reelection fight of Francisco I. Madero in 1910.[8]

For the next few years, Alvarado fought many successful battles and rose within the revolutionary ranks. He became a major in 1911, first serving with the forces of Juan Cabral in Sonora, and after Madero's assassination in 1913, attaining the rank of colonel under Alvaro Obregón's command. Alvarado became a brigadier general in 1914 after helping to assure several military victories for the Constitutionalist forces. Soon afterwards, on November 25, 1914, First Chief Venustiano Carranza promoted Alvarado to the position of military commander of Mexico City. He would not pass much time there, however, as Carranza designated Alvarado to be the governor and military commander of Yucatán on February 27, 1915.[9] As head of the Constitutionalist army, Carranza sent Alvarado to the state, determined to snuff out emerging counterrevolutionary rebellions while bringing stubborn local henequen planters into the revolutionary fold.[10] Certainly Yucatán was a valuable asset to the revolutionary government, supplying millions of pesos in taxes to Mexico City from its lucrative henequen production.[11]

Putting down rebel movements, Alvarado and his seven thousand troops entered the capital of Mérida on March 19, 1915. Although the Mexican Revolution began in 1910, Yucatán had remained largely untouched by revolutionary struggles until the entrance of Alvarado and his subsequent reforms that sought to restructure Yucatecan society.[12] Integral to his grand plan for Yucatán's future was the releasing of all women from their "traditional" position of servitude and the freeing of Maya women laborers from slave-like working conditions. Alvarado specifically addressed the issue of Maya women and children when he enforced a 1914 decree that canceled debt labor, including that of domestic servants.[13] Alvarado refined laws for women workers, delineating work hours, mandating rest periods for pregnant women, and establishing health standards.[14] He also created Decree Number 20, issued on April 24, 1915, which prohibited the use of domestic servants without pay or written contract.[15]

As Yucatecan workers were often Maya women and children who had worked in households for years with little compensation except for food and clothing, Alvarado set minimum wages and maximum hours for these servants, stating that such domestic servitude amounted to real slavery.[16] It is interesting to note, however, that chapter nine of the 1918 Work Code, dedicated exclusively to women and children, prohibited "unhealthy and dangerous labors for women in general and for youngsters less than 18 and older than 15 years of age."[17] Lumping women and children together, the code further restricted women and youngsters from working at night or in dangerous environments, and also from employment in those places which served as hubs for immorality, such as beer halls, casinos, cafes, or houses of prostitution.[18]

While Alvarado directed many reforms at women, they participated in the revolution as well, especially through women's use of the military tribunals. These "Tribunals of the Revolution" acted as courts and were an important aspect of Alvarado's judicial system during the preconstitutional period. Placing the tribunals in each of the sixteen *partidos*, or districts of the state, Alvarado ensured that all of Yucatán would have access to justice.[19] And during their time in use, from 1915 until 1917, the military commanders resolved more than 3,600 cases.[20]

The tribunals were to pass judgments quickly, without the complicated procedures that could intimidate the "poor and ignorant."[21] To this end, the military courts operated with the commander and his secretary only. The exclusion of lawyers was quite purposeful, as Alvarado prohibited any intervention by a third party, and especially by lawyers.[22] Certainly Alvarado revealed a marked dislike of attorneys, writing that with "very rare exceptions, they dedicate themselves body and soul to obtain from their profession the greatest gain possible."[23] In this manner the governor demanded that justice be streamlined and swiftly carried out with little legal muck to slow down the process.

Beginning in 1915, women actively took advantage of the revolutionary tribunals. Specifically addressing the needs of "widows and dispossessed orphans, poor people miserably robbed, and innocent women affronted and abandoned," Alvarado obligated the revolutionary judicial system to make reparations to those previously ignored.[24] And responding to this opportunity for greater legal representation, elite and poor Maya women alike appeared before the revolutionary tribunals. Overall, the military tribunals could be effective in making a difference in the everyday lives of women. For many women, the courts created a space where they could address prior wrongs and indeed have them recognized as such.

For instance, in the summer of 1915, Narcisa Alcocer, who came from the small town of Tinún, appeared before a military tribunal in Valladolid to declare that Francisco Gil had begun to pursue her when she was barely fourteen years old. He asked her to marry him, and, although Narcisa quickly accepted, it would seem that the proposal was actually a ploy to seduce her. Narcisa resisted his advances until the death of her father, when Francisco finally "trapped her in his net," and she surrendered so that he could take "the satisfaction of his instincts." Francisco followed Narcisa night and day, and when she attempted to resist his advances, he raped her. She eventually gave birth to a baby who died three days later. Despite Francisco's ill nature, Narcisa still wanted him to honor his proposal of marriage, something that he continued to oppose year after year. During the eight years that this relationship continued, Narcisa complained two times to local authorities of her pueblo without obtaining results. Yet when Alvarado and the Mexican Revolution arrived in Yucatán, Narcisa appealed to the newly established revolutionary courts, stating that "now there is justice without distinction of classes." Narcisa asked that Francisco pay her two hundred pesos for "damage he made to her because of not being married with her," and "making her lose her honor." When he first offered one hundred pesos, she threatened to complain until she received all that she asked. Not surprisingly, Francisco changed his mind, and Narcisa won her full amount.[25]

The fact that Narcisa and other women came forward at this point attests to the significance of Alvarado's reforms in the lives of many Yucatecan women. Narcisa's case further illustrates that many women were becoming aware of increasing possibilities throughout the state. Of course, not all welcomed revolutionary changes, especially those that concerned the church. And as revolutionary officials soon discovered, the closing of the state's churches would become one of the most contentious points between Alvarado and Yucatán's socially conservative population.

ALVARADO AND THE CHURCH

Soon after his arrival in Yucatán, Alvarado took aim at the Catholic Church. Many of Alvarado's decrees, such as those that prohibited bosses from imposing their religious beliefs upon their servants, reflected his concern that women could fall easily under the influence of the church.[26] While Alvarado may have wished to reduce the church's control over women, he nonetheless sought to replace religious concepts of morality with his own revolutionary version. Although an atheist, in many ways Alvarado promoted even greater restrictions over the moral lives of the Yucatecan people. For instance, the governor limited popular vices for the "good" of the people, including the enforcement of laws that prohibited the sale of liquor to minors and women.[27]

In accordance with revolutionary ideology, Alvarado vowed to break the chains of "religious fanaticism" that kept Yucatecan women under a "cloud of terror and superstition."[28] To accomplish this task, Alvarado removed physical evidence of the Church by sending priests away from the state, closing churches, and confiscating all relicts from inside the temples.[29] Departments of the government then utilized the shell of the churches for various purposes. For instance, Mérida's Santa Lucía church held materials from the Yucatecan Museum, the Divine Teacher was a depository for construction materials for the Office of Public Works, and the municipal band occupied the Jesus María church. Bundles of henequen filled many of the empty churches, and revolutionary officials established schools in others to take advantage of the large structures' open spaces.[30]

Alvarado argued that Maya women particularly were vulnerable to the allure of the church. Although the revolutionary governor promptly promised to free all women from this avowed enemy of the revolution, he nonetheless presumed that elite women were less devoted to religion and more secular than Maya women.[31] Alvarado's perception of Maya women derived partially from his belief that the Maya were tied to the traditions of their ancestors and thus unable to participate fully in a more modern Yucatán.[32] He further considered the rural Maya population's loyalty to local priests to be particularly destructive because workers, under the threat of eternal suffering, learned to be submissive to the more powerful.[33]

While Alvarado claimed that religious authorities prayed upon the Maya population, he still perceived *every* woman as vulnerable and in need of reeducation in the correct ways of revolutionary thinking. Indeed, revolutionary newspaper articles and leaflets commonly reflected this attitude. For instance, in 1916 the official Constitutionalist newspaper in Yucatán, the *Voz de la Revolución*, published a pamphlet concerning the "defanaticizing" of the Yucatecan population, arguing that revolutionary teachers should wage a systematic war in the schools against fanaticism and superstition. Yet the struggle over the minds of the women and children, the author also suggested, should employ various other approaches outside of the school. These methods included holding periodic lectures in local schools and replacing religious saints with patriotic and historical figures. According to the piece, speakers at the meetings were to provide a thorough explanation of true patriotic behavior, as well as a condemnation of religious customs. Moreover, civic and patriotic festivals would replace religious holidays, and festivals honoring modern culture would substitute for those dedicated to patron saints.[34]

Not all women agreed with the revolution's view of the church, and many women adamantly protected their local cathedrals. For instance, in 1916, a group of women headed by Magdalena Medina appeared before the military commander of Ticul. While there, the women requested that government officials open the doors to the principal church of the city and allow local priests to dedicate the building once again to the Catholic religion. The commander already had received orders from his superiors to unlock the doors of this church, but only those leading to the main ceremonial room and only during the hours as prescribed by law. After agreeing to these restrictions, the government official returned the keys to the twenty-one women.[35] In a similar case, Valladolid's military commander reported that December 29, 1916, would be an unforgettable day for the "old women" of the town. For on that date eighty-one women appeared before the military commander to demand the return of the churches and priests. Señora María Escalante spoke for all present, first asking for the town's major cathedral. Although the commander warned the women that there were very few powerful Catholics left in the area, he nonetheless agreed to their request. Still, he refused when the women also solicited the restoration of the Candelaria Cathedral, saying that the government would release only one church. The group of women conceded to this modified plan, and then gave *las gracias*. In the end of his report, the military commander wrote that all of the "old" women went away quite happy, and that the mothers of the community would once again be involved in their religious activities.[36]

The interactions of the women of Ticul and Valladolid with the military commanders suggest a give-and-take by both parties. The women demanded and regained control of at least one or part of the churches they desired, thus allowing priests to carry out religious services once again. Unlike the orderly gathering of the women of Ticul and Valladolid, there were also many near-riots and violent protests against Alvarado's strict anticlericalism. In response, by the early months of 1917, Alvarado allowed the return of some priests to the region.[37] In the process of pressing their demands, Yucatecan women not only contributed to an informal political process, but they also persuaded Alvarado to lift the ban on some church services. Beyond their informal participation, however, women also played important roles in more official and organized revolutionary activities. For example, in 1916 women came together to agitate for their rights during Yucatán's feminist congresses, and in the process they left an indelible mark on Mexico's history.

FEMINIST CONGRESSES

On October 29, 1915, the *Voz de la Revolución* proudly announced the convocation of Yucatán's feminist congress, which soon would take place in Mérida. Indeed, this was the first feminist congress in the history of Mexico, and only the second in Latin America.[38] According to the newspaper, the government's support of the women's gathering was yet more proof of the progressive spirit that animated revolutionary Yucatán during the Alvarado era. The article further promised that not only would participants discuss crucial issues relating to women's place in society, but they also would resolve essential problems during the congress. Women's emancipation was vital, the author reported, because up to this point Yucatecan women had surrendered themselves to their home and obligations, hiding as recluses within the four walls of their home and living their lives without aspirations for a different kind of liberty. In response to the "dire" needs of women, congress officials vowed to introduce women to aspirations other than the "conquest of bread." After all, the *Voz de la Revolución* argued that the Revolution "ha[d] manumitted women, conceding to them rights that they did not have before."[39] In other words, after freeing women, the revolution could now teach them a new way to live with the congresses as a guide.

Acting in his capacity as governor and military commander of the state, Alvarado signed the order for the two feminist congresses, the first held in January 1916 and the second in November of the same year. And whether or not the idea for the congresses originated with Alvarado, he managed the plans for the meetings with a tight rein.[40] For Alvarado, the meetings would not only educate women in a more progressive way of life, but they would also serve as an alternative to the activities of the church. Utilizing the popular belief that women could relate to other women better than men could, just as in religion, Alvarado hoped that the feminists would establish a larger revolutionary base.[41] While Alvarado attempted to reach out to women throughout the state, he nonetheless conceptualized the Yucatecan feminist congress with a certain type of woman in mind. This would be a congress of elite women only, since an educational requirement effectively eliminated the possibility of Maya involvement.[42] Without the participation of Maya women, more than six hundred delegates, mostly women teachers, participated in the national feminist gathering on January 13, 1916, in Mérida. They arrived from all parts of Yucatán, with their travel and lodging expenses paid for by the state.[43] Each participant received ten pesos daily, a free train ride to Mérida, and lodging in the city's various public schools. To encourage participation, state officials even suspended classes for the period of the congresses.[44]

Word of the congresses spread throughout Mexico and around the world. Hermila Galindo, one of the most prominent and controversial feminists from Mexico City and Carranza's secretary, was involved in the congresses from the beginning.[45] As the editor of the Mexico City feminist journal *Mujer Moderna*, Galindo worked with Carranza to promote his revolutionary doctrine. In response to Galindo's inquiries, Alvarado sent her names and descriptions of the congress participants as well as copies of *La Voz de la Revolución* which described the daily events of the meetings.[46] Organizers even chose Galindo's paper, "Women in the Future," as the opening presentation for the feminist meetings, although she did not personally attend. Besides feminists from Mexico, Alvarado also received requests from various international organizations for information about Yucatán's feminist gatherings.[47] For instance, Mary Sheepshanks, secretary of the International Woman Suffrage Alliance, whose president was Carrie Chapman Catt, wrote to Alvarado asking for information about the congresses. She mentioned that her organization followed Mérida's first feminist congress in the press, and that the convention was an important step forward for Mexico. Responding to the letter, Alvarado answered that he was sympathetic to the feminist cause, and he also sent her a book that contained the texts of the first congress.[48] Jane Addams, by then chair of the International Congress of Women, also expressed interest in Alvarado's feminist reforms, as well as in the feminist congress. In her correspondence with Alvarado dated April 3, 1917, Addams outlined issues discussed at the 1915 International Congress of Women at The Hague. As she explained, women from all over Europe and the United States traveled to the Netherlands to attend the conference, even in the middle of World War I. At the International Congress, the women constituted an International Committee for Lasting Peace with a resolution to find permanent peace in Europe. The congress also demanded that women receive the right of suffrage in every country throughout the world, and that governments resolve all international disputes by peaceful means.[49]

The four themes of Yucatán's feminist congress reflected an obsession with modernity and education. As such, the *Voz de la Revolución* proudly announced that the work of the congress was to "[f]ree the woman from the old traditional yokes and convert her so as to be prepared for life and truth."[50] Fittingly, the first theme of the congress discussed the various ways to liberate women from the past. Francisca García Ortiz spoke to this subject when she claimed that women "hold modern ideas which tend towards the improvement of our condition. . . . The yoke [of tradition] is disappearing and we can make it vanish completely, by educating society."[51] Thus, the revindication of women through an emphasis on primary education provided the basis for the second goal. The third sought to prepare women for the dynamic life of modern society through education in the arts and various occupations. Lastly, congress organizers hoped to urge women to participate in public life as a means to achieve a guiding role in society.[52]

Women expressed a number of different viewpoints throughout the congress, producing a lively mix of discussions and presentations veering from the conservative to the radical. Some espoused the traditional Catholic view of women and argued that women could never be the equals of men and should not hold public office.[53] Other participants countered that women should serve in all areas of civil life because they were no different from men intellectually.[54] Even the discussion of the first theme on ways to free women from the yoke of tradition generated disagreement. For instance, the *Voz de la Revolución* printed as a headline a quote taken from a dissenting member of the congress that read, "We should not shake off the yoke of men to fall under the yoke of other women."[55] The opening speech, taken from Hermila Galindo's "Women of the Future," provoked the greatest controversy during the congress. In her talk, read by César A. González of the Department of Public Education, Galindo argued that women were the sexual and intellectual equals of men, and, as such, should be allowed the same sexual freedom as men.[56] Galindo also endorsed sex education in the schools and the right of women to divorce, and she railed against religion.[57]

After the reading of the speech, Isolina Pérez argued that the congress organizers should destroy Galindo's talk, a statement which generated both
applause and protests.[58]

The feminists further produced a report responding to the four themes of
the congress. First, in the quest to free women from the yoke of tradition,
participants recommended that women should occupy jobs previously held
only by men, and that government officials should modify the Civil Code
to give women more rights and freedoms. They also promoted equal education for women, as well as secular education in general. In this area
women argued for the prohibition of religious instruction for children less
than eighteen years of age since they lacked rational thinking. For the second goal, the revindication of women through an emphasis on primary education, the women suggested the establishment of public meetings between teachers and parents to discuss the noble ends of rational education,
and that existing schools be substituted with rational instruction. In the
third area, which sought to prepare women through their education in the
arts and various occupations, congress members suggested creating an academy of the arts for painting, sculpture, decorating, and other arts, offering
classes in photography and ceramics, encouraging women to enter into the
field of medicine, and creating a love of literature. Lastly, to urge women to
participate in public life, the participants proposed that women should be
allowed to occupy all public offices, since no difference existed between
women's and men's mental capacities.[59]

The first feminist congress was a milestone for Yucatecan women in many
respects. Throughout the meetings, women gathered together to redefine
possibilities for their lives at home or in public. Many feminists struggled
to move beyond the traditional boundaries that defined women's proper
roles in society, demanding that the revolutionary government provide
them with greater opportunities in education and civil service. Women also
pushed for changes in the laws that covered family issues, such as marriage
and divorce. Even though women at the meetings revealed radically dis-
similar aspirations for women's place in Yucatán's future, the feminist congress still provided a space for women to speak out publicly and to demand
that government officials listen. Ultimately, citizenship may have meant different things to different women, but most participants called for a revision
in Yucatán's constitution to allow them the right to vote in municipal elections, as well as to run for statewide municipal offices.

The momentum for revolutionary change in Yucatán slowed soon after
the first feminist congress, but Alvarado still garnered enough support to
convoke the second feminist congress in November of 1916. The topics of
discussion remained similar to the first: freeing women from the yoke of
tradition, disseminating scientific knowledge, and extolling the merits
of education.[60] Nonetheless, this gathering was not as well attended as the

first, and the second congress was indicative of the loss of support for social reforms in general. Several factors contributed to this more stagnant
political atmosphere: falling henequen prices, continued political turmoil, and the passage of a bill that disqualified Alvarado from running
for reelection on the grounds that he failed to meet the residency requirement of five years.[61]

CONCLUSION

Governor Alvarado permanently left Yucatán in November 1918, although
he had spent little time living in the state during his last eighteen months
as governor. This was certainly not what Alvarado desired, as he struggled to
remain in the state where he carried out his revolutionary visions. Nonetheless, in 1917 Carranza ordered Alvarado to supervise southeastern Mexico
as chief of military operations, thus requiring Alvarado to spend many
months away from Mérida.[62] Surely this forced exile was no surprise to Alvarado, especially since his relationship with Carranza and the central government had been fraught with tensions throughout his term as governor.
While Carranza may have maintained a more hands-off approach while
henequen prices were high, he consistently attempted to rein in Alvarado's
more radical amendments, especially in the area of land reform.[63] Alvarado
remained active in Mexico's revolutionary politics during the years following his term as Yucatán's governor. In 1924, though, Alvarado's life was cut
short when he died from a bullet wound while supporting the failed Adolfo
de la Huerta rebellion in central Mexico.[64]

Alvarado's legacy in Yucatán continues to loom large. Certainly he argued
for women's access to the courts, education, right to enter politics, and
greater freedoms within the household. And with state support, women organized as feminists during the era of Alvarado, including Mexico's first
feminist congresses in 1916. An examination of Alvarado's term as governor further reveals that women were not simple pawns of the revolutionary
state. For instance, many women, including Maya and poor women, became adept at utilizing the revolutionary court system to present their cases
before the revolutionary tribunals. In their testimonies, women demanded
"revolutionary justice," and often won restitution for past wrongs.

In the end, utilizing gender as a category of analysis expands our understanding of the complex nature of revolutionary changes during the era of
Alvarado. By examining state formation through the lens of gender, and by
analyzing the interactions of Alvarado and the women of Yucatán, it be-
comes possible to understand the revolution as a process forged by Alvarado's reforms directed at women, and women's revolutionary demands
in return. While women would have to wait for many years to be able to

participate fully as citizens in Mexico's political process, they nonetheless contested their place within revolutionary society and in the process improved their lives on an everyday level.

NOTES

From *Gender and the Mexican Revolution: Yucatán Women and the Realities of Patriarchy* by Stephanie J. Smith (Chapel Hill: University of North Carolina Press, 2009). Used by permission.

1. Archivo General del Estado de Yucatán (AGEY), Fondo Municipio (FM) Valladolid, Juzgado (J), caja 387, vol. 48, p. 18, Aug. 27, 1915.

2. *Diccionario histórico y biográfico de la Revolución Mexicana*, vol. 7 (Mexico, D.F.: Instituto Nacional de Estudios Históricos de la Revolución Mexicana Secretaría de Gobernación, 1992), 544.

3. Salvador Alvarado, *Mi actuación revolucionaria en Yucatán* (Paris and Mexico: Librería de la Vda. de Ch. Bouret, 1918), 46.

4. Salvador Alvarado, *La reconstrucción de México: Un mensaje a los pueblos de America*, vol. 2, 2nd ed. (Mérida, Yucatán: Ediciones del Gobierno de Yucatán, 1980), 107, 110.

5. Alvarado, *La reconstrucción de México*, 2:112.

6. Alvarado, *Mi actuación revolucionaria en Yucatán*, 45.

7. Salvador Alvarado, *Antologia ideológica* (Mexico City, D.F.: SepSetentas, 1976), 7.

8. For more information on Alvarado's early career, see Gilbert M. Joseph, *Revolution from Without: Yucatán, Mexico, and the United States, 1880–1924* (Durham, NC: Duke University Press, 1988), 99. Also see the introduction, written by Héctor R. Olea, to Salvador Alvarado's *Mi sueño* (Hermosillo: Universidad Autónoma de Sinaloa and Instituto de Investigaciones, Económicas y Sociales Colección, Rescate 21, no year given), 1–8, and *Yucatán en el tiempo, enciclopedia alfabética*, 1998 ed., s.v. "Alvarado Rubio, Salvador." For Alvarado's firsthand account of his early years and his political awakening, see Alvarado, *La reconstrucción de México*, vol. 1, 16–29. For information on Alvarado during the revolution, see Alan Knight, *The Mexican Revolution*, vol. 2, *Counter-revolution and Reconstruction* (Cambridge: Cambridge University Press, 1986). Also, many thanks to Jürgen Buchenau for his helpful insights on Alvarado.

9. Knight, *Mexican Revolution*, vol. 2.

10. Allen Wells and Gilbert M. Joseph, *Summer of Discontent, Seasons of Upheaval: Elite Politics and Rural Insurgency in Yucatán, 1876–1915* (Stanford, CA: Stanford University Press, 1996), 275–85.

11. Wells and Joseph, *Summer of Discontent*, 261.

12. Gilbert M. Joseph and Allen Wells, "Yucatán, Elite Politics and Rural Insurgency," in *Provinces of the Revolution, Essays on Regional Mexican History, 1910–1929*, ed. Thomas Benjamin and Mark Wasserman (Albuquerque: University of New Mexico Press, 1990), 122.

13. Joseph, *Revolution from Without*, 105.

14. Shirlene Soto, *Emergence of the Modern Mexican Woman: Her Participation in Revolution and Struggle for Equality, 1910–1940* (Denver, CO: Arden Press, 1990), 71. Also see Anna Macías, *Against All Odds: The Feminist Movement in Mexico to 1940* (Westport, CT: Greenwood Press, 1982), 66.

15. AGEY, Fondo Poder Ejecutivo (FPE), Sección Gobernación (G), Serie Diario de la Revolución, caja 487, 1915. Also see Macías, *Against All Odds*, 66.

16. Alvarado, *Mi actuación revolucionaria en Yucatán*, 46. Also see Soto, *Emergence of the Modern Mexican Woman*, 72.

17. 1918 Codigo del Trabajo y sus reformas, from *Leyes y decretos del gobierno socialista del estado de Yucatán* (Mérida, Yucatán: Pluma y Lapiz, 1924), 90–91.

18. 1918 Codigo del Trabajo, 90–91.

19. Joseph, *Revolution from Without*, 112.

20. *Breves apuntes acerca de la administración del General Salvador Alvarado, como gobernador de Yucatán, con simple expresión de hechos, y sus consecuencias* (Mérida de Yucatán: Imprenta del Gobierno Constitucionalista, 1916), 16. Also see the *Diccionario histórico y biográfico de la Revolución Mexicana*, vol. 7, 797.

21. Salvador Alvarado, *Carta al pueblo de Yucatán* (Yucatan, Mexico: Maldonado Editores, 1988), 50. This letter was first published on May 5, 1916.

22. Alvarado, *Mi actuación revolucionaria en Yucatán*, 75.

23. Alvarado, *La reconstrucción de México*, vol. 2, 136.

24. Alvarado, *Mi actuación revolucionaria en Yucatán*, 77.

25. AGEY, FM Valladolid, J, caja 387, vol. 48, p. 12, Aug. 25, 1915.

26. AGEY, FPE, G, Serie Diario de la Revolución, caja 487, 1915.

27. AGEY, FPE, G, Serie Diario de la Revolución, caja 487, 1915.

28. Alvarado, *Mi actuación revolucionaria en Yucatán*, 55.

29. Joseph, *Revolution from Without*, 106.

30. AGEY, FPE, G, Serie Relación de los Templos, caja 628, 1918.

31. Joseph, *Revolution from Without*, 109.

32. Alvarado, *Mi actuación revolucionaria en Yucatán*, 39.

33. Alvarado, *Mi actuación revolucionaria en Yucatán*, 57.

34. Lorenzo Méndez, *Criterio revolucionario desfanatización* (Mérida: Yucatán, 1916).

35. AGEY, FM Ticul, vol. 136, caja 81, 1916.

36. AGEY, FPE, G, caja 589, 1917.

37. Joseph, *Revolution from Without*, 106.

38. The first feminist congress was held in Argentina in 1910. Macías, *Against All Odds*, 71.

39. *La Voz de la Revolución*, Oct. 29, 1915.

40. There is some controversy over who originated the idea for the feminist congresses. See Macías, *Against All Odds*, 70–71.

41. AGEY, FPE, Sección Alvarado, caja 475, 1915.

42. *La Voz de la Revolución*, Oct. 29, 1915. The requirement was "Al Congreso Feminista podrán asistir todas las mujeres honradas de Yucatán, que posean cuando menos los conocimientos primarios." Also see Alejandra García Quintanilla, *Los tiempos en Yucatán: Los hombres, las mujeres y la naturaleza (siglo XIX)* (Mexico, D.F.: Claves Latinoamericanas, 1982), 155.

43. *La Voz de la Revolución*, Oct. 29. 1915. Also see *La Voz de la Revolución*, Jan. 13, 1916.

44. *El primer Congreso Feminista de Yucatán, anales de esa memorable asamblea* (Mérida, Yucatán, México: Talleres Tipograficos del "Ateneo Peninsular," 1916), 47.

45. For information on Hermila Galindo, see Laura Orellana Trinidad, "'La mujer del provenir': Raices intelectuales y alcances del pensamiento feminista de Hermila Galindo, 1915–1919," *Signos Históricos* 5 (Jan.–June 2001): 109–37.

46. AGEY, FPE, Congreso Feminista, caja 519, 1916.

47. Intellectual trends and events from Europe and the United States influenced Alvarado's feminist discourse. Alaide Foppa, "The First Feminist Congress in Mexico, 1916," trans. Helene F de Aguilar, *Signs Journal of Women in Culture and Society* 5 (Autumn 1979): 193.

48. AGEY, FPE, Congreso Feminista, caja 519, 1916.

49. AGEY, FPE, G, caja 561, 1917.

50. *La Voz de la Revolución*, Nov. 17, 1915.

51. Foppa, "First Feminist Congress in Mexico," 194.

52. *La Voz de la Revolución*, Oct. 29, 1915. Also see Soto, *Emergence of the Modern Mexican Woman*, 73.

53. Macías, *Against All Odds*, 77.

54. *La Voz de la Revolución*, Jan. 17, 1916.

55. *La Voz de la Revolución*, Jan. 15, 1916. "No debemos sacudir el yugo de los hombres para caer bajo el yugo de otras mujeres."

56. Francesca Miller, *Latin American Women and the Search for Social Justice* (Hanover, NH: University Press of New England, 1991), 76. Also see Soto, *Emergence of the Modern Mexican Woman*, 74.

57. See Macías, *Against All Odds*, 74.

58. *Primer Congreso Feminista de Yucatán*, 69–70. Galindo would speak at the Second Feminist Congress, where she defended her first speech against those who called her work "a propaganda of immorality." Hermila Galindo, *Estudio de la Srita. Hermila Galindo con motivo de los temas que han de absolverse en el Segunda Congreso Feminista de Yucatán, Noviembre 20 de 1916* (Mérida, Yucatán, Mexico: Imprenta del Gobierno Constitutionalista, 1916), 555.

59. *Primer Congreso Feminista de Yucatán*, 129–30.

60. Soto, *Emergence of the Modern Mexican Woman*, 79.

61. Joseph, *Revolution from Without*, 114.

62. Joseph, *Revolution from Without*, 114.

63. Joseph, *Revolution from Without*, 130–31.

64. Joseph, *Revolution from Without*, 363–64, n. 11. Joseph argues that "Alvarado regarded Obregón as a bar to his own national political ambitions," and it was for this reason, more than ideology, that Alvarado supported de la Huerta during the rebellion.

4

Plutarco Elías Calles of Sonora

A Mexican Jacobin

Jürgen Buchenau

In May 1917, governor-elect Plutarco Elías Calles gave a rousing speech on the plaza of Nogales. The speech declared his intention to install a government "more radical than ever." The proletariat had elected him, Calles declared, and he therefore had a mandate to carry out a socialist program. A former provisional governor and ally of president Venustiano Carranza, he promised that his government would represent the people as opposed to the privileged classes. The enemies of the government, Calles assured the crowd, should expect no mercy from him.[1]

A bystander unfamiliar with the dynamics of the Mexican Revolution might well have assumed that Calles was a radical socialist within Carranza's victorious Constitutionalist coalition. To the contrary, the speech was evidence of a leadership that blended pragmatism with firebrand rhetoric. Even as Calles portrayed himself as the candidate of the oppressed, he assured U.S. agents that his speech was a mere "sop to the Mexicans," and that they could expect a much more conservative administration than his oration suggested.[2] Calles's years as the dominant political figure in Sonora therefore displayed the revolution's contradictions between popular aspirations and elite rule, between promises and betrayal, and between nationalist visions and capitalist reality.

A look at the Calles era in Sonora challenges historian Adrian Bantjes's assertion that "it was not until the 1930s . . . that revolutionary change came to Sonora."[3] It also qualifies another historian's broad condemnation of the Calles regime as one that came to power with the help of "military victory, sweeping repression, and the support of the U.S. government."[4] In revolutionary Sonora, reform and repression were two sides of the same coin, a dress rehearsal for Calles's career at the national level.

"LAND AND BOOKS FOR ALL"

The child born in the port city of Guaymas as Plutarco Elías Campuzano on September 25, 1877, was the product of a temporary liaison between two Sonorans of prominent birth who had seen decline into a middle-class existence. His father, Plutarco Elías Lucero, was a drifter and alcoholic who never stayed too long in any one place. After the death of his mother when he was three, Plutarco was raised by a maternal uncle, Juan Bautista Calles, from whom he adopted the last name by which he is most commonly known. Following an unsteady life as a teacher, hotel manager, farmer, and mill operator, Calles had followed Madero's campaign against Díaz (November 1910–May 1911) as a sympathetic observer rather than a participant. In July 1911, however, he became *comisario* (sheriff) of the border town of Agua Prieta, where he got firsthand experience with revolutionary violence during the uprising of the Chihuahuan rebel Pascual Orozco. It was on that occasion that he met fellow Sonoran Alvaro Obregón. After rejecting the February 1913 coup d'état of General Victoriano Huerta, Calles spent the next two years following Obregón's faction to national prominence. During the war between the factions, his forces defeated those of former governor José María Maytorena, a member of the Conventionist alliance led by Pancho Villa and Emiliano Zapata. On August 4, 1915, Carranza installed him, a relative unknown, as provisional governor and military commander of Sonora.

Calles soon found out that governing Sonora was an arduous task. A Conventionist governor still held sway in Villista-held territory, and Villa himself readied a major attack on Calles's provisional government in Agua Prieta. It was not until early November 1915 that the Callistas repelled Villa's last major offensive during the war of the factions. Moreover, much of Sonora lay in ruins following years of intense warfare. The warring bands had sacked towns and villages, raped women, and dragged young conscripts into battle. Countless fields lay abandoned, without the human effort and water necessary to make them produce. Food was scarce, and the major U.S.-owned copper mines of Cananea and Nacozari intermittently suspended operations whenever warfare threatened to draw near.[5] Complicating Calles's task, Sonorans remembered the pledges made by both sides during the war. Copper miners, who had fought for better working conditions in the Cananea strike of 1906, still found their basic needs unmet. Constitutionalist soldiers who had put their lives on the line for Calles demanded an irrigable plot of land and their share of the spoils of war. Facing continued water shortages, farmers in the Yaqui Valley knew that the Compañía Constructora Richardson, a U.S. corporation, enjoyed privileged access to the water of the Yaqui River. Making his job even more difficult, Calles needed to avoid friction with U.S. investors. As a border state rich in copper deposits, Sonora had a disproportionately large share of the country's foreign investment, and U.S.-owned firms such as the Richardson and the Cananea Consolidated Copper Co. (CCCC) played dominant roles in its economy. Although these companies paid minimal taxes, the state depended on them, as taxes on workers' wages and consumption constituted its greatest revenue source. Adding to these difficulties were looming conflicts with the central government headed by Carranza. Engaged in a quest to centralize government authority, Carranza infringed upon state and local sovereignty and even toppled several governors who did not follow his lead.

Aware that he was more vulnerable to local demands than to those from Mexico City, Calles took a bold approach to this array of contradictory pressures. His program, he declared, was about "the reality itself of a glorious people that has irrigated with its blood the soil on which the well-being and greatness of Mexico will thrive. . . ."[6] Calles stated his commitment to public morality, human rights, effective suffrage, local autonomy, and an independent judiciary, all Liberal tenets dating back to Madero's movement, which understood itself as a continuation of nineteenth-century Liberal reforms. But unlike the Maderistas, Calles did not stop at political reform. The new governor emphasized the need for public schooling in each community exceeding five hundred inhabitants, as well as his intention to require all mining and industrial companies to establish schools at their expense. He outlined his plans for the first teacher's college in Sonora. He called for the division of hacienda land, an equitable system of taxation, and "broad protection for workers." Calles closed his manifesto with the words "land and books for all"—a variation on Zapata's motto, "land and liberty."[7]

Decree Number 1, the Ley Seca, or dry law, indicated that Calles was serious about embracing modernity as he understood it. Just as neighboring Arizona entered the Prohibition era, the decree proscribed the production, importation, and distribution of alcoholic beverages.[8] This law was the most stringent of its kind in all of Mexico. It elicited favorable commentary from the consul in El Paso, who believed that Calles's anti-alcohol efforts in Agua Prieta could serve as a model for Ciudad Juárez, the troubled Mexican town across the border.[9] Opponents ridiculed the Ley Seca, given their new governor's own proclivities for wine and hard liquor such as *bacanora*, the highly potent liquor of the sierra. As one famous story had it, Calles celebrated this first decree with a good swig of brandy, and the following year, he was reportedly found to be in possession of a bottle of bacanora.[10]

Whether these stories are true or not, Calles's personal experience contributed to the decision to wage a campaign against drinking that still stands as one of the hallmarks of his governorship. His own father slowly drank himself to a death that arrived in 1917 in the form of cirrhosis of the liver. Plutarco, Jr., himself had spent years immersed in drinking and carousing. In addition, Calles believed that his campaign addressed one of the causes of poverty. In an August 1917 letter to the governor of Sinaloa, which had just abolished its own dry law, he vowed to "eliminate the disgusting vice of inebriation, the cause of the ruin and degeneration of our people."[11] No longer, Calles reasoned, would workers drink away their wages; and no longer would they miss work on San Lunes because of their hangovers. Calles was also concerned about the impact of Prohibition in the United States, which drove many drinkers to quench their thirst south of the border. As comisario of Agua Prieta, he had witnessed the ill effects of alcoholic tourism such as gambling, prostitution, and violent crime. To demonstrate that he meant business, Calles reportedly ordered the execution of a poor drunkard in Cananea.[12] Although the Ley Seca was impossible to enforce, it set the tone for an energetic governorship. Another decree outlawed gambling, which Calles portrayed as a source of vice and social disintegration.[13]

Over the next eight months, Calles also promulgated social reform legislation. One decree struck at large landowners by forbidding repurchase agreements. These agreements allowed hacendados to protect themselves from taxation and agrarian reform by holding large tracts of land that nominally remained the property of their former owners. Other measures slapped new taxes on landowners and mining companies and required them to exploit the natural resources in their possession.[14] This land tax, however, was modest compared to that imposed by Salvador Alvarado, the fellow Sonoran and new governor of Yucatán.[15]

Like Alvarado, Calles carried out a modest agrarian reform program. The division of large estates had never been a high priority for most Sonoran revolutionaries. Moreover, Carranza, who had called for the division of hacienda land at the height of the war between the factions, had backpedaled on land reform after his triumph over the Conventionists. Calles favored the *pequeña propiedad*, the family farm, as the basis of a U.S.-style society of yeoman smallholders. As he knew well, a plot of irrigable land could serve as a reward for lesser retainers. Therefore, he expropriated lands of his political enemies—and especially those owned by indigenous Yaquis allied with Maytorena and Villa—and distributed them among his supporters. Ironically, then, Callista land reform was directed *against* the native population of Sonora. This method allowed him to create a new group of loyal landowners.[16] In addition, Calles and his allies set up the first rural credit banks in Sonora.

In the area of gender relations and the family, Calles legalized divorce and moved to rein in the worst abuses committed by men. He outlawed the hiring out of wives for pay and, following a Carranza law on the national level, permitted divorce under certain circumstances. The decree retained the gender discrimination typical of its times. For example, a woman's adultery always constituted grounds for divorce, while a woman could only divorce an errant husband if he had either cohabited with his mistress, was guilty of adultery in the married couple's home, or behaved in such a manner as to bring public scandal or "dishonor" upon his wife.[17]

Calles's most important initiatives focused on rural education. The mainstays of the state's economy—cash crop agriculture and mining—drew workers into remote areas, where children remained, in the governor's words, "without the elementary education that the law requires."[18] As a result, one decree authorized the establishment of municipal libraries and evening schools for adults; another followed up on his campaign promise to set up the state's first normal school for teachers; and yet another forced large companies to establish schools to educate the workers' children.[19] A year later, the state budget committed more than 1.5 million pesos to public education, or almost 58 percent of total expenditures. This budget included funds for public libraries and adult education, another important Calles initiative.[20] In sum, while Calles could not eradicate the widespread illiteracy, he put in place an infrastructure for future improvements in rural education. By 1918, his policies had resulted in the construction of more than one hundred new schools, and student enrollment had doubled since 1910.[21]

Calles's greatest innovation in education was the establishment of the "Cruz Gálvez" school, an institution for orphans of the revolution in Hermosillo. This new boarding school was designed to impart practical skills as well as literacy and math at no cost to the students.[22] The Cruz Gálvez school had two separate sections for boys and girls, and a small "correctional" section for delinquents. The boys' section received the most funding, and education in the school followed strict gender lines: boys learned carpentry and other crafts while girls learned sewing and cooking.[23] Both private and public funds helped make these schools a success: in Calles's words, "there was not a town or a family which failed to give. As fast as the money came in, we began to build."[24] In the 1917 state budget, Cruz Gálvez absorbed 7 percent of the allotment for education.[25] The expenditure repaid itself in more ways than by educating the young. Cruz Gálvez soon became an industrial venture, a wholly Mexican-owned institution that stimulated the local economy. Calles's own upbringing as an orphan abandoned by his one living parent most likely played a role in making the school a priority.[26]

This reform program cost money at a time when years of fighting had depleted the state treasury. The obvious target for refilling state coffers was the foreign-owned mining companies. Unfortunately, these companies claimed to have suffered serious financial losses after the war between the factions. Calles, however, was not easily thwarted and insisted that foreign companies should be treated on equal terms with Mexican ones, which implied full payment of all taxes. Aware that even a modest production tax could fund all of his programs and restore the fiscal health of his state, Calles levied a 1.5 percent tax on all mining production.[27]

The flip side of Calles's reform program was a fierce campaign against his enemies. In particular, the governor turned against the Yaquis, an indigenous community from central Sonora that had always fiercely protected its independence. From their base in the Sierra de Bacatete near Guaymas, the Yaquis carried out raids into areas that had once been theirs—lands among the most fertile in Sonora. On January 29, 1916, Calles deprived the Yaquis of the right of citizenship except for those who left their support system for the white man's world.[28] The governor also took action against the Catholic Church, a relatively insignificant element, as Sonora's population of 260,000 people contained no more than thirty-five priests.[29] On March 16, 1916, Calles ordered all priests expelled from the state because he considered them spies and enemies, "bad elements" who meddled in state politics.[30] An early example of the anticlericalism that marked his national political career, the measure reflected the governor's innermost aversion to organized Catholicism. In a comparative context, however, Calles was not the country's only anticlerical governor, as Manuel Diéguez demonstrated in Jalisco, one of the strongholds of Catholic authority.[31]

THE SONORAN MAXIMATO

Just at the moment when Calles appeared to have consolidated his position, the specter of a large-scale U.S. military intervention forced him into a new role. Pancho Villa's attack on Columbus, New Mexico, on March 9, 1916, put the entire border region on red alert. U.S. president Woodrow Wilson responded to this attack by sending a "Punitive Expedition" into Chihuahua, provoking fears that Wilson might take this opportunity to send troops into other border states as well. To make matters worse, the trouble on the border encouraged the Yaquis to rebel. As a result, on March 29, 1916, Secretary of War Obregón appointed Calles *jefe de operaciones militares* (chief of military operations) in Sonora.[32] Between April and July 1916, the same leader who had just begun to demobilize the militias that had laid waste to Sonora toured the state in search of recruits and oversaw the Yaqui campaign.[33] On May 16, 1916, Carranza appointed Calles's close friend Adolfo de la Huerta provisional governor of Sonora.

As Carranza found out soon enough, however, Calles's political strength did not depend on holding the position of governor. In fact, Calles followed the first chief's orders confident in his continued influence in the state government. Indeed, U.S. intelligence agents described the new era as a bicephalous system with a "military" and a "civilian" governor. As one of these officers remarked shortly after the transition of power, "Sonora now [has] two governors. One, de la Huerta, has the name and absolutely no power. Calles, the 'deposed' governor, possesses all the pay, powers, and emoluments of the office."[34]

In his new role as strongman behind the scenes, Calles relied upon his army officers. Many of the officers came from middle-class origins and ad- mired Calles for his administrative skills and his reform program. They re- membered that the Constitutionalist movement had supplied them with food, clothing, and ammunition across the U.S. border while their adver- saries withered in starvation and used outdated weaponry. These officers had enjoyed a streak of victories under Calles that had given them ample opportunities for enrichment. They continued to depend on their patron at a time when political stability had not yet been restored, and more so than ever in the crisis of 1916. Calles's campaign against the Yaquis, though un- successful overall, offered a chance to reward Constitutionalist soldiers with land. Supported by the new rural credit banks and a favorable tax structure, these troops turned into yeoman farmers were Calles's greatest loyalists.[35]

The political network that sustained Calles's informal power rested upon the civil servants he had recruited to the state bureaucracy and the provisional governor himself. De la Huerta combined integrity with a sharp intellect, and unlike Calles and Obregón, he held a high school degree from Mexico City and had even pursued some university studies in accounting and music. As a civilian, he displayed an abiding respect for constitutional rule, which en- deared him to Carranza. De la Huerta had not yet built up an independent power base in the state and stressed his "intimate . . . friendship" with Gen- eral Calles, whose "unconditional approval" had helped him assume the po- sition.[36] Calles sometimes tired of the solicitude of his friend, chiding de la Huerta on one occasion for his "childish" endeavors to explain his conduct to him.[37] Such solicitude, however, should not be mistaken for submission. As governor, de la Huerta possessed negotiating skills that Calles lacked, and during his term of governor, he even negotiated a temporary truce with the Yaquis after the failure of Calles's campaign. The Sonoran Maximato was thus a system of shared governance rather than a dictatorship.[38]

First and foremost, Calles and de la Huerta needed to pay attention to the implications of World War I for the border region, as the Wilson adminis- tration gravitated toward the western Allies. While Carranza left no doubt about his desire to keep Mexico out of the conflict, his own rise to power had been intertwined with Great Power rivalry. Working at cross-purposes, both the United States and imperial Germany ended up supporting Car- ranza when his victory over Villa appeared inevitable. Even before the pub- lication of the Zimmermann telegram in February 1917 conjured up the possibility of an alliance between Carranza and the Kaiser, Mexicans were concerned about their country's role in case of war between the United States and Germany.[39]

The war scare constituted both a challenge and an opportunity for Calles and de la Huerta. As revolutionary politicians, they called for an end of all remaining special privileges of foreigners in Sonora. On the other hand, the threat of another U.S. invasion earned them popular support at a time of patriotic rallying behind the leaders. On the national level, Carranza applied this lesson by mixing nationalist rhetoric with pragmatic actions, and Calles and de la Huerta did the same in Sonora. This pragmatism was most appropriate. Both politicians knew from experience that the copper companies could resist compliance with any law by simply shutting down operations. These firms had never accepted Calles's decree that terminated all Porfirian concessions, and Calles and de la Huerta were fortunate that rising copper prices in the World War I era had made the copper companies amenable to paying production taxes. As military commander, Calles therefore adopted a cooperative approach toward U.S. citizens and investors while guarding a nationalist image. After his appointment as military commander, for example, he informed Obregón that the main purpose of his presence in the border region was to protect the copper mines, a message that most likely referred to the threat posed by the Punitiva.[40] Six months later, he demonstrated that such "protection" meant cracking down on labor organizers. When the election of several nationalists to the town council in Cananea led to an attempt to hold all U.S. residents in jail until General John J. Pershing withdrew from Chihuahua, Calles sent a contingent of soldiers and ordered the execution of five of the delegates.[41] The saber-rattling was not in vain: the CCCC and the other copper companies drastically increased earnings over the next year as the world war dragged on, and the production taxes paid by these firms finally stabilized the state treasury.[42]

Nonetheless, de la Huerta's most significant measure as governor—the establishment of the Cámara Obrera (Workers' Chamber) in October 1916—had the potential of upsetting this precarious balance. De la Huerta charged the Cámara Obrera, a body that consisted of workers' leaders from the state's largest companies, with "studying" issues relating to workers. The decree also asked the new chamber to issue workers' compensation judgments for those injured on the job. The Cámara Obrera practically became an arm of the state government, a legislature with distinct responsibilities. Its representatives received a monthly stipend, and they were enjoined to avoid strikes by means of mediating labor disputes. De la Huerta thus envisioned the Cámara as an instrument to mitigate class conflict and find negotiated solutions to labor disputes. Indeed, the foundation of the Cámara Obrera constituted the type of paternalistic measure that would characterize the Sonorans' approach to organized labor at the national level.[43] Protected by the state, the chamber successfully proposed several decrees designed to improve working conditions. These decrees established the right of collective bargaining, set up impartial boards of arbitration for labor disputes, prescribed maximum work hours and minimum wages, and mandated employer-funded health care as well as indemnities for workplace injuries.[44]

The Cámara Obrera's objectives received a boost from the promulgation of a new federal constitution in Querétaro in March 1917. For several months, a constitutional convention had deliberated a new document that would take the place of the Constitution of 1857. This convention consisted of both civilian and military representatives of Carranza's and Obregón's factions, with the latter dominant due to their greater numerical weight within the victorious coalition. While a majority of the Carrancistas merely desired to update the old constitution, many Obregonistas and reform-minded Carrancistas such as Pastor Rouaix viewed the meeting as an opportunity to enshrine their economic and social objectives. These delegates successfully pushed for a clause that kept the Catholic Church out of political life (Article 3), made land and the subsoil the patrimony of the Mexican nation, for private use only as a government concession (Article 27), and established the right of collective bargaining for workers, as well as a six-day work week, an eight-hour work day, and the employees' right to indemnity payments in case of injury (Article 123). Legislation that had existed in Sonora and other states thus became a part of the national Constitution.[45]

For Calles, the new constitution entailed both a triumph and a significant setback. The delegates at Querétaro had codified many of the most important points of the Sonoran reform program. Nonetheless, one of the pet projects of Calles—Prohibition—was not included in the document, and in the following summer, the newly elected state congress refused to incorporate the Ley Seca into the Sonoran constitution. Even more significantly, the constitution also shifted the formulation of social reform to the federal government, which had the power to interpret and limit the provisions of the new constitution by means of *leyes reglamentarias*, or enabling legislation. Without a ley reglamentaria, a constitutional provision essentially remained a dead letter. While the states could still enact social reforms, the federal government would again require compliance with its dictates. The constitution also undermined a spoils system crucial to Calles's success. Officials loyal to Calles had long administered the customs and port authorities, and control of these institutions presented a great opportunity for corruption and smuggling.[46] For example, in October 1916, de la Huerta imposed a prohibitive duty on cattle passing from Sonora to Arizona. When Calles outlawed the grazing of cattle within twenty-five miles of the border, ostensibly to prevent smuggling, rumors flew that he wanted the smuggling business to himself, and that ten dollars per head went to his bank in the United States.[47] A further element in the spoils system—the practice of parceling out the land of the enemies among loyal subordinates—had also flourished in Calles's first governorship. Now, the decisions of Calles and de la Huerta were subject to federal review, and the two leaders saw several of their land expropriations overturned by the National Agrarian Commission.

This erosion of Calles's authority followed an open challenge to his power in October 1916. Recognizing the failure of his plan to rein in Calles by reassigning him to the post of military commander, Carranza asked Obregón to replace him as jefe de operaciones in Sonora with his undersecretary, General Francisco Serrano. In a move that indicated that Carranza had struck a deal with Obregón, the president also ordered de la Huerta and Calles to Mexico City for reassignment to other duties.[48] This step was designed to clear the way for Obregón's brother José in the upcoming gubernatorial elections. Calles was consternated by this bald attempt to clip his power. As Serrano reportedly told a Constitutionalist officer, he "gave every indication of being a whipped man. He was sullen and morose . . . [, and] he asserted that he was at a loss to explain his recall."[49] On the strength of his clientelist networks, however, Calles outlasted this challenge to his bailiwick, and in January 1917, Calles announced his candidacy for governor.[50]

In the statewide elections of June 1917, Calles won an overwhelming triumph over José Obregón to become the first state governor elected under the new political order. Obregón had received only lukewarm support from his brother once the caudillo realized the extent of Calles's influence in his home state. In poor health and temporarily retired from politics, Obregón had finally recognized that he needed Calles more than he needed Carranza. Thus, out of the failed ouster grew a firm alliance that would progressively undermine Carranza in future years. The election made Calles constitutional governor, a post with much greater authority than the provisional governorship. He was not again seriously threatened in his hold over the state.[51]

CONSTITUTIONAL GOVERNOR

Calles's period as constitutional governor began with a surprise. On June 22, 1917, the managers of the CCCC halted production and took their movable equipment across the border. The measure was a bold step to force Calles to come to terms with the copper companies. From the perspective of the firm's managers, they were responding to a combination of higher production taxes and labor agitation promoted by the Cámara Obrera. Without tax revenue, the managers reasoned, the Sonoran government would have to give in to the CCCC. The crisis tested the Callistas' mettle in dealing with powerful foreign investors and a suddenly desperate populace in Cananea. Within days, Cananea authorities reported a critical food shortage and recommended the transport of the town's six thousand miners to other areas. Calles faced a stark alternative: give in to the copper barons and lose face politically, or stand his ground and risk a crisis of enormous proportions.[52]

The governor dealt with the crisis on two fronts. Publicly, he lambasted the copper companies and maintained steadfastly that he would not change Sonora's laws for their benefit. Most importantly, he called the bluff of the CCCC and removed the miners from Cananea so that they would not cross into the United States in search of work, where they, he believed, would "encounter a difficult situation shameful to our race."[53] Indeed, soon thereafter, Arizona authorities broke a strike at the Copper Queen mines in Bisbee, detaining twelve hundred miners, including many Mexican immigrants, in inhumane conditions. Calles believed that he could convince the miners to become agriculturalists. However, there was not enough irrigable land to provide six thousand miners with a new livelihood; the miners lacked experience as farmers; and many of them had no interest in farming.[54]

Behind the scenes, however, Calles was more conciliatory. He sought mediation through the services of a W. D. King, a former lobbyist for the copper companies. To coordinate his strategy with Carranza, the governor took a leave of absence and traveled to Mexico City in what was only his second trip to the capital. This leave of absence ultimately turned into an entire year. Compared to de la Huerta, interim governor Cesáreo Soriano was a Calles stooge, entirely dependent on his mentor.[55] Conveniently for Calles, it fell to Soriano to take the unpopular steps needed to come to a negotiated solution with the CCCC. On Calles's instructions, he held firm in the matter of the reform laws. But his first act as governor—the closure of the Cámara Obrera—amounted to a significant concession to the copper companies. To justify this step to the Sonoran public, Soriano argued that the promulgation of Article 123 made the Cámara a superfluous institution. In fact, however, closing the Cámara was in the interest of both the copper companies and the state government, as Calles regarded the Cámara as too radical.[56] Ultimately, the removal of the Cámara cleared the way for the return of the CCCC: on November 17, 1917, the company resumed operations without having achieved its principal objective of modifying de la Huerta's workplace laws.[57]

The resolution of this conflict left Calles free to pursue his enemies. By August 1917, he had returned to his post of jefe de operaciones to once again take on the Yaquis.[58] He and Soriano vowed to pursue an "energetic, definitive, and, if necessary, terrible campaign against that relatively insignificant group of individuals who are hostile to any civilizing influence." The best solution to the problem, they believed, was "the complete extermination" of the Yaquis.[59] However, this campaign was no more successful than the previous one. In August 1918, Calles finally abandoned the Yaqui campaign and returned to the post to which he had been elected.[60]

By contrast, Calles softened his position regarding the church. After the expulsion of the priests in March 1916, he had resisted a series of demands for their return. In a small concession, he did allow priests to enter Sonora temporarily to administer baptisms and last rites to the dying. Ultimately, however, the governor recognized the enormous political cost of his anti-clerical policies, which had antagonized not only Carranza, but also many of his own supporters. In April 1919, Calles signed a new law that allowed one priest for every ten thousand inhabitants—a total of twenty-six priests for the entire state.[61]

Likewise, Calles displayed an ambivalent attitude toward the large Chinese population of his state, most of which was active as small merchants, moneylenders, and shopkeepers. Sonoran nationalists targeted the Chinese as an undesirable ethnic group. Unlike U.S. investors, the Chinese competed with native capitalists and found themselves the target of envy and racist stereotypes. In Cananea, for example, the Chinese population of some eight hundred residents dominated local commerce. As immigrant non-whites, the Chinese became pariah capitalists in an increasingly xenophobic society. In 1916, a schoolteacher and entrepreneur from Magdalena, José María Arana, led a statewide movement to rid Sonora of the Chinese. As Arana stated, "when the first Chinese came to Mexico they were humble and miserable; but now they have enriched themselves, and we can stand them no longer."[62]

This movement placed the state administration in a predicament. On the one hand, joining the anti-Chinese fray would have enhanced its populist credentials. On the other hand, a campaign against the Chinese would have harmed a sector of society that paid its taxes and conducted its business exactly as the Callistas desired of all Sonorans. Moreover, Calles intended to show foreigners in Sonora that if they were expected to follow Mexican law, they would also be protected by it. As Soriano instructed local authorities in December 1917: "the truly democratic character of our institutions . . . absolutely rejects any type of persecution against individuals, groups, or classes."[63] One year later, Calles told the presidente municipal of Magdalena: "you, as the authority, are required to give protection to those foreigners . . . [who] are protected by our laws like those of any other nationality."[64] Nonetheless, he also suppressed further Chinese immigration into Sonora and pressured Chinese merchants to employ Mexicans rather than their own relatives.

A similar ambivalence marked Calles's approach to World War I, and particularly the issue of German activities in Sonora. As U.S. military intelligence records illustrate, Calles was friendly to German interests although loath to assist German schemes designed to provoke a war between

the United States and Mexico. As would become obvious later on, he ad-
mired Germany for reasons ranging from that country's well-organized
military to its social security and medical insurance for all workers. Calles
allowed German espionage free rein: his military trainer was also a German imperial agent, and the governor furnished another agent with
money and a firearm.[65] Like his superiors Carranza and Obregón, however,
Calles would not embroil Mexico in a conflict with the United States that
held no benefits for either the central government or his own ambitions.
Cited by the historian Friedrich Katz, the testimony of German agent Anton Dilger to the effect that he and Calles prepared an attack on the United
States in 1918 must therefore be regarded as implausible.[66] Neither U.S.
military intelligence sources nor Mexican documents corroborate Dilger's
boast to German diplomats that he could provoke a war between the
United States and Mexico "by having General Calles attack the United
States."[67] Mindful of his need to procure supplies and weapons from the
United States, Calles took pains to assure U.S. officials of his friendly atti-
tude toward the United States.[68]

Calles's final significant act as governor was the codification of the reform
decrees from the preceding four years in three seminal 1919 laws: the "Ley
de Gobierno" (Government Law), the "Ley de Trabajo" (Work Law), and
the "Ley Agraria" (Agrarian Law). The Ley de Gobierno defined the responsibilities of the governor and the state legislature and affirmed the principle
of the *municipio libre* (free municipality). The Ley de Trabajo ensconced the
right of collective bargaining, the right to strike, and the laws regarding
boards of arbitration and workers' compensation. It also outlawed long-
term debt service and the *tienda de raya*, the infamous company store in
which workers could exchange scrip for goods at inflated prices. Finally, the
Ley Agraria sought to foster smallholding, entitling agricultural workers to
their own parcels of land and fixing the upper limits of landownership. If
carried out to the letter, the Agrarian Law would have eliminated most large
estates in Sonora.[69] However, Calles never intended to break up all large estates. To him, Sonora's future lay in farmers such as the ones organized in
Obregón's new league of chickpea producers, most of whom farmed small
to mid-size plots.

Having thus assured his political legacy, Calles neared the conclusion of
his term aware of the fact that the new constitution prohibited the reelection of presidents and state governors. In May 1919, he accepted Carranza's
nomination as secretary of Industry, Commerce, and Labor, to begin September 1. On that day, de la Huerta took office as constitutional governor,
and Calles entered a new phase in his life as a player in national politics.[70]

Reform and repression marked the Calles era in Sonora. During this period, the state stood at the forefront of state-sponsored social reform. Like
several other states during the turbulent 1910s, Callista Sonora served as a

dress rehearsal for reform at the national level. By 1919, the state government had achieved marked advances in elementary school enrollment and
the working conditions of mine workers. Calles and de la Huerta had also
reversed two decades of generous concessions in favor of U.S.-owned mining companies and forced them to share at least some of their revenue. Finally, in expropriating the properties of their enemies, Calles and his allies
had helped craft a new landowning class that competed for power with the
notable families. But these advances came at a high price. Yaquis and May-
torenistas paid for their opposition with their lives and their lands; the Chinese community found itself attacked by xenophobic mobs; Catholic
priests had to beg to gain readmittance to the state; Calles reined in labor
protests that did not suit his interests; and liberal democracy remained as
elusive as in the Porfiriato. In particular, the Yaqui campaigns served as a
bloody reminder of the cost of Callista reforms.

NOTES

1. Louis L. Van Schaick, "Weekly Border Report," Nogales, May 19, 1917, National Archives, Washington, D.C. (hereafter NA), RG 165, Military Intelligence Division (hereafter MID), box 1943, 8536-241. A previous version of this chapter was
published in Jürgen Buchenau, *Plutarco Elías Calles and the Mexican Revolution* (Lanham, MD: Rowman and Littlefield, 2007), 55–80.
2. Louis L. Van Schaick, "Weekly Border Report," Nogales, May 19, 1917, NA,
MID, box 1943, 8536-241.
3. Adrian A. Bantjes, *As If Jesus Walked on Earth: Cardenismo, Sonora, and the Mexican Revolution* (Wilmington, DE: Scholarly Resources, 1998), 3.
4. Ignacio Almada Bay, *Breve historia de Sonora* (Mexico City: Fideicomiso Historia de las Américas, 2000), 138.
5. Cynthia Radding, "El triunfo constitucionalista y las reformas en la región,
1913–1919," in *Historia General de Sonora*, vol. 4. *Sonora moderno, 1880–1929* (Hermosillo: Gobierno del Estado de Sonora, 1997), 265–66.
6. Plutarco Elías Calles, *Decretos, circulares y demás disposiciones dictadas por el
C. Gobernador y Comandante Militar del Estado de Sonora, General Plutarco Elías Calles,
durante el año de 1915* (Hermosillo: Imprenta de Gobierno, 1915), 3.
7. Calles, *Decretos 1915*, 3–9.
8. Calles, *Decretos 1915*, 11–12.
9. Andrés García to Carranza, El Paso, Oct. 19, 1915, Archivo CONDUMEX,
Mexico City, Archivo Venustiano Carranza, carpeta 55, leg. 6240. García encloses a
press clipping with his remarks to the *El Paso Times*.
10. Edward M. Farmer, "Plutarco Elías Calles and the Revolutionary Government
in Sonora, Mexico, 1915–1919" (Ph.D. diss., Cambridge University, 1997), 185, n.
24, and 195.
11. Calles to Iturbe, Nogales, Aug. 18, 1917, Archivo Histórico General del Estado de Sonora (hereafter AHGES), vol. 3124, "Bebidas"; Iturbe to Calles, Culiacán,

Aug. 19, 1917, Fideicomiso Archivos Plutarco Elías Calles y Fernando Torreblanca (hereafter FAPEC), Archivo Plutarco Elías Calles (Anexo), gav. 8, exp. 129.

12. Calles, *Decretos 1915*, 11–12.

13. AHGES, vol. 3072, and Calles, *Decretos 1915*, 15–17.

14. Plutarco Elías Calles, *Decretos, circulares y demás disposiciones dictadas por el C. Gobernador y Comandante Militar del Estado de Sonora, General Plutarco Elías Calles, durante el año de 1916* (Hermosillo: Imprenta de Gobierno, 1916), 51–57 and 86–87.

15. Gilbert M. Joseph, *Revolution from Without: Yucatán, Mexico, and the United States, 1880–1924*, 2nd ed. (Durham, NC: Duke University Press, 1988), 134.

16. Farmer, "Plutarco Elías Calles," 182.

17. Calles, *Decretos 1915*, 34–41.

18. Calles, *Decretos 1915*, 20.

19. Calles, *Decretos 1915*, 19–21, 41–45, 47–48.

20. "Ley de Egresos," *Boletín oficial: órgano del gobierno constitucionalista de Sonora* 4, nos. 2–6 (Jan. 13–27, 1917).

21. Farmer, "Plutarco Elías Calles," 339.

22. Calles, *Decretos 1915*, 45–46.

23. Calles, *Decretos 1915*, 45–46.

24. Robert H. Murray, trans. and ed. *Mexico before the World: Public Documents and Addresses of Plutarco Elías Calles* (New York: Academy Press, 1927), 217.

25. "Ley de Egresos," *Boletín oficial* 4, no. 2 (Jan. 13, 1917): 2.

26. Engracia Loyo, *Las escuelas J. Cruz Gálvez: Fundación y primeros años, Boletín No. 40* (Mexico City: Fideicomiso Archivos Plutarco Elías Calles y Fernando Torreblanca), 12–13.

27. Farmer, "Plutarco Elías Calles," 238–41; Calles, *Decretos 1915*, 54.

28. Calles, *Decretos 1916*, 62–64.

29. Carlos Macías Richard, *Vida y temperamento: Plutarco Elías Calles, 1877–1920* (Mexico City: FAPEC and Fondo de Cultura Económica, 1995), 200–202.

30. Calles to Moreno, Hermosillo, Mar. 19, 1916, AHGES, vol. 3129.

31. Farmer, "Plutarco Elías Calles," 204.

32. Alvaro Obregón to Enrique Estrada, Querétaro, Mar. 28, 1916, Archivo de la Secretaría de la Defensa Nacional (hereafter ASDN), Archivo de Cancelados, exp. XI/III/1–44, vol. 1, p. 69.

33. Cándido Aguilar to Obregón Querétaro, July 28, 1916, and Calles to Obregón, Empalme, Aug. 3, 1916, ASDN, Archivo de Cancelados, exp. XI/III/1–44, vol. 1, pp. 93 and 96.

34. Commanding Officer to Commanding General, Southern Department, Douglas, May 20, 1916, NA, MID, box 1940, 8534-84.

35. Héctor Aguilar Camín, *La frontera nómada: Sonora y la Revolución Mexicana* (Mexico City: Siglo Veintiuno Editores, 1977), 430–36.

36. De la Huerta, "Informe," May 19, 1917, AHGES, vol. 3132.

37. Soriano, "Informe," Sept. 24, 1917, AHGES, vol. 3071; Calles to de la Huerta, Hermosillo, Aug. 9, 1918, APEC (Fondo Especial), gav. 4, exp. 7.

38. Pedro Castro, *Adolfo de la Huerta: La integridad como arma de la revolución* (Mexico City: Siglo XXI Editores, 1998), 12.

39. Friedrich Katz, *The Secret War in Mexico: Europe, the United States, and the Mexican Revolution* (Chicago: University of Chicago Press, 1981), 306–14.

40. Obregón to Jesús Acuña, Querétaro, Apr. 6, 1916, ASDN, Archivo de Cancelados, exp. XI/III/1–44, vol. 1, p. 75.

41. Bigelow to Commanding General, Douglas, Oct. 2, 1916, NA, MID, box 1941, 8534-138.

42. *Boletín Oficial* 3, no. 3 (July 15, 1916): 2.

43. The decree can be found in Roberto Guzmán Esparza, *Memorias de don Adolfo de la Huerta, según su propio dictado* (Mexico City: Ediciones Guzmán, 1957), 117–22.

44. For versions of these decrees codified as state law in 1918, see FAPEC, Fondo Plutarco Elías Calles, serie 010201, exp. 2, inv. 38 "Elías Calles, Plutarco (Gral. Gob.)," leg. 3.

45. Peter H. Smith, "La política dentro de la Revolución: El congreso constituyente de 1916–1917," *Historia Mexicana* 22, no. 4 (Apr. 1973): 363–95; and E. Victor Niemeyer, Jr., *Revolution at Querétaro: The Mexican Constitutional Convention of 1916–1917* (Austin: University of Texas Press, 1974).

46. Macías, *Vida y temperamento*, 263–69.

47. Bigelow to Commanding General, Douglas, Oct. 5, 1916, NA, MID, box 1941, 8534-140.

48. Calles to Obregón, Empalme, Son., Oct. 21, 1916, and Obregón to Calles, Mexico City, Oct. 24, 1916, ASDN, Archivo de Cancelados, XI/III/1–44, vol. 1, pp. 105–7.

49. Commanding General to Chief of Staff, Nogales, AZ, Oct. 30, 1916, NA, MID, box 2163, 9700-42.

50. Knabenshue, "Weekly Border Report," Nogales, Jan. 20, 1917, NA, MID, box 1943, 8536-156.

51. Van Schaick, "Weekly Border Report," Nogales, May 19, 1917, NA, MID, box 1943, 8536-241.

52. Farmer, "Plutarco Elías Calles," 264–80.

53. Quoted in Linda B. Hall and Don M. Coerver, *Revolution on the Border: The United States and Mexico, 1910–1920* (Albuquerque: University of New Mexico Press, 1988), 39.

54. Hall and Coerver, *Revolution on the Border*, 39–40.

55. Farmer, "Plutarco Elías Calles," 280–301.

56. Lawton to Secretary of State, Hermosillo, Sept. 12, 1917; border report, Nogales, Sept. 29, 1917, NA, RG 59, 812.00/21282, 21312.

57. Edward Farmer, *Un nacionalismo pragmático: El gobierno callista en Sonora y el capital extranjero*, Boletín 31 (Mexico City: Fideicomiso Archivos Plutarco Elías Calles y Fernando Torreblanca, 1999), 8–9.

58. J. A. Castro to Calles, Mexico City, Aug. 4, 1917, ASDN, Archivo de Cancelados, XI/III/1–44, vol. 1, p. 114.

59. Quoted in NA, MID, box 1944, 8536/280/1.

60. Macías, *Vida y temperamento*, 251–54.

61. Farmer, "Plutarco Elías Calles," 205–8; "Ley que fija el número de ministros de cultos religiosos que deberán ejercer su ministerio en el Estado," Apr. 24, 1919, FAPEC, Fondo Plutarco Elías Calles, serie 010201, exp. 2, inv. 38 "Elías Calles, Plutarco (Gral. Gob.)."

62. Quoted in Farmer, "Plutarco Elías Calles," 198.

63. Circular, Cesáreo Soriano, Dec. 4, 1917, FAPEC, Fondo Plutarco Elías Calles, serie 010203, exp. 1, inv. 40 "Soriano, Cesáreo, G."

64. Calles to presidente municipal, Hermosillo, Jan. 2, 1919, FAPEC, Archivo Plutarco Elías Calles (Anexo) gav. 15, exp. 262.

65. Calles to Carranza, Hermosillo, Oct. 22, 1917, FP, serie 0201, gav. 83, exp. 4, inv. 713, "Elías Calles, Plutarco (Gral.) 1917"; Joel A. Lipscomb to Southern Department, Nogales, Feb. 8, 1918, MID, box 1444, 8536-297.

66. Katz, *Secret War in Mexico*, 431.

67. United States Senate, *Investigations of Mexican Affairs: Preliminary Report and Hearings of the Committee on Foreign Relations, United States Senate, Pursuant to S. res. 106, Directing the Committee on Foreign Relations to Investigate the Matter of Outrages on Citizens of the United States in Mexico* (Washington, DC: Government Printing Office, 1920), 1:460; German military attaché to Auswärtiges Amt, Madrid, July 8, 1918, Politisches Archiv, Auswärtiges Amt, Berlin, Germany (PAAA), R 16917.

68. See NA, MID, files 10541-367 and 473.

69. FAPEC, Fondo Plutarco Elías Calles, serie 010201, exp. 2, inv. 38 "Elías Calles, Plutarco (Gral. Gob.)," legs. 9–10.

70. Farmer, "Plutarco Elías Calles," 382; Macías, *Vida y temperamento*, 255.

5

Adalberto Tejeda of Veracruz

Radicalism and Reaction

Andrew Grant Wood

An enthusiastic participant in the revolution and advocate for radical change in the congressional debates that followed, Veracruz governor Adalberto Tejeda Olivares presided over a number of bold social reforms during his two terms in office (1920–1924, 1928–1932), including one of the most significant agrarian reforms in the nation. Not surprisingly, many of his initiatives sparked significant defiance from conservative elements of Veracruz society. Following a brief portrayal of Tejeda's formative years, I will discuss some of the most controversial of the governor's policies and the intense political negotiation that played out during his tenure.[1]

BACKGROUND

Adalberto Tejeda was born on March 28, 1880, in the northern sierra town of Chicontepec, Veracruz, a traditional crossroads in the Huasteca for the region's diverse ethnic populations. Tejeda's mother, Eutiquia Olivares, came from an indigenous family who owned a small general store. Adalberto's father, Luis Tejeda, hailed from neighboring Jalacingo. A fairly well-to-do family, the Tejedas enjoyed a close affiliation with a distinguished real estate and credit broker, Braulio Melesio de Jesús Guzmán, who acted as a political patron to Adalberto's father.

In the 1880s, Tejeda's uncle Pedro served as a deputy to the Veracruz state legislature and National Congress. Around the same time, Luis Tejeda worked as the canton's *jefe político* for president Porfirio Díaz. As the chief federal administrator in Jalacingo, Luis oversaw political and commercial affairs for the municipalities of Altotonga, Atzalán, Jalacingo, Martínez de la Torre, Las Minas, Perote, and Tlapacoyan.[2]

The death of Tejeda's father in the early 1890s left the family with limited economic resources. As a result, Eutiquia took Adalberto and his sister Dolores to Mexico City. There, Tejeda first entered the Escuela Nacional Preparatoria and then attended engineering school (Escuela Nacional de Ingenieros), where he familiarized himself with the opposition journalism of Ricardo Flores Magón and others who dared criticize the administration of Porfirio Díaz. He married María Tejeda Perdomo in 1911 and subsequently returned to the Veracruz Huasteca, where he took a job in the town of Huayacocotla as a surveyor. In the years that followed, Tejeda became embroiled in the civil war following Victoriano Huerta's 1913 coup d'état in February and the subsequent assassination of Madero. In the weeks following the coup, Tejeda helped form a volunteer corps in his native Chicontepec. By June, Venustiano Carranza had forged the Constitutionalist coalition and he soon assigned his son-in-law, the Veracruzano revolutionary general Cándido Aguilar, to the Huasteca region. That October, Aguilar formed the Eastern Division (*División de Oriente*), and by December, Tejeda had enlisted.[3]

On April 21, 1914, U.S. Marines invaded and occupied the port of Veracruz following a diplomatic confrontation regarding the arrest of nine visiting U.S. soldiers in Tampico, Tamaulipas. The Marines turned the city over to Venustiano Carranza and his Constitutionalist forces later that year, helping the Constitutionalists defeat their rivals during the bloody conflict between the revolutionary factions. Well connected to Carranza's political network, Tejeda prepared to travel to the Constitutional convention in Querétaro in early 1917. At the last minute, the death of his mother prevented him from attending.[4] Not long out of the spotlight, the young politician was elected by Veracruzanos to serve as senator in the national congress. A staunch defender of Mexico's oil reserves because of his familiarity with the resource-rich Huasteca region, Tejeda often spoke out against granting concessions to foreigners. In doing so, he earned a considerable reputation. Along with several other lawyers and engineers who took a stand against foreign oil, Tejeda claimed he opposed the companies because they expressed little interest in the long-range environmental and economic interests of the nation.

Making a passionate appeal to the Senate in early October 1919, Tejeda argued for tight controls over the oil industry by referring to various laws protecting subsoil resources in Romania, Russia, and the United States.[5] A renewed threat of military conflict with the Yankees, however, forced lawmakers to compromise.[6] Nevertheless, Tejeda remained committed to the idea of full national control over oil resources, causing some foreign diplomats and businessmen to consider him in a negative light. The British consul in Tuxpan remarked that the Veracruz senator appeared to be "the aggressive and rude type of Mexican" who "possessed a strong character (and seemed) extremely anti-foreign."[7] To many Mexicans, however, he appeared to be upholding the fundamental ideals of the revolution. The following year, Tejeda would build upon this notoriety in his campaign for governor.

In April 1920, Alvaro Obregón announced his opposition to Carranza's plan to appoint his own successor. Later termed the Agua Prieta revolt, the rebellion spread rapidly and forced Carranza to flee Mexico City. A short while later an assassin's bullet ended his life. Sonoran Adolfo de la Huerta temporarily assumed office until Alvaro Obregón was declared the winner of national elections held in the fall of 1920.

In Veracruz, the Agua Prieta revolt played out with chief of military operations Guadalupe Sánchez and Adalberto Tejeda occupying leading roles. For his part, Tejeda commanded a force largely composed of members of the civil guard. Stationed in Jalapa, he worked under Sánchez, who coordinated action throughout the state. By June 1920, Sánchez, Tejeda, and others opposed to Carranza had also forced ex-governor Cándido Aguilar (who had left office to become minister of foreign relations in the Carranza administration) to leave the country. Filling the vacancy, Sánchez nominated the relatively unknown Antonio Nava to serve as interim governor until elections could be held. By July 1920, Tejeda, Veracruz senator Gabriel Gavira, and Jacobo Rincón had emerged as the three leading candidates.

Tejeda's participation in the Agua Prieta revolt, along with his earlier stance against the foreign oil companies, made him an attractive associate of the new regime in Mexico City. Nevertheless, he faced stiff competition from Gavira, who enjoyed greater prestige and political connections. Jacobo Rincón also hailed from Orizaba, but he differed from Gavira in that his support came largely from the old elites: landowners, businessmen, and clergy. When Obregón and Sánchez named him the candidate of the Partido Liberal Constitucionalista (PLC, or Liberal Constitutionalist Party) for governor, Tejeda's fate was largely sealed, as the PLC was then the nation's dominant party. Still, Tejeda also needed to deal with other important figures in state politics, including caudillo Manuel Peláez, who commanded a formidable army that patrolled the Huastecan oilfields.[8]

When the unofficial election results appeared in October, a sharp division in the state legislature between Tejedistas and followers of Rincón and Gavira (who by then had formed an alliance) emerged, with the former enjoying only a slight advantage. On October 12, the port of Veracruz daily newspaper *El Dictamen* reported that in Jalapa, two warring legislatures sought legitimacy. While supporters of Tejeda hunkered down in the legislative chamber, the Rincon-gavistas congregated in the main auditorium of city hall.[9] The Veracruz Electoral Commission eventually confirmed that Tejeda had won. Reflecting the still bitter rivalry between the two factions, the new governor assumed power on December 1, 1920, as federal troops stood by. Behind the scenes, powerful figures such as Veracruz military commander Sánchez as well as President Obregón harbored doubts about Tejeda's ability to keep the peace. Immediately seeking to develop an independent political base, one of the first things the new governor did was to end prohibitions on mass political organizing in the state. Not surprisingly, this move alienated certain powerful regional elites who resented the resulting ascendancy of peasant and worker groups. Complicating matters was the fact that Tejeda also faced a significant economic challenge, as a recession plagued both the state and the nation as a whole.

While the country had broken new records for silver exports the previous year, the price of precious metals had fallen off by the end of 1920. In the aftermath of World War I, other key exports, including cattle and henequen, experienced a similar drop. Luckily, the downturn would have proven much worse if not for the fact that the petroleum industry registered some of its highest revenue totals ever recorded. Yet this situation remained precarious as the imposition of a new petroleum export tax caused the oil companies to cease operations in protest. Uncertain about the nation's future, Tejeda emphasized his strong desire to stabilize the Veracruz economy in his first address to the state legislature on May 5, 1921.[10]

Meantime, Tejeda established his own security force to collect information and extend his influence throughout the state. In certain cases he did not hesitate to employ a creative tallying of votes to secure his preferred candidate in local elections. Tejeda used this technique to such a degree that by the end of the first six months of his term, over half of the state's mayors and town councils had been replaced with individuals loyal to the new administration in Jalapa. Wary of Tejeda's manipulations, some local officials resisted. Politicians ousted by the governor in the towns of Puerto México, Huatusco, Tuxpan, San Juan Evangelista, and the port of Veracruz, for example, complained vehemently.[11]

Early in 1921, members of the Chamber of Commerce and the Property Owners' Association, as well as the editors of *El Dictamen*, found themselves in common cause against the governor. Giving voice to a growing conservative force against Tejeda, the newspaper's editors attacked, describing him as an "agitator," "cannibal," "without culture," and "incompetent" while deriding him at length in their editorials. To counter opposition from hostile elites, Tejeda bolstered the state's civil guard. The governor ostensibly did this to establish an armed force independent of military commander Guadalupe Sánchez.[12] Tejeda also launched his first major popular initiative that sought to win the backing of organized labor. It was a state profit-sharing measure titled the Ley de Utilidades.[13]

Tejeda's bill stipulated that workers would receive approximately one month's additional salary from their employer after working for one year.[14]

Supervision of this process would be entrusted to local commissions under the guidance of the state labor relations board (Junta Central de Conciliación y Arbitraje). Although the governor provided additional details that sought to guard against excessive action being taken by either "Capital" or "Labor," his opponents vehemently criticized the proposal. Some legislators went so far as to denounce the bill as "Bolshevik communism." The editors at *El Dictamen* followed suit by characterizing the measure "The Hunger Law" and arguing that it "would bring the ruin of industry and commerce."[15] An editorial noting the governor's presence at a labor gathering in Jalapa sarcastically asked if Tejeda wanted to turn Veracruz into "another soviet."[16]

In June and early July 1921, public debate over the profit-sharing initiative grew more intense both inside and outside of Veracruz. A letter to President Obregón from a concerned Mexico City law firm argued against the measure by stating that "[it] created a grave situation [especially since] no other state has proposed such a law." The writer went on to suggest that "a solution to labor's problems should be sought without injuring the interests of capital."[17] Others from around the country wrote to the president suggesting that Tejeda's proposal be completely withdrawn from consideration.[18] Two representatives in the State legislature published a letter in *El Dictamen* that argued that, if approved, the proposed law "would encourage capital flight to other states thereby endangering the needed economic growth in Veracruz."[19]

Although it seemed that Tejeda would not have the votes, the legislature passed the bill on July 6, 1921.[20] In response, business interests moved quickly to block its implementation. Employers in Veracruz filed an assortment of *amparos* (legal stays) against the new law. They based their grievance on the assertion that profit sharing violated their constitutional right to private property.[21] Moreover, they objected strongly to a section that required them to compensate their workers from 1917.

After considering arguments against the Ley de Utilidades, the Mexican Supreme Court blocked application of the law. In a communication to Tejeda, President Obregón defended the action and stated "the sovereignty of the Court and the Constitution must be respected."[22] He further suggested the law only favored a "small minority" and instead proposed a moderate worker security measure be added to existing labor legislation as an alternative.[23] Adding fuel to growing anti-Tejedista fires in the state, *El Dictamen* then whipped up opposition a few weeks later by again claiming that the law would bankrupt industry and commerce.[24]

By this time, the controversy had gained the attention of several national elite groups, as members of the Industrial Association and National Commercial Association met with the president to discuss the matter. They told Obregón they might have to relocate factories and businesses out of

Veracruz if a resolution in their favor could not be negotiated. The chief executive then contacted Tejeda and insisted a settlement with business owners be reached immediately. Finding the idea of a compromise utterly unattractive, the governor told Obregón that he saw no reason to revise the law. Representatives from the textile industry in Orizaba, Tejeda pointed out, had not even bothered to discuss the matter with him.

Tensions rose as influential Veracruz businessmen moved to circumvent the governor's program by creating various ad hoc committees in the port of Veracruz, Orizaba, Córdoba, and Jalapa. Hundreds of small business owners throughout the state, including many hotel, restaurant, and retail interests, also rallied against the law. Further complicating matters for the new governor, opposition in the press continued unabated during the summer of 1921. As a result of coordinated efforts opposing the profit-sharing law, nearly 130 amparos had been granted by the Supreme Court by the end of 1921. Facing a statewide opposition, the legislative support needed to enforce the measure quickly dwindled. Seeing this, the governor turned to the problem of urban housing in order to gain support from the inhabitants of the state's cities.

In the years before Tejeda took office, a growing number of Veracruz residents had complained about deteriorating conditions and the high price of rental housing. And while temporary measures imposed in 1917 had provided some relief, governor Antonio Nava's August 1920 reversal of reform legislation lifted restrictions on rent increases. At the time, several residents petitioned officials in Jalapa, calling the move an "unjustified and shameful" act.[25] That same month, the Mexico City newspaper *El Universal* noted a significant rise in rents in the port which, they claimed, "exceeded that of the interior of the country."[26] Upon taking office, Tejeda faced what many considered a crisis in urban popular housing.

Residents in the port of Veracruz asked that the governor take action against specific individuals—including the two Cuban brothers Manuel and Antonio Cangas—who managed a number of crowded tenements. After city officials had issued a number of warnings without much result, the governor helped coordinate legal action to deport the two foreigners. Yet despite these efforts, official proceedings failed.[27]

By the beginning of 1922, renters took matters into their own hands by organizing a housing strike. The protest began in late January as women living in the port's red light district presented their complaints against their landlords to Veracruz mayor Rafael García. As a member of the Worker Party sympathetic to the plight of tenants, García declared that landlords should be advised to lower their rents as soon as possible and warned that strict measures would soon be taken by the city government if they failed to act.[28] On February 2, a handful of concerned citizens called a public meeting in the People's Library. After an enthusiastic exchange, the next few days saw *porteños* form an association they termed the Revolutionary Syndicate of Tenants. One of the organization's first acts was to declare a citywide rent strike to protest housing conditions.[29] Led by charismatic, one-eyed tailor Herón Proal, protesters demanded that landlords annul individual contracts with tenants and draw up new agreements supervised by the renters' union. With the backing of countless residents, Proal and his associates called for a reduction of rents to 1910 levels as well as a determined cleanup of local tenements. Before long, tenants in dozens of tenements across town had joined the boycott.[30]

Following several months of exuberant protest, conflict arose between rival factions within the movement. Tragically, the split provided a pretext for federal repression which took place on the night of July 5. After a skirmish between tenants early in the evening, a deadly showdown between members of the revolutionary syndicate and the military took place. In the melee, countless tenants were killed or injured. By the next morning, *El Dictamen* reported that nearly 150 members of Proal's syndicate had been arrested and taken to the city's Allende Jail.

Shocked by the violence, lawmakers in Jalapa sought to mediate the situation. Local representative Carlos Palacios petitioned Governor Tejeda and President Obregón for the immediate release of tenant prisoners. While neither politician complied with the congressman's demand, the governor did move to expedite passage of state housing reform legislation. In the wake of the July massacre, the Veracruz legislature debated a groundbreaking housing reform law, eventually approving it in May 1923. The measure incorporated several key tenant demands in its calling for a reduction in rent to slightly more than 1910 levels and provision for the supervision of landlord/tenant relations. Legitimated by Article 27 of the Constitution, Tejeda's rent law made provisions for the expropriation of urban lands for the purposes of new housing construction. Yet while the tenant movement had achieved moderate gains for renters, the protest had deeply frustrated Tejeda in his desire to gain control of Veracruz's mass urban movements. As a result, he soon turned his attention to rural areas and, specifically, began working with peasant organizers as a way to bolster his political base.

The rent strike had temporarily brought together several important popular organizers in the Veracruz region. The most noteworthy of these were Úrsulo Galván Reyes and his colleague Manuel Almanza García. After a stint in the Constitutionalist Army both Galván and Almanza briefly aligned themselves with the House of the World Worker and for a time organized laborers in northern Veracruz. They then spent time creating an agrarian cooperative in the small town of Anton Lizardi before relocating to the port of Veracruz, where they participated in a radical reading group known as Antorcha Libertaria.[31] An informal association of young men (both foreign and national) then living in the port, many (including Rafael García and tenant leader Herón Proal, as well as Galván and Almanza) went on to play leading roles in establishing a Veracruz branch of the Mexican Communist Party and the subsequent shaping of the state's social history over the next two decades. Lively exchanges with his colleagues helped Galván sharpen his ideological views while also deepening his commitment to the idea of "liberating" the Mexican peasantry.

In early February 1923, Galván and Almanza had convinced members of the Revolutionary Syndicate of Tenants to fund a delegation (composed of active *agraristas* Sóstenes Blanco, Marcos Licona Lara, and José María Caracas, as well as a handful of tenants and other communists) to accelerate peasant organizing efforts throughout the state. Visiting with rural workers in a number of communities, Galván was convinced that he had the necessary support to establish an independent peasant movement.

Midway through his term, Tejeda faced increasing pressure from General Guadalupe Sánchez as well as conservative business and landholding interests affiliated with the National Cooperatist Party. Sánchez and his associates blamed Tejeda's populist politics for social unrest in Veracruz cities and throughout much of the countryside, where peasants regularly clashed with landowners' private police (*guardias blancas*).[32] On certain occasions conflict reached deadly proportions, as was the case on March 9, 1923, when seven died and four were seriously wounded in a clash between state civil guard members and individuals associated with the security force of the landowning Lagunes family in the town of Puente Nacional. When reported in *El Dictamen*, the incident sent a shock wave across Veracruz as it had become clear that a showdown between Tejeda and Guadalupe Sánchez (who in fact had been helping to arm various guardias blancas throughout the state) was inevitable. Although Obregón sought to mediate the conflict, he sided with Sánchez and criticized the Veracruz governor for allowing municipal officials in Puente Nacional to employ the services of the civil guard. When Obregón called for the disbanding of the civil guard and a halt to all agrarista activity in the state, Tejeda realized he was in serious trouble.[33]

Looking for support, the governor turned to minister of government Plutarco Elías Calles as well as to various labor unions and peasant organizations. Tejeda also invited Galván to Jalapa. The two convened a statewide agrarista congress in late March 1923. With delegates from over one hundred communities, participants founded the Veracruz League of Agrarian Communities and Peasant Unions (*Liga de Comunidades Agrarias y Sindicatos Campesinos del Estado de Veracruz*). Úrsulo Galván, Antonio Carlón, José Cardel, Carolino Anaya, and Adalberto Tejeda served as the principal leadership. Following the establishment of the league, the stage was set for a series of dramatic struggles between a formidable Tejedista coalition on one side and a powerful assortment of conservative forces on the other.[34]

Landowners quickly countered with an organizing drive of their own. By late November, a "union of farmers" had been established to combat Tejeda's State Agrarian Commission efforts to redistribute land throughout the region through petition drives and, sometimes, outright force. Tension continued to build as Tejeda accelerated land reform in November 1923.[35]

Meantime, a larger political crisis was in the making. In early December 1923, a collection of powerful individuals associated with the National Co-operatist Party, including Guadalupe Sánchez, General Enrique Estrada in Jalisco, and General Fortunato Maycotte in Oaxaca, joined with former minister of finance Adolfo de la Huerta to stage a revolt against the Obregón government. They were unhappy with the president's management of the army, agrarian reform, and the selection of Calles as Obregón's sucessor. The insurrection was particularly heated in the state of Veracruz—rebels took control of the port of Veracruz and Jalapa, where they had driven off a small military force as well as a collection of approximately two hundred workers and peasants stationed to defend the state capital. Armed patrols operating at the behest of the landowners hunted down and killed several Veracruz agraristas and labor leaders, including José Cardel and José Fernández Oca. Defying Tejeda, the rebels chose Veracruz Senator José Pereyra Carbonell to serve as their "governor"; he subsequently sought to win over a portion of the peasantry by issuing a specious statement on agrarian reform that El Dictamen printed in early 1924.[36]

While those loyal to Tejeda had been caught off guard by the rebellion, they soon mobilized against the Delahuertistas. Peasant organizers formed a number of guerrilla squadrons which traveled across central Veracruz. Initially on his way to a conference in Moscow, Úrsulo Galván hurried home to join in the action. Also out of the state on business in Mexico City, Adalberto Tejeda reaffirmed his loyalty to Obregón before rushing back to Veracruz. On January 28, 1924, General Eugenio Martínez captured several key rebel commanders and booted de la Huerta and Sánchez out of Veracruz. Over the course of the next few weeks, armed agraristas in cooperation with members of the federal forces under General Heriberto Jara gained the upper hand.[37]

As the de la Huerta uprising came to an end, so, too, did Tejeda's term. Preparing for the upcoming elections, he designated his friend Enrique Meza to succeed him. The more popular candidate, however, was Heriberto Jara, who enjoyed renewed popularity across the state and in Mexico City because of his successful campaign against the rebels. When endorsed by presidential candidate Calles, Jara easily won the governorship.

Jara's term saw a continued strengthening of the Veracruz peasant movement despite the fact that the new governor did not court peasants with quite the same enthusiasm as Tejeda had. During the mid-1920s, many intimately associated with the movement, including Úrsulo Galván, Manuel

Díaz Ramírez, and Manuel Almanza, continued their close relationship with the Mexican Communist Party. They also kept in close contact with Tejeda, who had been selected by President Calles to serve in his cabinet— first as minister of communications and then as minister of government.

Although Tejeda benefited from the patronage of Calles, he nonetheless maintained a certain distance from the *jefe máximo*. Attending concerts and plays and tending to his wife and two children, the former Veracruz governor acted as an important liaison between the federal government and his Veracruz allies. As minister of government under Calles, he helped promulgate anticlerical measures during the Cristero Rebellion (1926–1929). Justifying these actions, Tejeda claimed he was not against religion per se, but only religious "fanaticism." Nevertheless, he often spoke out against the "ominous work of the clergy" in perpetuating "superstitious belief and ignorance among the common people." In response, supporters of the religious cause branded him "one of the most terrible and unforgiving [enemies] of the Catholic faith."[38]

In 1927, Tejeda sought another term as governor of Veracruz and gained the endorsement of Calles. With the former governor making his move, some in the state argued that Tejeda should not be allowed to hold office a second time. But when supporters of Obregón revised the federal constitution in November 1927 so that he could run again for president, lawmakers in Veracruz followed suit by legitimating Tejeda's bid for another term.

On July 17, 1928, the assassination of Alvaro Obregón by a young Catholic militant named José de León Toral shocked the nation. Calles responded to the crisis by installing former Tamaulipas governor Emilio Portes Gil as president, but only after Tejeda and a number of other influential politicians had insisted on the selection. In September 1928, Calles informed Congress of his determination to end the "era of caudillos" and followed this declaration with the founding of a national political party (the Partido Nacional Revolucionario, or PNR) in 1929. From the outset, Tejeda made clear his unwillingness to cooperate with party officials in establishing the PNR in Veracruz. Delegates to the party convention that March selected Pascual Ortiz Rubio as the official candidate for president despite sharp criticism from Tejeda and others present. In response, several *obregonista* generals, including José Gonzalo Escobar and Jesús Aguirre, staged a military revolt. Tejeda once again realigned himself with the regime in Mexico City and mobilized forces to put down the rebellion. He galvanized a collection of loyal associates, including Úrsulo Galván, who commanded a powerful agrarian guerrilla force.[39]

Following the rebel defeat, Tejeda requested that Galván sever his relationship with the Mexican Communist Party in exchange for government support for the Veracruz Peasant League. When Galván agreed, many accused him of selling out. The governor then saw to the election of several agraristas to political office at municipal and state levels—even in highly contested areas such as the port of Veracruz where resistance to Tejeda was strongest.[40] For his part, Galván served as a state senator while peasant military leader Manuel Jasso assumed a post as federal deputy. The formation of what was soon termed the Tejeda-peasant political bloc wielded considerable power while an independent force of loyal agrarian guerillas helped enforce the terms of Tejeda's renewed agrarian reform.[41]

In this regard, Tejeda's second term proved especially significant as the number of requests for land surpassed that of any other state in the union. In fact, the total property redistributed amounted to more than that of all other previous governors combined (beginning in August 1914 under Cándido Aguilar).[42] Not content with simply dividing up old estates, the governor saw to the supplying of necessary irrigation, roads, credit, machinery, and training. Reform initiatives established cooperatives at each *ejidal* community to administer this critical flow of resources from state agencies to peasants. Motivated by personal experience, a desire to address social injustices, and his strategy to strengthen his political base, Tejeda presided over this massive undertaking. Bolstered by the passage of new legislation between 1929 and 1932, his far-reaching programs were enforced by a state civil guard and powerful peasant guerilla army (approximately 7,000 strong by 1931).

Tejeda's reforms also impacted urban properties. Approved in May 1932, Law 66 provided for the expropriation and redistribution of urban lands to provide housing for workers. Despite this, the governor never sought to establish any type of Veracruz labor confederation that would operate under his command. Instead, he tried his best to deal with unions affiliated with the existing CROM (Confederación Regional Obrera Mexicana—Regional Confederation of the Mexican Worker), and CGT (Confederación General de Trabajadores—General Confederation of Workers).[43]

Tejeda's commitment to social progress proved unwavering during his two administrations. Like many of his generation, he believed strongly in the power of education and dedicated considerable resources to the building of rural schools. Starting during his first term, Tejeda dedicated unprecedented portions of the state budget to education. He pushed for training in agriculture, industry, art, and business while also strengthening primary and secondary education throughout the state. Special schools for peasants offered up-to-date training in agricultural techniques. As he saw it, public education could provide peasants with the tools necessary to escape the negative influence of prejudice and superstition. In turn, it would also turn them into more productive workers better able to contribute to the national economy.

Rounding out his social agenda, Tejeda generally took a dim view toward alcohol—seeing it as the cause of both physical and moral degeneration.

Taking action, he ordered his rural police to crack down on pulque trafficking. In late July 1929, the governor imposed a ban on the establishment of new cantinas and vigorously sought to limit the sale of alcoholic beverages. Businessmen across the state complained vehemently to officials in Mexico City, claiming that the governor had no right to intervene in their commercial affairs.

On another front, Tejeda joined national leaders in seeking to limit the influence of the clergy.[44] Not surprisingly, most church officials deeply disliked the governor. Nevertheless, Veracruz bishop Rafael Guízar y Valencia assumed a relatively moderate position in regard to official political programming. For a time, Tejeda toned down his campaign against the church after Obregón declared his desire to seek reelection in June 1927.[45] Nevertheless, following President Portes Gil's negotiations to end the Cristero conflict in mid-1929, the Veracruz leader stepped up pressure on religious officials by denouncing the compromise while applying anticlerical legislation with renewed vigor. This meant, in part, that foreign-born priests would no longer be allowed to practice in the state. In the meantime, Tejeda made every effort to encourage other clergy to break from Rome.

Tejeda pressed for what he viewed as "defanaticization" in public schools and supported the work of the statewide Revolutionary Anticlerical League.[46] His efforts caused an uproar, as conservative elements across the state criticized the governor for his "radicalism." Proof that church-state relations had reached a boiling point came in the spring of 1931 when a bomb mysteriously exploded in the Jalapa cathedral.[47] The subsequent passage of legislation limiting the number of priests to one for every hundred thousand residents in mid-1931 (the infamous "Law of the Thirteen" because the total number of priests amounted to thirteen for the whole state) further incensed church loyalists. Complaints reached President Ortiz Rubio, who warned Tejeda that his law could easily provoke conflict elsewhere in Mexico. Despite this, Tejeda remained steadfast in his convictions, arguing that the church diverted millions of pesos from the people each year for "frivolous projects."

Tension between church and state in Veracruz continued well into the summer of 1931. On July 25, a young seminarian tried to assassinate the governor in Jalapa. Hearing the news, some took matters into their own hands by defacing churches in the state capital, in the port of Veracruz, and in other areas. In one of the bloodiest conflicts, fifteen died and nearly thirty were wounded on October 17, 1931, when a mob in the town of Tlapacoan attacked municipal leaders loyal to Tejeda after someone had burned down the parish church. Gradually, clergy compromised their position as orders came from Rome that urged priests to avoid confrontation and to work within limitations imposed by the government.

Still, it would not be until 1937 that churches closed during Tejeda's second administration were reopened.[48]

Yet while Tejeda enjoyed impressive control over Veracruz during his second administration, divisions within his political coalition (composed largely of an assortment of regional peasant and liberal middle-class groups) were always evident. In fact, the state leader's failure to win significant favor with the powerful Veracruz labor movement caused him many difficulties.[49] In the meantime, feuding between communists, members loyal to President Calles's PNR, and Tejedistas led by Galván significantly weakened the governor's power.[50] When Galván died while receiving treatment at the Mayo Clinic in Minnesota for a leg tumor in July 1930, the Veracruz peasant movement suffered a tremendous blow from which it would never recover.[51]

Tejeda also faced a growing political challenge from rival leaders in the state such as Senators Manlio Fabio Altamirano and Arturo Campillo Seyde, who struggled for control of the Veracruz PNR affiliate.[52] Added to this were persistent attacks coming from commercial, military, and church groups across the state whose interests were regularly articulated in *El Dictamen*. Their criticism grew more virulent in mid-1930, when Tejeda imposed new taxes on oil and certain other commercial enterprises as a way to combat the growing impact of the Great Depression.[53]

Over time, federal officials working to consolidate their rule through the incorporation of regional leaders and various popular groups into the PNR increasingly viewed the situation in Veracruz with suspicion. Most agreed that Tejeda's political machine had amassed too much power. Not coincidentally, this judgment came midway through the governor's second term, just as Tejeda began making his aspirations for president known. Turning up at peasant, labor, and national party meetings outside the state, Tejeda generated growing support. Of course, his politics contrasted sharply with the increasingly conservative policies of the PNR.[54] Seeking to counter any potential challenge Tejeda might muster, soon-to-be-president General Abelardo L. Rodríguez (1932–1934) and Calles hatched a plan to undermine the Veracruz governor's bid for executive office. One stiff challenge to Tejeda's power came in October 1932, when delegates attending the PNR national convention sought to purge the party of what the national press had dubbed its "Bolshevik" elements. Tejeda and his supporters were effectively marginalized during the meeting. At the same time, Calles and his allies moved to stop further land reform. Federal officials crafted legislation that declared current land reform efforts throughout the nation to be in violation of 1929 revisions to agrarian law.[55] This measure essentially called for a reversal of revolutionary land reform policies by ending any further redistribution of land parceled out as communal plots (*ejidos*). To bring about this change and force renegade politicians like Tejeda to comply, Calles formed a special military directorate composed of five generals. Subsequently, president Abelardo L. Rodríguez (who had assumed office in September 1932) sent military engineers to Veracruz in early November 1932.[56]

Veracruz voters elected Tejeda's hand-picked successor, Gonzalo Vázquez Vela, in December of that year, despite the mounting challenge to his power. Almost immediately, officials in Mexico City (including recently appointed minister of war Lázaro Cárdenas) claimed that conditions in rural areas had changed so that independent militias such as the Veracruz Security Forces were no longer necessary. Despite initial objections from Tejeda, federal forces moved to disarm the formidable agrarista guerillas by dispatching several battalions to the state. Outmaneuvered, Tejeda instructed his followers to avoid violence and cooperate with federal forces. In early January 1933, he watched as some 7,000 federal troops fanned out across Veracruz to confiscate the guns and ammunition of militant peasants.[57]

Still enjoying significant control over organized peasants in Veracruz as well as certain radical factions within the National Peasant League, the ex-governor remained one of the most prominent "leftist" politicians in Mexico at the time. Nevertheless, pressure from the national palace seeking to weaken Tejeda's political base eventually took its toll. In February 1933, the state agrarian movement divided as *campesino* delegates attended competing conventions held in Jalapa. On the one side, Tejeda loyalists under the leadership of José García gathered after learning that President Rodríguez wanted García to resign. Meantime, another faction loyal to Rodríguez convened nearby. Headed by former communist Sóstenes Blanco and composed of approximately 1,300, including Governor Vázquez Vela (who had been issued an ultimatum by the president), ranking officials of the PNR, and President Rodríguez's official representative, this group represented an outright challenge to Tejeda and his followers. Bitter relations between the two factions persisted even after President Rodríguez called representatives from each league to Mexico City to negotiate a truce and consolidate the formation of a neutral, third league (termed "yellow") made up of elements from both the rival "red" (Tejeda) and "white" (Blanco) factions.[58]

Under the banner of the newly formed Socialist Party of the Left (PSI), Tejeda campaigned full-time for the presidency throughout the latter half of 1933.[59] He denounced the corruption and crony capitalism of the PNR (whose candidate would soon officially be Lázaro Cárdenas). In response, PNR officials sought to dismantle further Tejeda's political machine, first at the local level, then in the state legislature, and finally in the state and federal courts. After expelling lawmakers loyal to Tejeda in both the state and national legislatures, party goons then turned to hunting down radical agraristas in Veracruz.

With his political base crumbling, Tejeda lost ground in late 1933. He nevertheless remained true to his political ideals and persisted in his criticism of the national party. Soon, however, health concerns limited his ability to campaign in the final months. As a result, Tejeda made only a modest showing in the polls as Lázaro Cárdenas won handily in July 1934.

Tejeda retired from political life until Cárdenas assigned him to a diplomatic post in France in July 1936. Over the next two decades the former Veracruz governor served his country as ambassador to Spain (1937–1939) and then Peru (1942–1947) before returning to Mexico to take a position in the Veracruz state government of Adolfo Ruiz Cortines in December 1950. He was subsequently honored with a promotion to brigadier general upon his official retirement from active military service in May 1948. In September 1960 Tejeda died in Mexico City.

Adalberto Tejeda's career in public service produced a lasting, albeit highly contentious legacy. Details regarding his careful negotiation with the national postrevolutionary regimes reveal much in regard to the often violent reconsolidation of national power during the first half of the twentieth century. As the political and social history of Veracruz during the Tejeda era attests, the 1920s and early 1930s were critical years for Mexicans as the ideals of their revolution were either co-opted or significantly compromised by a powerful central government determined to neutralize all independent political opposition that stood in its way.

*I extend special thanks to Heather Fowler Salamini for her warm collegiality and pioneering work on Veracruz.

NOTES

1. Portions are drawn from Andrew Grant Wood, *Revolution in the Street: Women, Workers and Urban Protest in Veracruz, 1870–1927* (Lanham, MD: SR Books/Rowman and Littlefield, 2001), 51–63. On the history of Tejeda and the agrarian movement in Veracruz, see Heather Fowler Salamini, *Agrarian Radicalism in Veracruz, 1920–38* (Lincoln: University of Nebraska Press, 1971); Heather Fowler Salamini, "Orígines laborales de la organización campesina en Veracruz," *Historia Mexicana* 20, no. 2 (Oct.–Dec. 1970), 235–64; Heather Fowler Salamini, "Los orígenes de las organizaciones campesinas en Veracruz: Raíces políticas y sociales," *Historia Mexicana* 85, no. 1 (July–Sept. 1972), 52–76; Heather Fowler Salamini, "Revolutionary Caudillos in the 1920s: Francisco Múgica and Adalberto Tejeda," in *Caudillo and Peasant in the Mexican Revolution*, ed. David A. Brading (Cambridge: Cambridge University Press, 1980), 169–92; Romana Falcón, *El agrarismo en Veracruz: La etapa radical, 1928–1935* (Mexico City: Colegio de México, 1977); Carlos Martínez Assad, "La lucha de los campesinos en Veracruz entre 1923 y 1934: Un intento de organización

independente," *Cuadernos Agrarios* 5 (1977): 38–56; José Rivera Castro, "Veracruz: Organización y radicalismo campesino," in *Actores sociales en un proceso de transformación: Veracruz en los años veinte*, ed. Manuel Reyna Muñoz (Jalapa: Universidad Veracruzana, 1996), 191–222; as well as Olivia Domínguez Pérez, ed., *Agraristas y agrarismo: La liga de comunidades agrarias del estado de Veracruz* (Jalapa: Gobierno del Estado de Veracruz/Liga de Comunidades Agrarias y Sindicatos Campesinos del Estado de Veracruz, 1992).

2. Romana Falcón and Soledad García Morales (in collaboration with María Eugenia Terrones), *La semilla en el surco: Adalberto Tejeda y el radicalismo en Veracruz, 1883–1960* (Mexico City: Colegio de México/Gobierno del Estado Veracruz, 1986), 34–38. Related information pertaining to the state's jefe politicos can be found in Soledad García Morales and Jose Velasco Toro, eds., *Memorias e informes de jefes políticos y autoridades del régimen porfirista, 1877–1911* (Jalapa, Veracruz: Gobierno del Estado de Veracruz/Universidad Veracruzana, 1991).

3. For a concise history of Veracruz during the revolution see Karl Koth, *Waking the Dictator: Veracruz, the Struggle for Federalism, and the Mexican Revolution, 1870–1927* (Calgary: University of Calgary Press, 2002).

4. Falcón and García Morales, *La semilla en el surco*, 70.

5. "Discusión en la H. Cámara de Senadores del proyecto de Ley del Petroleo presentado por el C. Senador Tejeda, sesión del dia 10 de Octubre 1919," in Secretaria de Industria, Comercio y Trabajo, *Documentos relacionados con la legislación petrolera mexicana*, vol. 2 (Mexico City: Talleres Gráficos de La Nacion, 1922).

6. On the 1919 intervention crisis see Manuel A. Machado and James T. Judge, "Tempest in a Teapot? The Mexican-U.S. Intervention Crisis of 1919," *Southwestern Historical Quarterly* 74 (1970): 1–23.

7. British Viceconsul in Tuxpan to Hohler, Apr. 26, 1916. Quoted in Falcón and García Morales, *La semilla en el surco*, 97.

8. On Peláez see Soledad García Morales, "Manuel Peláez y Guadalupe Sánchez: Dos caciques regionales," *La Palabra y El Hombre* 67 (Jan.–Mar. 1989): 125–36.

9. *El Dictamen*, Oct. 12, 1920.

10. Adalberto Tejeda, "Informe que rinde el ejecutivo del estado libre y soberano de Veracruz-Llave ante la H. Legislatura del mismo por el período comprendido del 16 del octubre de 1920 al 5 de mayo de 1921," in *Estado de Veracruz: Informes de sus gobernadores, 1826–1986*, ed. Carmen Blázquez Domínguez, vol. 10 (Jalapa: Gobierno del Estado de Veracruz, 1986), 5423.

11. Falcón and García Morales, *La semilla en el surco*, 124–25.

12. Tejeda replaced Abraham Sánchez (older brother of Guadalupe Sánchez) with two of his longtime associates.

13. For discussion of this period see Soledad García Morales, "Adalberto Tejeda y la intervención federal en la política de Veracruz (1920–1923)," *La Palabra y El Hombre* 42 (Apr.–June 1982), 43–50, and also Sergio Florescano Mayet, "Veracruz y Adalberto Tejeda ante los movimientos populares (1920–1922)," *La Palabra y El Hombre* 74 (Apr.–June 1990), 57–81.

14. The 1918 Veracruz Labor Law provided the most immediate legal precedents to Tejeda's bill but did not provide for their implementation and enforcement. My discussion of the Ley de Utilidades controversy follows Olivia

Domínguez Pérez, *Politica y movimientos sociales en el tejedismo* (Jalapa: Universidad Veracruzana, 1986), 40–45.

15. *El Dictamen*, Dec. 26, Mar. 9, 1921.

16. *El Dictamen*, Mar. 11, 1921.

17. Fernando Duret, Gustavo Suzarte Campos, and Luis F. Contreras. Archivo General de la Nación (hereafter AGN), Obregón-Calles, 243-VI-L-2, July 25, 1921.

18. See various petitions both for and against in AGN, Obregón-Calles, 243-V-L-2.

19. *El Dictamen*, July 2, 1921.

20. *El Dictamen*, July 7, 1921.

21. The identity of several businesses who joined in this effort are revealed in the records of the Junta Central de Conciliación y Arbitraje de Veracruz, housed in the state archive Archivo General del Estado de Veracruz (hereafter AGEV) in Jalapa.

22. Quoted in Domínguez Pérez, *Politica y movimientos sociales en el tejedismo*, 45.

23. Later, the court decided that the issue would be better resolved by somehow adding the workable aspects of Tejeda's proposals to existing labor legislation.

24. *El Dictamen*, July 21, 1921.

25. See, for example, Juan L. Sánchez to Antonio Nava, Aug. 2, 1920, AGEV, gobernación, 1920.

26. *El Universal*, Aug. 1, 1920.

27. AGEV, gobernación, 1920.

28. *El Dictamen*, Jan. 29, 1922.

29. *El Dictamen*, Feb. 6, 1922. For a full treatment of the tenant movement, see Wood, *Revolution in the Street*.

30. *El Dictamen*, Mar. 7–9, 1922.

31. Fowler Salamini, *Agrarian Radicalism in Veracruz*, 29–31.

32. Another key piece of legislation that would be approved by Veracruz lawmakers that summer was an important worker safety law (*ley de enfermedades profesionales y no profesionales*). See Domínguez Pérez, *Política y movimientos sociales en el tejedismo*, 46–56.

33. Fowler Salamini, *Agrarian Radicalism in Veracruz*, 37–49; Falcón and García Morales, *La semilla en el surco*, 152–54.

34. Falcón and García Morales, *La semilla en el surco*, 158.

35. Falcón and García Morales, *La semilla en el surco*, 162–63. In September, electricians had gone on strike in the port of Veracruz and soon countless others turned the situation into a general strike that paralyzed the city.

36. Fowler Salamini, *Agrarian Radicalism in Veracruz*, 41–43; Falcón and García Morales, *La semilla en el surco*, 164–67.

37. Fowler Salamini, *Agrarian Radicalism in Veracruz*, 44–45. For a full account see Soledad García Morales, *La rebellion delahuertista en Veracruz, 1923* (Jalapa: Universidad Veracruzana, 1986).

38. Falcón and García Morales, *La semilla en el surco*, 169–71.

39. Fowler Salamini, *Agrarian Radicalism in Veracruz*, 62–65; Falcón and García Morales, *La semilla en el surco*, 182–87.

40. See Falcón and García Morales, *La semilla en el surco*, 194–99.

41. Fowler Salamini, *Agrarian Radicalism in Veracruz*, 69–73; Falcón and García Morales, *La semilla en el surco*, 187–91.

42. Falcón and García Morales, *La semilla en el surco*, 225-28.

43. Eitan Ginzberg, "Ideología, política y la cuestión de las prioridades: Lázaro Cárdenas y Adalberto Tejeda, 1928-1934," *Mexican Studies/Estudios Mexicanos* 13, no. 1 (Winter 1997): 77-79, 63.

44. The history of the state and church conflict in Veracruz is detailed in John B. Williman, *La iglesia y el estado en Veracruz, 1840-1940* (Mexico City: Sep-Setentas, 1976) and William John Backer, "Church and State in Veracruz, 1840-1940: The Concord and Conflicts of a Century" (Ph. D. diss., University of St. Louis, 1971).

45. Fowler Salamini, *Agrarian Radicalism in Veracruz*, 68.

46. On this history from a national perspective see Adrian Bantjes, "Idolatry and Iconoclasm in Revolutionary Mexico: The De-Christianization Campaigns, 1929-1940," *Mexican Studies/Estudios Mexicanos* 13, no. 1 (Winter 1997): 87-120.

47. Falcón and García Morales, *La semilla en el surco*, 258; Fowler Salamini, *Agrarian Radicalism in Veracruz*, 92.

48. Falcón and García Morales, *La semilla en el surco*, 265-67.

49. Fowler Salamini, *Agrarian Radicalism in Veracruz*, 73-74.

50. Falcón and García Morales, *La semilla en el surco*, 288-92.

51. Sóstenes Blanco, *Ursulo Galván (1893-1930): Su vida—su obra* (Jalapa: Liga de Comunidades Agrarias y Sindicatos Campesinos del Estado de Veracruz, 1966), 30.

52. Falcón and García Morales, *La semilla en el surco*, 272-82, 292-95.

53. Falcón and García Morales, *La semilla en el surco*, 303-10.

54. See Fowler Salamini, *Agrarian Radicalism in Veracruz*, 108-14, for comparisons between Cárdenas and Tejeda, as well as Ginzberg, "Lázaro Cárdenas y Adalberto Tejeda, 1928-1934," 55-85.

55. Falcón and García Morales, *La semilla en el surco*, 321.

56. Fowler Salamini, *Agrarian Radicalism in Veracruz*, 115; Falcón, *El agrarismo en Veracruz*, 112.

57. Of course not everyone lamented the disarming of Tejeda's political force. Rival agrarian groups such as the Veracruz "white league" led by Sóstenes Blanco supported the program, as they allied themselves with President Rodríguez. Falcón, *El agrarismo en Veracruz*, 115-22; Fowler Salamini, *Agrarian Radicalism in Veracruz*, 115-17; Falcón and García Morales, *La semilla en el surco*, 320-26.

58. Fowler Salamini, *Agrarian Radicalism in Veracruz*, 122-25.

59. He officially declared his candidacy in September 1933.

6

José Guadalupe Zuno Hernández and the Revolutionary Process in Jalisco

María Teresa Fernández Aceves

In December 1920, the Catholic press *Restauración* sarcastically described the violent participation of José Guadalupe Zuno Hernández (1891–1980) and José María Cuéllar in the electoral process for governor and state congressmen.[1] For the Catholic press, Zuno lacked honor, and it accused him of promoting the drinking of alcohol and the stealing of votes. In this election, two political groups clashed—the conservative Partido Nacional Jalisciense (PNJ), affiliated with the Partido Nacional Cooperatista, and the Confederación de Partidos Liberales de Jalisco (CPLJ), an Obregonista populist and progressive force. Zuno, as deputy and president of the CPLJ, led Basilio Vadillo's electoral campaign to become governor.

According to the press, Zuno and Cuéllar burst into a voting booth because the CPLJ was losing. They demanded the public electoral officials give them the voting files. Both factions struggled to keep the votes, but Cuéllar shot and killed Gudelio L. Jiménez, vice president of the PNJ and secretary of a voting booth.[2] This was a bloody electoral dispute in which both parties took over votes by using "gun shots, blows, slaps, and flying chairs."[3] After the election, the leaders of the PNJ tried to impeach Zuno and Cuéllar as state deputies and claimed they had won. In the end, the Jaliscan Obregonista group, the CPLJ, obtained the legal recognition as winners of the elections. Zuno and his faction were ready for the next political struggles.

This brief description of events during the 1920 statewide elections illustrates why Zuno was one of the most controversial political figures in Jalisco. Zuno's career has elicited strongly divergent opinions not only from those around him, but also from historians. On one hand, the Catholic and conservative press portrayed Zuno as a politician who did not respect the legal system and was determined to reach and maintain power by any means. In 1937, the U.S. consul in Guadalajara, who had served in this capacity since 1920, described Zuno as an "extraordinarily astute politician, remarkably intelligent and extremely corrupt."[4] On the other hand, Zuno's own memoirs,[5] one of his followers' chronicles,[6] and most of the revisionist Jaliscan historiography about the revolutionary process have lauded his role in the defense of regional autonomy at the municipal and state levels, and his anticlerical, labor, agrarian, and educational policies.[7]

FAMILY, THE CENTRO BOHEMIO, AND THE RISE OF POLITICS

José Guadalupe Zuno's life history and political trajectory illustrate how a young generation challenged the political system of the Porfiriato and sought radical changes during and after the Mexican Revolution. His case clearly illustrates how these processes were experienced in Jalisco. Zuno was born in the hacienda de San Agustín in the municipality of Jamay, Jalisco, in 1891. He came from a rural lower-middle-class family. His father, Vicente Zuno Estrada, was a *tenedor de libros* and a rural teacher, and his mother was María Trinidad Hernández Gómez. The Zuno Hernández family migrated to Guadalajara in 1893, where they owned a small grocery store.[8]

Zuno was given a public liberal and anticlerical education with a nineteenth-century tradition that valued the patria, the constitution, people, freedom, independence, and equality. His grandfather and uncles were Juarista Liberals opposed to Díaz's dictatorship. His grandfather participated in the Reform War (1858–1861) and was an anticlerical.[9] During his school years, he learned the principles and impact of the long struggle between federalism and centralism in Mexican history, and he grew to appreciate the importance of the separation of church and state for maintaining autonomy and the equilibrium of powers.[10] Zuno attended the Liceo de Varones, where he soon developed the drawing skills that allowed him to join the *reyista* newspaper *El Perico* as a cartoonist. In 1908, together with Rafael Buelna, he initiated the anti-reelectionist campaign inside the liceo. Like Madero would soon do on the national level, Zuno and Buelna gave new impetus to nineteenth-century liberal ideas. The authorities of the liceo did not tolerate their political activities, so they were expelled before finishing the last year of high school. Then Zuno migrated to Mexico City, where he met other artists and intellectuals with progressive and revolutionary ideas, among them José Clemente Orozco and Gerardo Murillo (Dr. Atl). Here, he began to work at the maderista newspaper *El Constitucionalista*.[11] In 1912, he returned to Guadalajara with other painters such as Carlos Sthal and Xavier Guerrero. They established their own painting workshop, which soon became known as the Centro Bohemio.[12] This center was the most prolific and vibrant political and cultural site of Guadalajara because it gathered artists and writers that later would become political and social leaders. Zuno was its most important social, political, and cultural reformer. Therefore, the Centro Bohemio developed the intellectual base of Zunismo.[13]

At the end of 1912, Zuno returned to Mexico City and soon thereafter experienced the coup d'état of Victoriano de la Huerta. After the arrival of the Constitutionalist General Manuel M. Diéguez in Guadalajara in 1914, he returned and participated in the provisional governor's implementation of revolutionary and anticlerical social reforms. Zuno started working as a cartoonist for the *Boletín Militar* and was state inspector for drawing for the Secretaría de Educación. Later, he helped to establish a political and revolutionary association, Amigos del Pueblo, where the members of Centro Bohemio and other radical and iconoclast intellectuals such as the schoolteacher Atala Apodaca (1884–1977) collaborated.[14] Amigos del Pueblo campaigned in favor of the Constitutionalists and the revolution.[15]

During this period, Zuno and Alfredo Romo, another member of the Centro Bohemio, joined the revolution by taking the military train led by Carlos Roel, with the destination of Saltillo, Coahuila.[16] This military experience allowed Zuno to reestablish his relationship with Rafael Buelna, a former classmate of the liceo who had become a general and *comandante* of the military post in Tepic.[17] Buelna connected Zuno and Alfredo Romo with the Sonoran group—Álvaro Obregón and Benjamín Hill. In 1914, Zuno met Obregón in Guadalajara. This was the beginning of an important relationship for both Obregón and Zuno that was crucial for their rise in politics. They developed a reciprocal friendship and loyalty that transcended political ties by establishing family bonds through *compadrazgo*.

After two electoral defeats as an independent candidate for deputy in the district of Los Altos in 1916 and 1917, Zuno affiliated with the Partido Liberal Jalisciense and published critical articles in the newspaper *Gil Blass* to challenge the decadent Carrancismo in Jalisco.[18] During the Constitutionalist Convention in Querétaro, Zuno initially used cartoons to represent his nineteenth-century liberal ideas—ideas focused on political democracy rather than social reform. However, he soon recognized the significance of the interaction among revolutionary caudillos, artists, workers, artisans, peasants, and women in the process of drafting the 1917 Constitution. This revolutionary milieu gave impulse to his political career and movement.[19] By 1919, Zuno and the Centro Bohemio actively supported Obregón's campaign for president and mobilized autonomous progressive forces—workers, artisans, teachers, women, and peasants.[20] Thus, the rise of Obregonismo from 1919 to 1923 galvanized the revolutionary process in Guadalajara and Jalisco and created a coalition of popular forces to promote secular, land, labor, and educational reforms.

THE RISE OF RADICAL STATE POLITICS

As indicated at the beginning of this chapter, Zuno participated in the problematic Badillo campaign and in the recognition of this electoral process. Basilio Badillo was a radical Obregonista but weak Jalisco governor who sought the politicization of workers through Marxist and Leninist ideas and technical education at the Universidad Obrera (1921–1922).[21] The significant violence between Catholics and the revolutionaries, as well as Badillo's lack of strong alliances with workers, local politicians, and legislators, contributed to his fall. His failed attempt to politicize workers showed that the radicalization of workers could not be directed and planned from above. In fact, labor forces were more radical than the weak revolutionary state.

Zuno and his group won the elections for mayor of Guadalajara in 1922 and for the state and federal deputies. As mayor, he worked on legal reforms to encourage the autonomy of municipalities and promoted urban transformations regarding the distribution of water. This was a strategic position because he had the opportunity to mobilize quickly to the next level: the governorship. He was only mayor of Guadalajara for three months because he decided to run for governor and was elected in December of 1922.

Thus, as the leader of the CPLJ, as mayor of Guadalajara (1922), and as governor of Jalisco (1923–1926), Zuno allied with teachers, professionals, artists, artisans, industrial and service workers, and sectors of the peasantry to build a secular, populist movement that would defeat the Catholics, implement a program of social justice, and secure regional autonomy.[22] He promoted social reform regarding agrarian and labor matters as well as in the areas of university education, relations with the Catholic Church, gender, and general welfare.

Although he was associated with president Álvaro Obregón, Zuno opposed the ambitions of the Mexico City–centered Confederación Regional Obrera Mexicana (CROM) to organize and dominate the local labor movement. Zuno created broad coalitions with male peasants and male and female urban workers. Many of the latter were organized in women's political groups. At the CPLJ, Zuno established an office to orient peasants in land claims and appointed a well-known *agrarista* leader, Secudino E. Delgadillo, to represent rural communities in their claims for land.[23]

In 1922, Zuno signed a pact with workers of the Grupo Acción of Jalisco, in which artisans and industrial and service workers gave their support in exchange for fulfillment of their labor demands.[24] To give more autonomy to workers and counteract the intrusion of the CROM, on September 17, 1924, Zuno created the Confederación de Agrupaciones Obreras Libertarias de Jalisco (CAOLJ) out of the Grupo Acción. In 1925, Zuno invited Mexico City communists, among them David Alfaro Siqueiros, Amado de la Cueva,

Hilario Arredondo, and Roberto Reyes Pérez, to participate in the labor movement. They worked closely with electrical, textile, and mine workers to expand the rank-and-file of the CAOLJ, in which artisans and service workers predominated.[25]

Through the Liga de Comunidades Agrarias de Jalisco and the CAOLJ, the two main peasants' and workers' organizations, Zunistas fought on different fronts. To counter the strong Catholic social action movement, Zuno declared that his government would recognize only secular labor organizations. He outlawed all Catholic labor organizations. In response to the central government's efforts to repress his activities, Zuno also decreed the autonomy of municipalities, the legislature, and the courts. The Guadalajara-based CAOLJ promoted independent unions, strikes, and struggles against CROM strikebreakers and the authoritarian policies of the federal Ministry of Industry and Labor—an agency headed by CROM leader Luis Napoleón Morones. Zunistas and their communist allies also fought against the exploitation of workers by local and foreign companies. In 1927, Zunistas and communists united organized labor in Jalisco into the Confederación Obrera de Jalisco.

Like other revolutionary leaders, Zuno believed that education was the main avenue to modernize the country because it would form productive and disciplined citizens. His most important educational project was the establishment of the Universidad de Guadalajara (UdeG) in 1925. Zuno and other professionals and intellectuals conceived the UdeG as a popular, nationalist, and liberal state university.[26] Zuno's university project was in line with his position regarding the normal schools, or *normales*. At the time, the normales were under the direction of the federal Secretaría de Educación Pública (SEP, or Secretariat of Public Education). By having the normales, teachers, and students under his domain, the governor was able to expand his base and to indoctrinate them in the values of social justice. As in the labor realm, there were disputes over who should control it: the federal or state SEP or the university.

Like Salvador Alvarado in Yucatán, Zuno recognized that women could be an important force in his group. He had dialogued with feminists and social reformers such as the North American Jane Addams when she visited Guadalajara in 1925. He had also visited with a founder of the progressive Hull House in Chicago, and he worked with local feminists like Atala Apodaca and María A. Díaz (1896–1939) to understand and negotiate women's issues.[27] By including women, he did not seek to reduce male power or upset traditional gender roles, but he favored their incorporation into the political and social life of the state with a view of expanding his own power base.[28]

Radical women who organized into female or mixed-sex unions—textile workers, teachers, and food workers—joined Zuno's labor organization, the

CAOLJ.[29] Just like working men, working women demanded the implementation of their labor rights under the Constitution of 1917. In doing so, however, they encountered resistance from their male superiors who ridiculed the constitution because it had not been fully implemented by means of federal *leyes reglamentarias*, or enabling legislation. For instance, the textile worker María A. Díaz asked Zuno to draft a state labor law to protect workers and end the extreme exploitation.[30] Working women became advocates of Zuno's labor policies such as the first labor law of August 13, 1923,[31] the establishment of the Boards of Conciliation and Arbitration at the Labor Department, the Ley de Sindicato y Sociedades Mutualistas of 1924, and a *colonia obrera* (workers' colony) in 1925.[32] Zuno's laws derived from the Constitution of 1917, which benefited women workers by granting them the rights to have child care centers, a minimum wage, maternity leave, and equal wages to those of men. Different types of women workers—textile workers, tortilla makers, service workers, clerks, and teachers—claimed the right to have a job, to receive a minimum wage, to organize a union, and to have their labor contracts fulfilled. Furthermore, Zuno needed radical liberal women to offset strong Catholic women organizations, including the Asociación de Damas Católicas and the Liga Protectora de la Obrera. Consequently, Zuno created similar organizations to the Catholics to fulfill the needs of workers and tried to solve the problems faced by working-class women. He established the Casa Amiga de la Obrera (CAO, a day care center and school) in 1925 to follow up on the postulates of Article 123 of the Constitution and the state labor law of 1923.

The CAO was part of the public beneficence and opened its doors in the former convent of Saint Theresa. Zuno envisioned it as a center for women workers' children where boys and girls would receive meals and lessons and be taught personal hygiene.[33] In less than a week, the CAO received many applications from women requesting places for their children; some even asked if they could leave their newborn babies in the facility. Faced with such a response, Zuno ordered measures to restrict the entrance of children. For example, working-class mothers needed to prove that they were single, poor, and employed. These criteria were also applied to widowed male workers.[34] Like the Catholic soup kitchens, the CAO provided children with four meals, one of which included meat. Parents were required to pick up their children in the afternoon and take care of them afterwards.

Unlike the Catholic organizations based on charity, the CAO was part of a secular program that also sought to create a new social order, a secular society, in which the state would provide certain services to the masses because they had some rights. The revolutionary state was sensitive to working-class women's needs, in part because secular pioneer women teachers and textile workers became part of state bureaucracy at the normal school and the labor and health departments. They pushed within the state for improvement on issues such as education and welfare institutions for women workers and children. These women were significant in the expansion and implementation of social rights.

ZUNO AND THE DE LA HUERTA REBELLION IN JALISCO

The year 1924 marked the rising strength of the state government of Jalisco as well as the recovery of the federal government from the devastating Adolfo de la Huerta rebellion during the first part of the year. In Jalisco and elsewhere, the church had supported the rebellion, and both the state and federal government took advantage of their victory to move to repress the church. The defeat of the rebellion helped to reconfigure political power at the national and regional levels. After the uprising, some anti-Zunistas and Callistas—Félix Robles and José García de Alba—claimed that Zuno had supported it. Obregón helped exonerate Zuno from these charges. Still, presidential candidate Calles began actions to reduce Zuno's power because of the governor's affiliation with Obregón, his independent political strength, and his opposition to the CROM and its leader, the Calles ally Morones. The anti-Zuno campaign included an instigated rural revolt against him on June 4, 1924; an election in which Zunistas and CROMistas came to blows, ending in the killing of a Zunista deputy; accusations that Zuno had assassinated agraristas during the de la Huerta rebellion; and actions led by the Moronista senator Gonzalo N. Santos, representative of the Bloque Socialista.[35] A few days after the rural insurrection, Morones publicly announced the fall of Zuno.[36]

To counterbalance these actions, Zuno selected members of his group to run as candidates for the next state elections. They won all the electoral districts. By the end of 1924, Zunismo controlled state deputies, the municipality of Guadalajara, and state magistrates. During that time, Calles, as elected *presidente*, made it clear to Zuno that he was his foe and was ending his support to Obregón.[37] Immediately, Calles appointed Zuno's enemies to important public posts such as the *jefe de operaciones militares* and removed Zuno's friend, General Lázaro Cárdenas.

In 1925, it was clear that the battle of the federal government against Zuno was underway. Calles pressured federal Jaliscan deputies to break with Zuno, and Morones claimed that Zuno attempted to assassinate him.[38] Toward the end of this year, Santos and Morones approached the federal deputy, Alfredo Romo, and suggested that he suspend his political relationship with Zuno in exchange for their support as a candidate for governor. The Zunistas had already chosen their own candidate for governorship: José

M. Cuéllar. Both Cuéllar and Romo were Zunistas and had been members of the Centro Bohemio. Romo and eight other deputies broke with Zuno.[39] This small group established its own legislature, disowned Zuno as governor, and demanded Calles's presidential recognition. Zuno responded with popular mobilizations and the state legislature petitioned to the federal congress for its legal recognition. Finally, Zuno dismissed CROMistas from public offices, including the rector of the Universidad de Guadalajara, Enrique Díaz de León, and impeached Jaliscan Callista deputies.[40]

For his part, Zuno radicalized his labor and his anti-church policies in order to fight both Calles and the Catholic social action movement. He believed that the church had supported conservative generals in the de la Huertista movement. To punish the church, he prohibited the meetings of the Knights of Columbus, the Asociación Católica de Jóvenes Mexicanos (Male Youth Mexican Catholic Association), and Catholic trade unions. He called these "actos delictuosos" (criminal acts). The Catholic press protested these prohibitions, yet Zuno continued his attack. On December 22, 1924, he ordered the Seminarios Mayor y Menor to be closed, allegedly for "lack of hygiene."[41] Immediately, Catholics mobilized to denounce these unfair policies as violating their individual rights.

Both Zuno and Calles radicalized their anticlerical policies by closing private schools, convents, and seminaries, and by restricting the number of priests. Catholics saw these anticlerical policies as religious persecution. Between 1925 and 1926, the church and state conflict steadily escalated. As Catholics responded with more protests and mobilizations, Zuno and Calles repressed more, and consequently, violence increased on both sides. Church-state relations drastically deteriorated during these years, finally exploding in 1926.

THE IMPEACHMENT

While Calles continued working on the implementation of radical anticlerical measures, Zuno was under investigation by the federal congress. Zuno was charged with the dissolution of municipal governments, political assassinations, and not respecting the federal pact. Before the federal congress judged Zuno's charges and removed him from his public post, Zuno resigned as a governor of Jalisco to preserve the state's sovereignty and to block Calles's plan to impose a Callista local executive.[42] Zuno continued his control of state politics, defended state regional autonomy, and stopped the Callista centralist policies. The next governors—Clemente Sepúlveda and Silvano Barba González, both of whom ruled but a short period of time—the state congress, the Supremo Tribunal de Justicia, the Confederación de Partidos Revolucionarios de Jalisco, and the CAOLJ were Zunistas. However, Zuno could not hold a public post or be elected for seven years.

The aggression against Zuno prompted mobilizations against the Callistas' interventionist tactics, mobilizations that ended in violent clashes between Zunistas and Callistas on the streets and in the next elections for governor, in which Romo—now a Callista—confronted the Zunista Cuéllar and another candidate. Each one of these contenders accused the others of electoral fraud. When the state's electoral authorities recognized Cuéllar as the winner, Calles ordered the attorney general to begin a criminal investigation against Cuéllar.[43] Thus, the state legislature was forced to disqualify Cuéllar as governor. Immediately, Cuéllar blamed Zuno for his political defeat. He later reestablished his relationship with Calles, who made possible the closing of Cuéllar's criminal investigation and later made him governor during the Maximato.[44]

In light of the ongoing political discord, the local factions negotiated and agreed that the next governor would be Margarito Ramírez (1927–1929). With this political deal, the Jaliscan Obregonismo and Zunismo recovered, radicalizing its labor, agrarian, and church policies within a context of warfare because of the Cristiada (1926–1929). Ramírez created the Red Guard, formed by agraristas and miners, and incorporated Zuno, Romo, and Cuéllar into the War Commission. This unity of the local political leaders ended because Ramírez and Zuno each tried to assume complete control of the state. Thus, Ramírez became an anti-Zunista and began to campaign against Zuno's manipulation of town councils. Zuno decided to retreat from politics to finish high school and study law. This decision left Zunismo without a leader and facilitated its fragmentation. Instead of protecting regional autonomy from the centralist policies of Calles, Ramírez focused on controlling and ending the Cristero war. The July 1928 assassination of Obregón—a murder that removed Zuno's primary mentor on the national scene—dealt a serious blow to Zunismo and facilitated the strengthening of Callista policies in Jalisco during the Maximato.[45]

Zuno played a significant role even after the decline of his faction. Even as Callismo reigned in Jalisco in the 1930s, Zuno, as a lawyer, continued to defend workers and unions.[46] In 1936, he unsuccessfully ran for senator. Free of Calles's shadow, President Cárdenas appointed him as *consejero de la presidencia* and *apoderado general* of Ferrocarriles Nacionales Mexicanos in 1937. Zuno returned to Guadalajara in 1947, where he held different public posts in the state bureaucracy and at the Universidad de Guadalajara. In 1974, the Fuerzas Revolucionarias Armadas del Pueblo kidnapped Zuno and demanded that president Luis Echeverría Alvarez, Zuno's son-in-law, release *guerrilleros* in exchange for his release. The president did not enter into negotiations with the rebels, and Zuno was freed. In 1980, he died at the age of 91.

FINAL CONSIDERATIONS

Zuno's movement was the most important popular and progressive force in Jalisco in the 1920s and 1930s. Zuno built a broad coalition and implemented social policies that improved the living, labor, and social conditions of workers, peasants, women, and teachers. All of these policies became more radical during the struggle for regional autonomy, the church-state conflict, and the revolutionary process of state-building. Zuno's movement was an autonomous political force that helped to give voice to subaltern groups. By allying with them, he consolidated a base that supported him as a mayor and as a governor. Like other revolutionary caudillos, he seized the opportunity to rise quickly in politics; in this case not because of his military achievements in the armed movement, but rather because his of political artwork. Like other revolutionaries, Zuno had a radical discourse in relation to labor, agrarian, and church matters, but he modernized a traditional gendered ideology by allowing women to have access to higher education. For him, politics was mainly a male activity. The revolutionary process had mobilized and politicized diverse social actors, among them women. Zuno encountered them in his political struggles and perceived that women could be important auxiliaries for his own goals. This alliance permitted radical women to participate in state bureaucracy as labor, health, and educational inspectors.[48]

Unfortunately, Zuno's movement depended heavily on his personality. After his resignation from the governorship, Zunismo started fragmenting amid the conflict about who would be his long-term successor. Neither Zuno nor Calles had won a decisive victory. Zuno, however, had saved state sovereignty by resigning, and he continued controlling state and local political machinery until 1930. Without a doubt, Zuno's family remained important political players. They later consolidated a *cacicazgo* in southern Jalisco, and in 1970, Zuno's son-in-law, Luis Echeverría, became president of Mexico.[49]

NOTES

1. Biblioteca Pública del Estado de Jalisco (hereafter cited as BPEJG) "Zuno se defiende," *Restauración*, Dec. 23, 1920, 6.

2. BPEJG, "El diputado al Congreso general, José María Cuéllar, asesinó al señor Gudelio L. Jiménez, secretario de una casilla electoral," *El Informador*, Dec. 20, 1920, 1.

3. José Guadalupe Zuno Hernández, *Reminiscencias de una vida*, 2 vols., *Biblioteca de autores jaliscienses modernos 2*, 4 (Guadalajara: n.p., 1958).

4. George H. Winters (American Consul) to Secretary of State, Guadalajara, Nov. 11, 1937, National Archives, Record Group 59 (hereafter NA, RG 59), 812.00 Jalisco/200.

5. Zuno wrote more than twenty books in which he traced the influences and developments of his liberal, anticlerical, political, revolutionary, and artistic family background. Throughout these books, Zuno emphasized his male conception of politics. They are not testimonies from the buoyant political period he lived through and promoted; rather, they are his memories thirty years after he was forced to resign his governorship. José Guadalupe Zuno Hernández, *Anecdotario del Centro Bohemio* (Guadalajara, Jal.: n.p., 1964); José Guadalupe Zuno Hernández, *Historia de la revolución en el estado de Jalisco* (Mexico: Instituto Nacional de Estudios Históricos de la Revolución Mexicana, 1964); Zuno Hernández, *Reminiscencias de una vida*.

6. J. Angel Moreno Ochoa, *Semblanzas revolucionarias, 1920–1930* (Guadalajara, Jal.: Galería de Escritores Revolucionarios Jaliscienses, 1959).

7. Mario A. Aldana Rendón, *Jalisco desde la revolución* (Guadalajara: Gobierno del Estado de Jalisco, Universidad de Guadalajara, 1987); Elisa Cárdenas et al., *José Guadalupe Zuno Hernández: Siete facetas de su vida* (Guadalajara: Universidad de Guadalajara, 1992); Javier Hurtado, *Familias, política y parentesco: Jalisco, 1919–1991* (Guadalajara: Fondo de Cultura Económica, Universidad de Guadalajara, 1993); Fidelina G. Llerenas and Jaime E. Tamayo Rodríguez, *El levantamiento delahuertista: Cuatro rebeliones y cuatro jefes militares, colección fin de milenio. Biblioteca movimientos sociales* (Guadalajara: Universidad de Guadalajara, 1995); José María Murià, *Historia de Jalisco*, 4 vols. (Guadalajara, Jalisco, Mexico: Unidad Editorial del Gobierno de Jalisco, 1980); Leticia Ruano et al., *José Guadalupe Zuno Hernández: Vida, obra y pensamiento* (Guadalajara: Universidad de Guadalajara, 1992); Jaime Tamayo, *El movimiento agrario y la revolución maderista (Jalisco, 1910–1913): El movimiento agrario y la Revolución Mexicana: Dos momentos cruciales en Jalisco, colección investigadores*, 7 (Guadalajara: Centro de Estudios Históricos del Agrarismo en México, 1983); Jaime Tamayo, *El movimiento obrero jalisciense y la crisis del '29: La última batalla de los rojos, colección aportaciones* (Guadalajara: IES, Universidad de Guadalajara, 1987); Jaime Tamayo and Laura Romero, *La rebelión estradista y el movimiento campesino, (1923–1924), colección investigadores* (Guadalajara: Centro de Estudios Históricos del Agrarismo en México, 1983); Jaime Tamayo and Patricia Valles, *Anarquismo, socialismo y sindicalismo en las regiones, colección fin de milenio. Biblioteca Movimientos Sociales* (Guadalajara: Universidad de Guadalajara, 1993); Jaime E. Tamayo Rodríguez, *La conformación del estado moderno y los conflictos políticos, 1917–1929*, ed. Mario A. Aldana Rendón, vol. 2, *Jalisco desde la revolución* (Guadalajara: Gobierno del Estado de Jalisco, Universidad de Guadalajara, 1988). There are new works with a post-revisionist analysis for this period; see Robert Curley, "Slouching towards Bethlehem: Catholics and the Political Sphere in Revolutionary México" (Ph.D. diss., University of Chicago, 2001), and María Teresa Fernández-Aceves, "Political Mobilization of Women in Revolutionary Guadalajara, 1910–1940" (Ph.D. diss., University of Illinois, 2000).

8. Universidad de Guadalajara, *Jalisco en el siglo 20: Perfiles* (Guadalajara: Universidad de Guadalajara, 1999), 101; Moreno Ochoa, *Semblanzas revolucionarias, 1920–1930*, 53; José Guadalupe Zuno Hernández, *Reminiscencias de una vida*, 2nd ed., vol. 2 (Guadalajara: n.p., 1973), 8.

9. Hurtado, *Familias, política y parentesco*, 54–55.

10. José Guadalupe Zuno Hernández, *Nuestro liberalismo* (Guadalajara: Ediciones Centro Bohemio, 1956).

11. Misael Gradilla Damy, *El juego dell poder y del saber: Significación, norma y poder en la Universidad De Guadalajara. Socioanálisis de una institución en su conflicto* (Mexico: El Colegio de México, 1995), 122–23; Universidad de Guadalajara, *Jalisco en el siglo 20: Perfiles*, 101; Hurtado, *Familias, política y parentesco*, 55; Tamayo Rodríguez, *La conformación del estado moderno*, 232; Zuno Hernández, *Anecdotario del Centro Bohemio*, 1.

12. According to Zuno, the members of the Centro Bohemio were Martinez Valadez, Amado de la Cueva, Carlos Orozco Romero, Enrique Diaz de Leon, Juan de Dios Robledo, Hernandez Galvan, Jesus S. Soto, Alfaro Siqueiros, Alfredo Romo, and Antonio Cordova. Hurtado, *Familias, política y parentesco*, 57; Zuno Hernández, *Anecdotario del Centro Bohemio*, 12–13.

13. Universidad de Guadalajara, *Jalisco en el siglo 20: Perfiles*, 101–2; Moreno Ochoa, *Semblanzas revolucionarias, 1920–1930*, 53; Tamayo Rodríguez, *La conformación del estado moderno*, 235–36.

14. María Teresa Fernández Aceves, "Educación secular: El caso de Atala Apodaca," in *Cátedras y catedráticos en la historia de las universidad e instituciones de educación superior en México*, ed. Lourdes Alvarado and Leticia Pérez Puente (Mexico: UNAM-CESU, forthcoming).

15. Fernández Aceves, "Educación secular"; Universidad de Guadalajara, *Jalisco en el siglo 20: Perfiles*, 103.

16. Zuno Hernández, *Reminiscencias de una vida*, 135–36.

17. Hurtado, *Familias, política y parentesco*, 55, 57, 60; Moreno Ochoa, *Semblanzas revolucionarias, 1920–1930*, 53.

18. Universidad de Guadalajara, *Jalisco en el siglo 20: Perfiles*, 103; Hurtado, *Familias, política y parentesco*, 59.

19. Zuno Hernández, *Reminiscencias de una vida*, 136–37.

20. Fernández-Aceves, "Political Mobilization of Women," 172–75.

21. Alma Dorantes, María Gracia Castillo, and Julia Tuñón Pablos, *Irene Robledo García* (Guadalajara: Universidad de Guadalajara, Instituto Nacional de Antropología e Historia, 1995), 56–57; Ernest Gruening, *Mexico and Its Heritage* (New York: Century Co., 1928), 440–41; Tamayo Rodríguez, *La conformación del estado moderno*, 103–66; Hurtado, *Familias, política y parentesco*, 62–64.

22. Tamayo Rodríguez, *La conformación del estado moderno*, 97, 134, 71, 91, 99, 245–46.

23. Tamayo Rodríguez, *La conformación del estado moderno*, 135–36.

24. Tamayo Rodríguez, *La conformación del estado moderno*, 245–50. The group Acción belonged to the Federación de Agrupaciones Obreras de Jalisco, the local branch of the Confederación Regional Obrera Mexicana. It included iron workers, carpenters, hairdressers, corn mill workers, peasants, carriers (*cargadores*), clerks, bakers, shoemakers, tailors, shawlmakers, meat workers, mechanics, potters, janitors, bricklayers, jewelers, textile workers, and graphic art workers.

25. After the de la Huerta rebellion (1923–1924), Zuno radicalized his labor policies. Moreno Ochoa, *Semblanzas revolucionarias, 1920–1930*, 126, 41–44; Jaime E. Tamayo Rodríguez, *Los movimientos sociales, 1917–1929*, ed. Mario A. Aldana Rendón, vol. 5, *Jalisco desde la revolución* (Guadalajara: Universidad de Guadalajara, Gobierno del estado de Jalisco, 1988), 34–37.

26. Tamayo Rodríguez, *Los movimientos sociales, 1917–1929*, 38, 43.

27. Gradilla Damy, *El juego dell poder y del saber*, 123; Abel Mercado Martínez, "Influencias ideológicas de la Universidad de Guadalajara, 1925-1940" (B.A., Universidad de Guadalajara, 1986), 8.

28. Jane Addams, "Jane Addams's Dairy, 1925," in *Jane Addams at the University of Illinois–Chicago* (Chicago: 1925).

29. Susan K. Besse, *Restructuring Patriarchy: The Modernization of Gender Inequality in Brazil, 1914-1940* (Chapel Hill: University of North Carolina Press, 1996); Victoria De Grazia, *How Fascism Ruled Women: Italy, 1922-1945* (Berkeley: University of California Press, 1992); Mary K. Vaughan, *Cultural Politics in Revolution: Teachers, Peasants, and Schools in Mexico, 1930-1940* (Tucson: University of Arizona Press, 1997).

30. The female unions that joined the CAOLJ were Unión Social de Expendedoras de Masa, Unión de Trabajadoras en Molinos de Nixtamal, and Unión Libertaria de Galleteras. There were radical women in the Unión de Trabajadores de Molinos de Nixtamal y Anexos, Sindicato Evolucionista de Obreros de Río Grande, Sindicato Libertario de Obreros de Río Blanco, and Sindicato Libertario de Obreros de Atemajac. See Archivo Histórico de Jalisco (hereafter AHJ), Ramo de Trabajo, T-9-926, exp. no. 2132. María Teresa Fernández Aceves, "Once We Were Corn Grinders: Women and Labor in the Tortilla Industry of Guadalajara, 1920-1940," *International Labor and Working-Class History* 63 (2003): 84; Tamayo Rodríguez, *Los movimientos sociales, 1917-1929*, 34-37.

31. Similar demands were made by male textile workers from the late 1910s to early 1920s. AHJ, Ramo de Trabajo. Archivo Particular Guadalupe Martínez, "El como se realizó la Ley del Trabajo para el estado de Jalisco."

32. There was no consensus on the need to legislate Article 123, which gave labor rights to workers. For instance, on June 8, 1923, textile workers asserted that it was necessary to legislate Article 123 to avoid the exploitation of the working class. The Catholic workers rejected Zuno's labor law because it did not give legal status to Catholic trade unions. On July 12, 1923, the Union Sindicatos de obreros Catolicos (USOC) led one thousand workers of twenty different unions in the state to protest and argued that this law violated constitutional Articles 9, 13, and 123. They asserted that this law favored Bolshevik worker organizations that were patronized by the state government. The USOC demanded that its point of view be considered. Elite Catholic women, members of the Unión de las Damas Católicas Mexicanas (UDCM), regarded the law as killing Catholic trade unions. Zuno did not heed their petitions. Consequently, Catholics saw Zuno as a dictator, tyrant, and *cacique*. AHJ, Ramo de Trabajo, T-1-923, caja T-5 bis, exp. no. 6056; "Ley estatal del trabajo," T-4-923, caja T-20 bis "J," exp. no. 7958. Francisco Barbosa Guzmán, *La iglesia y el gobierno civil*, ed. Mario Alfonso Aldana Rendón, vol. 6, *Jalisco desde la revolución* (Mexico: Universidad de Guadalajara, Gobierno del Estado de Jalisco, 1988), 273-74, 76.

33. Zuno also enacted the Ley de Bienes Familiares to protect workers' patrimony. The Jaliscan Catholic Legislature (1912-1914) had already decreed a similar law called Ley Bien de Familia, which attempted to give land to rural people. Barbosa Guzmán, *La iglesia y el gobierno civil*, 177; Tamayo Rodríguez, *La conformación del estado moderno*, 248-50. Laura O'Dogherty Madrazo, *De urnas y sotanas: El partido Católica cacional en Jalisco* (El Colegio de México, 1999), 324.

34. BPEJG, "Hoy se inaugura la Casa Amiga de la Obrera," *El Informador* (Guadalajara), July 1, 1924, 1.

35. BPEJG, "Esta funcionando la Casa Amiga de la Obrera," *El Informador* (Guadalajara), July 7, 1925, 1; BPEJG, "Aumentan los asilados en la Casa Amiga de la Obrera," *El Informador*, July 10, 1925, 1.

36. For a detailed description of these Callistas actions against Zuno, see Tamayo Rodríguez, *La conformación del estado moderno,*259–79; Murià, *Historia de Jalisco*, 377.

37. Tamayo Rodríguez, *La conformación del estado moderno*, 264.

38. Tamayo Rodríguez, *La conformación del estado moderno*, 267; Zuno Hernández, *Reminiscencias de una vida.*

39. Tamayo Rodríguez, *La conformación del estado moderno*, 270.

40. Tamayo Rodríguez, *La conformación del estado moderno*, 270–72. The deputies were José Manuel Chávez, J. Rodrigo Camacho, Napoleón Orozco, Manuel Vidrio Guerra, Victoriano Salado, Joaquin Vidrio, J. Trinidad de la Torre, and Enrique Díaz de León.

41. Tamayo Rodríguez, *La conformación del estado moderno*, 272.

42. Barbosa Guzmán, *La iglesia y el gobierno civil*, 280; Muriá, *Historia de Jalisco*, 378; BPEJG, *El Informador*, Dec. 23 and 26, 1924; Antonio Rius Facius, *De don Porfirio a Plutarco: Historia de la ACJM* (Mexico: Editorial Jus, 1958), 271 .

43. NA, RG 59, 812.00/27735, 812.00/27740, 812.00/27743, 812.00/27744, 812.00/27745; Tamayo Rodríguez, *La conformación del estado moderno*, 270–77; Murià, *Historia de Jalisco*, 381.

44. Tamayo Rodríguez, *La conformación del estado moderno*, 291.

45. Murià, *Historia de Jalisco*, 313–14; Tamayo Rodríguez, *La conformación del estado moderno*, 292.

46. Gradilla Damy, *El juego dell poder y del saber*, 124–25.

47. José Guadalupe Zuno Hernández, "Demanda promovida por el Lic. José G. Zuno como apoderado de los sindicatos de obreros de las fábricas de Atemajac, Río Blanco y la experiencia en contra de la Cía. Ind. De Guad., S.A., " AHJ, Ramo de Trabajo, T-8-932, caja T-211, exp. no. 8313: 1932.

48. Fernández-Aceves, "Political Mobilization of Women."

49. Guillermo de la Peña Topete, "Populism, Regional Power, and Political Mediation: Southern Jalisco, 1900–1980," in *Mexico's Regions: Comparative History and Development*, ed. Eric Van Young (San Diego: University of California, 1992), 191–223.

7

Tomás Garrido Canabal of Tabasco

Road Building and Revolutionary Reform

Kristin A. Harper

In November of 2001, while conducting doctoral research in Tabasco, I had the good fortune to present my research findings at the First Annual Congress of Tabasco Historians. Housed in Villahermosa's historic Instituto Juárez, the congress included faculty and students from the Universidad Juárez Autónoma de Tabasco and other individuals interested in Tabascan history. My paper explored some of the beneficial domestic reforms that Tomás Garrido Canabal's regime had directed toward the poorer members of Tabascan society, and overall, the presentation was well received. Yet there were skeptics in my midst. A Tabascan professor I had had the pleasure of meeting prior to the congress stood up and challenged my paper's premise that, generally speaking, Garridismo had meant something positive for Tabasco's poor communities. Suddenly, and perhaps to his surprise as much as to mine, a group in the amphitheater seconded his criticism by bursting into applause. Momentarily at a loss for words, and then careful to marshal specific evidence to support my claim, I reiterated my belief that there were many laudable characteristics of the Garrido regime, especially when it came to material improvements for the laboring classes. At this point another group in the amphitheater vigorously applauded. Feeling at least partially vindicated by the second bout of clapping, I quickly realized that my rebuttal had only served to cement the impression that I was a "Garrido apologist."

Strictly speaking, I am not a Garrido apologist. I have simply become accustomed to the moral ambiguities of Mexican revolutionary reformism. Having dipped into the evidentiary cauldron of Tabascan revolution-era politics, I have come to accept that the coercive, even violent, aspects of a regime do not necessarily negate its gentler gestures. Authoritarian and

populist, the Garrido administration left in its wake both militant supporters and vociferous detractors—the polarized opinions of whom have contributed to, but also distorted, the historiography of the Garrido era.[1] This
article attempts to grapple with these competing schools of thought by examining a Garridista reform measure for which the coercive and beneficent
effects were equally palpable: road building.

Tomás Garrido Canabal, who, with one brief exception, wielded power in
Tabasco between 1923 and 1935, remains one of the most memorable figures of the Mexican Revolution.[2] Charismatic and forceful, he is most
widely remembered for his strident anticlericalism. Undertaken with
missionary-like zeal, the Garrido government's efforts at secularization involved knocking down churches, removing crosses from cemeteries, and encouraging Tabascans to eat beef on Fridays.[3] But revolutionary Tabasco
boasted other notable changes. During the Garrido era, scores of new
schools were created; women were given the right to vote, first in municipal
and then in state-level elections; thousands of Tabascans were mobilized
into labor leagues, anti-alcohol brigades, and student organizations; and
meaningful steps were taken to improve housing, transport, and communications. These reforms were impressive by a number of measures, and to the
extent that previously ignored groups entered into a social contract with
government, it can be argued that Garridista reformism widened the scope
of political participation in Tabasco. At the same time, the regime was not
shy about violating individual rights in the name of social progress.
Nowhere is this more clearly revealed than with Tabasco's 1925 Road Law.

Curiously, despite the controversy it stirred up at the time, revolutionary
Tabasco's Road Law, or *Ley Vial* in Spanish, rarely enters the realm of historical discourse today. Roads, admittedly, are less compelling than red-
shirted Garrido militants ceremoniously burning religious objects. Yet an
analysis of Tabasco's 1925 Road Law, which required men between the ages
of eighteen and fifty to donate twelve days of labor a year to road building,
encourages us to focus on some of the thorny issues of revolutionary state
formation. For one, it allows us to consider the relative ease with which regional administrations were able to forgo legal niceties in their pursuit of
revolutionary objectives. More specifically, road building sheds light on the
relationship between coercion and beneficence in Tomás Garrido Canabal's
Tabasco. Before turning to the Road Law, however, some background on the
Tabascan revolutionary *caudillo* is needed.

THE EARLY LIFE AND POLITICAL
RISE OF TOMÁS GARRIDO CANABAL

On September 20, 1890, Tomás Garrido Canabal was born to Josefa Canabal Brown and Pío Garrido Lacroix at his maternal grandparents' hacienda

in Palenque, Chiapas. The child of wealthy landowners (his family owned cattle ranches of considerable size in both Tabasco and Chiapas), Tomás Garrido attended private schools in Villahermosa and later studied in Veracruz. His political proclivities emerged early in life. In 1906, while a teenager studying at the Instituto Juárez in Villahermosa, Garrido joined a student protest against longtime Porfirian governor Abraham Bandala. Later, in 1912, he affiliated with a political movement in neighboring Campeche. It was also in Campeche that Garrido would earn a law degree and meet Dolores Llovera Sosa. From a prominent Campechana family, Dolores Llovera Sosa married Garrido in 1915. Together they had three children: Mayitzá Drusso, Soyla Libertad, and Lenin.[4]

By 1915, Garrido began to accumulate what would become an impressive list of revolutionary credentials, holding minor positions in the administration of General Salvador Alvarado in Yucatán and then returning to Tabasco to serve in the administration of Francisco Múgica (1915–1916).[5] Some have suggested that Múgica was suspicious of Garrido due to the latter's *latifundista* upbringing.[6] Whatever Múgica's true feelings were about the young Tabascan lawyer, Garrido was clearly influenced by the revolutionary program that Múgica initiated in Tabasco. A number of reforms undertaken by Múgica during his brief tenure as Tabascan governor—which included attempts to convert church buildings into schools and a controversial approach to road building—gathered new force during the Garrido era.[7]

Garrido's tenure as Tabasco's polemical strongman coincided closely with the leadership exercised at the national level by Alvaro Obregón and Plutarco Elías Calles—men to whom he was unquestionably loyal. First and foremost an Obregonista, Garrido strengthened his ties to Calles following Obregón's assassination in 1928.[8] A militant Callista during the next six years, Garrido also impressed presidential hopeful Lázaro Cárdenas, who showered praise on him during a campaign stop in Tabasco in 1934. Reflecting on the range of social reforms he had witnessed during an extensive tour of the state, Cárdenas averred that "the Mexican Revolution [has achieved] a profound social interpretation in Tabasco."[9] Indeed, the vigor with which the Garrido regime implemented revolutionary reform in the impoverished and waterlogged state of Tabasco compelled people to stand up and take notice.

But the Garridista approach to revolutionary reform sometimes involved arbitrariness, a fact noted by General Manuel Avila Camacho after he served a stint as Tabasco's chief military officer.[10] The Juventud Revolucionaria Tabasqueña (JRT), a virulently anti-Garrido organization based in Mexico City, put it in bolder terms. In a letter sent to president Abelardo L. Rodríguez in 1933, JRT members claimed that Tomás Garrido had turned Tabasco into his own "fiefdom" where laws were freely violated.[11] While characterizing Garrido-era Tabasco as a lawless fiefdom was taking it too far, a willingness to play fast and loose with constitutional principles was a fairly pronounced characteristic of the Garrido regime.[12] The Road Law passed by the Garridista-dominated legislature in 1925 is a case in point.

CUTTING CONSTITUTIONAL CORNERS EN ROUTE TO MODERNITY: TABASCO'S 1925 ROAD LAW

The Tabascan state legislature passed the Road Law in 1925 with the respectable purpose of improving Tabasco's badly compromised infrastructure. Part of a broad series of reforms designed to promote economic development, the law championed an issue of profound national concern: the creation and improvement of transport and communications.[13] From a local standpoint, road building was of utmost relevance. The paucity of land routes in Tabasco meant that farmers relied heavily—as they had for thousands of years—on the state's many rivers to move their goods. While rivers were an effective means of transport, roads promised to expand the transit options available to the state's residents. The economic and social benefits to be gained by improving Tabasco's dismal road system were beyond dispute.

Passed with the goal of better connecting Tabasco's seventeen municipalities, the Road Law required able-bodied men between the ages of eighteen and fifty, regardless of their nationality, to donate twelve days of labor a year to local road construction—ideally in their communities of residence.[14] The only way a man could be excused from his road shift was to find and pay for a substitute laborer.[15] Not surprisingly, the Road Law's labor provisions invited criticism. Indeed, just months after its passage, complaints about the Road Law prompted officials in Mexico City to launch an investigation into its constitutionality.[16]

The precipitating event occurred in July of 1925 when a group of Mexico City health workers on assignment in Tabasco's port city of Frontera were called upon to perform road duty. When the Health Department requested that its employees be exempt from road duty, inasmuch as they were federal workers with important health-related responsibilities to carry out, the municipal president of Frontera allegedly threatened the head of the sanitary delegation in Tabasco with arrest and expulsion from the state. Indignant, the chief of the health department, Bernardo J. Gastélum, informed an official at the Department of the Interior that his delegation leader in Tabasco had actually fled the state for fear of local authorities.[17]

In an attempt to deflect criticism away from the Road Law and onto the leader of the health delegation in Frontera, Tabasco's interim governor, Santiago Ruiz, dashed off his own telegram to the Department of the Interior. Governor Ruiz noted that whereas foreigners and federal authorities from other departments had complied with the newly passed Road Law, the medical delegate in Frontera had expressed "open opposition" to it, even dismissing one of his employees who had contributed to the road work. But his missive was unable to staunch official concerns. On August first, the sub-secretary of the Department of the Interior asked the governor to send him a copy of Tabasco's Road Law, which was promptly analyzed by a legal consultant.[18]

The lawyer's seventeen-page analysis of the law found that several of its provisions violated Article 5 of the Mexican Constitution. Article 5, which made its first appearance in the 1857 constitution as a safeguard against slavery, states that "nobody can be forced to render personal services without just recompense and full consent." An 1898 revision of the article allowed that there were certain public services that the government could demand of its citizens without the benefit of payment, such as jury duty, a principle upheld in the Constitution of 1917. But because roadwork was not specifically enumerated as a public service the government could demand of its citizens free of charge, the lawyer deemed the labor provisions of Tabasco's Road Law unconstitutional. He recommended that the law be repealed.[19]

FOR THE PUBLIC GOOD?
POPULAR RESPONSES TO THE ROAD LAW

Despite the legal consultant's opinion that three articles of Tabasco's Road Law were unconstitutional, the law stayed on the books until March 1928. Foot dragging in the Tabascan legislature, however, did not prevent local citizens from challenging the legality of forcing men to work without pay. In 1926, three men from the municipality of Comalcalco sought protection from a federal judge when the municipal president imprisoned them for failing to perform roadwork. In appealing to the district judge in Villahermosa, two of the men, Luis and Miguel Cordova, cited Article 5 in protesting the municipality's attempt to have them perform work "without just payment." Furthermore, they suggested that road duty was burdensome "because the poverty in which we live forces us to work daily in search of sustenance for our families." Meanwhile, municipal authorities in Comalcalco painted an unflattering portrait of the plaintiffs. According to documents submitted to the judge, not only had the plaintiffs thrice refused to cooperate with road cleaning, they had encouraged others in their community to do likewise.[20]

Acutely aware of the Road Law's unpopularity, Garridista officials no doubt took solace in citizen letters affirming the benefits of road construction. Writing to Garrido from the sizeable indigenous community of San Carlos, two local activists, Melesio Jimenez and José López, praised the speech a government representative had recently delivered there in favor of the Road Law. The visiting official, Luis Chable, had told the gathering that he was aware that "bad elements" in the pueblo were encouraging people not to perform their road duty. Underscoring the "transcendental importance" of roadwork, he urged them to come together and to respect the Road Law. The letter writers optimistically informed Garrido that Luis Chable's words had helped convince many individuals in San Carlos that road building represented an "improvement for [the] pueblo."[21]

Examples of official corruption, though, prompted some early supporters of the Road Law to later change their minds. A group of artisans and workers from Tenosique wrote Garrido to this effect in October of 1928. Indicating that they had initially welcomed the Road Law, it was nonetheless their opinion that over the years the Ley Vial had been "prostituted" by individuals who sought to make a profit from it. They were also unsatisfied with the conditions of the roads—quipping that given Tenosique's small size, and the fact that the Road Law had been in force for three years, the roadways "should be as clear as a good quality mirror." Perhaps most unsettling to the letter writers, though, was the fact that municipal authorities had never announced that the Road Law had been overturned.[22] Indeed, by the time they informed Garrido of the irregularities they had witnessed in Tenosique, the Road Law had been abolished for over six months.[23]

Within months of the Road Law's repeal, Garridista governor Ausencio Cruz decreed a 15 percent increase in property taxes as a way to finance roadwork.[24] Although presumably a portion of those funds was to be earmarked to pay road laborers, citizens of several municipalities continued to complain about unpaid roadwork. Just how widespread a practice this was in the post-1928 period is unclear. However, in a letter sent to president Lázaro Cárdenas in 1935, Sixto Quiroz, a federal rural schoolteacher working in Tabasco's sierra region, claimed that the municipal president of Tacotalpa was "the first to subdue the campesinos, imposing on them 2 or 3 days of [unpaid] roadwork."[25] Bartolo Pérez, a farmer from the Centro, also noted the burdensome demands of local authorities. In a 1934 letter to President Rodríguez, Pérez complained that he and six of his compañeros were "constantly pestered by the state police for not wanting to show up for the innumerable unpaid jobs that they daily assign us." Not only were they obliged to open paths two days a week, reported Pérez, but they were called upon to build kiosks for local fairs, dance halls, and even airplane landing fields.[26] Also disturbing were allegations from community members from Olcuatitán, Nacajuca, that because they had supported the candidates for deputy and senator run by the opposition party, El Partido Reconstructor Tabasqueño, they were being punished with two road shifts a week.[27]

If roadwork was a "constructive" way to punish the political opponents of Garridismo, it was also a convenient way for the government to gauge the support of its citizens. Consider for example, the correspondence between a sugar refinery owner named Ovidio Ruiz and Tomás Garrido in the fall of

1930. In a letter dated September 27, Ruiz complained that his workers were being ordered to perform two days of road duty in a location approximately ten leagues from the refinery. Though allegedly Ruiz had complied with the road requirement on an earlier occasion, he opined that the distance that his workers were presently being asked to travel meant they would miss four full days of work. This would force him to cease operations at his factory for an entire week. Garrido's blunt response called into question Ruiz's social convictions:

> It surprises me greatly that . . . you are concerned about the days your finca workers may miss [from work], since on the . . . occasions I have passed by your refinery I have seen people resting, whether for the patron saint day of Tacotalpa or Holy Week, with your permission and authorization. . . . [It does not seem right to me] that you grant permission to adore pieces of wood and . . . to kiss the priest's hand, and yet now refuse to contribute to the magnificent work [of] . . . BUILD[ING] ROADS."[28]

Complaints against the Road Law were rampant throughout the Garrido era. Yet somehow, despite popular protestations and refusals, roads were built. There is simply no question that the fear of punishment acted as a negative inducement to roadwork. According to Esperanza Marin Viuda de Castro, for whom memories of the Ley Vial also included the requirement that *finca* owners tend to the front of their properties, people who failed to comply with the law could be jailed or fined.[29] Other Tabascans, of course, heaved their machetes and picks against the thick brush of the Tabascan *campo* unreservedly, certain that roads would benefit them.[30] Eventually, perhaps, some Tabascans got paid for road labor. But whether they labored willingly or begrudgingly, with remuneration or without, Tabascans did expand the road network during the Garrido era.

THE ROADS THEMSELVES

Gauging the effectiveness of roads proves difficult because much of the information about them is filtered through partisan lenses. Today, for example, critics of Garridismo ridicule Garrido-era roads as little more than dusty paths, turned into impassible muddy quagmires during Tabasco's extended rainy season.[31] Certainly the fact that many of the state's roads remained unpaved lends credence to this assertion. But given the region's impoverished ground infrastructure—the 1930 census indicated that river routes were still predominant over ground routes in Tabasco—any and all gains in road construction had value.[32] As ninety-year-old Jorge Ruiz Andrade observed in an interview in November of 2001, the roads were of a rustic sort, "but they *were* built."[33]

Nor were Tabasco's roads hopelessly rudimentary. Manuel López Garduno, whom president Pascual Ortiz Rubio had sent to Tabasco on a business matter, praised the state of the roads in a 1931 memo. Informing the president of the "wide roads that [were] being built in the various municipalities of the state," López Garduno added that he had had the occasion to travel along some of them by car, finding the ride swift and without "obstacle."[34] And in a 1944 editorial commemorating the one-year anniversary of Garrido's death, a writer for _Rumbo Nuevo_ urged all Tabascans "to acknowledge the material progress" achieved by the Garrido regime. Among the accomplishments that the author attributed to the deceased leader were improvements in communications and transport.[35]

A PATH TO THEIR HEARTS?

Elderly Tabascans today frequently recall their personal interactions with Tomás Garrido during the 1920s and 1930s. Even those individuals who lived in what were at that time extremely remote villages and _ranchos_ remember how Garrido had visited their communities—sometimes with Mexico City dignitaries in tow. An airplane aficionado, Garrido was known to descend on small rural hamlets in his black and red plane, _El Guacamayo_. Moreover, he utilized the expanding network of roads to get up close and personal with the Tabascan people.

In April of 1931, for example, Garrido took advantage of the advances in road building to travel by car to the municipalities of Nacajuca and Jalpa de Méndez. Respectively eighteen and twenty-eight kilometers distant from Villahermosa, Nacajuca and Jalpa de Méndez had been difficult to reach just years before. Having paid a visit to the rural teacher training school "Plutarco Elías Calles" located in Jalpa de Méndez, Garrido and his entourage traveled to Nacajuca before returning to the state capital. The very next day, Garrido and a ten-car motorcade set out from the State House to inaugurate a new highway connecting the municipality of Macuspana to Villahermosa.[36]

It was probably on that exact stretch of road that Garrido was preparing to travel when he was approached by two boys from Macuspana, sometime around 1931. One of the boys was twelve-year-old Nicolás Sánchez Pascual, who recalled his interaction with Governor Garrido:

> Don Tomás Garrido . . . was in his car, a black car, his chauffer already at the wheel, and it occurred to my friend and me to speak with [Garrido] to see if he would [help us get more education].[37] Don Tomás was already inside his car, but he . . . saw that we were heading his way. . . . Don Tomás opened the door of his car and got out and he says:

"What do you want, boys?"
"Licenciado, we want to see if you'll take us [to get more schooling]."
"What's that? You want to study?"
"We want to study."
"Very good."

Right then and there, Garrido saw to it that the boys would continue their studies, arranging for them to attend the normal school in Jalpa de Méndez. To this day, Nicolás Sánchez, who went on to become a teacher, retains a deep affection for the man who allowed him to pursue his education. In the barbershop he runs in his retirement, Sánchez has a newspaper photograph of Tomás Garrido fastened to a supply cabinet. He explains: "I am infinitely grateful to Don Tomás Garrido, [for] what I am today. I tell you, my ambition was to be a schoolteacher, and way back when, Don Tomás helped send me to school."[38]

Certainly not all Tabascans were gratified by the visits that Garrido and his revolutionary entourage paid to their communities.[39] Those individuals who disagreed with the Garrido regime's approach to reformism, for example, were uninterested in adding another layer of official surveillance to what they already deemed a precarious existence. Scrutinized, in many cases, by the prying eyes of municipal authorities on the lookout for religious objects or clandestinely produced alcohol, some Tabascans wished that the revolutionary state would just go away.

CONCLUSION

The Road Law was passed in 1925 with the laudable goal of developing Tabascan transport and communications. One of many initiatives designed to promote economic development, the Road Law, its proponents hoped, would draw on the patriotic labor of Tabascans from all social classes.[40] There were, to be sure, regime enthusiasts who willingly contributed their musculature to the improvement and creation of roads. Yet, for many people, the unpaid labor method the Garridistas chose to achieve road construction presupposed a level of public-spiritedness that simply did not exist. For its detractors, then, the Road Law did not signify a "transcendental" investment in future prosperity, as much as it did a government abuse of their persons. In repealing the Road Law in 1928 the regime appeared to be conceding the point. Yet even as a dead letter, the Road Law had a lingering effect. In the post-1928 period, at least some Tabascans continued to perform roadwork without pay.

Its coercive effects notwithstanding, the Road Law did accelerate advances in Tabasco's ground infrastructure, creating an ever-expanding network of roads that facilitated the transport of goods and people. Moreover, roads gave Garrido officials in the capital greater access to the people of the state. An activist politician who tirelessly toured Tabasco evaluating the successes and failures of his administration's policies, Garrido took particular interest in the region's remote and impoverished communities. Just ask Francisco Sánchez Cruz, a lifelong resident of the Chontal community of Vicente Guerrero. Eighty-two years old when I interviewed him in 2001, Sánchez Cruz shared scores of memories about Garrido and his era. His was a balanced appraisal. Identifying both positive and negative characteristics of the regime, Sánchez Cruz nonetheless fondly remembered Garrido's many visits to Vicente Guerrero. Recalling Garrido's attendance at a community festivity, Sánchez Cruz commented, "Back then, the *licenciados* [came] and now they don't come."[41] So it would appear. Most of Vicente Guerrero's roads remained unpaved in 2001.

NOTES

1. Controversial leaders often inspire literature heavier in polemics than empirical fact, Juan Perón of Argentina being a prime example. For analysis of this phenomenon, see Cristián Buchrucker, "Interpretations of Peronism: Old Frameworks and New Perspectives," as well as his introductory essay in *Peronism and Argentina*, ed. James P. Brennan (Wilmington, DE: Scholarly Resources, 1998).

2. An increasingly important political player by 1919, Garrido served as interim governor several times before commencing his first term as the constitutionally elected governor in 1923. Garrido was elected to a second term in 1930, with a Garrido loyalist serving as governor in the intervening period. Since when Garrido himself was not occupying the governor's chair, his unconditional loyalists served in his stead, contemporary observers and historians alike have seen fit to characterize Tabasco between 1923 and 1935 as the Garrido era. Garrido was, however, briefly ousted from power during the national de la Huerta rebellion of 1923–1924, which manifested itself with particular force in Tabasco.

3. The best synthetic treatment of Garrido's anticlericalism can be found in Carlos Martínez Assad's widely cited study, *El laboratorio de la revolución: El Tabasco garridista* (Mexico: Siglo Veintiuno Editores, 1979), ch. 1. Also see Adrian A. Bantjes, "Idolatry and Iconoclasm in Revolutionary Mexico: The De-Christianization Campaigns, 1929–1940," *Mexican Studies/Estudios Mexicanos* 13, no. 1 (Winter 1997).

4. Baltasar Dromundo, *Tomás Garrido: Su vida y su leyenda* (Mexico: Editorial Guarania, 1953), 15–16; and John W. F. Dulles, *Yesterday in Mexico: A Chronicle of the Revolution, 1919–1936* (Austin: University of Texas Press, 1967), second printing, 612. Garrido, who carried on numerous extramarital affairs, fathered additional children outside of his marriage. A picture of one of these children appears in a photo essay assembled by Juan José González Martínez for his popular *Zona Luz* series. See *La Zona Luz: Tomás Garrido Canabal*, vol. 1 (Apr. 24, 2000).

5. Carlos E. Ruiz Abreu and Jorge Abdo Francis, *El hombre del sureste: Relación documental del archivo particular de Tomás Garrido Canabal*, vol. 1 (Villahermosa: Uni-

versidad Juárez Autónoma de Tabasco and Secretaría de Gobernación, Archivo General de la Nación, 2002), 9. This is the first volume of what will be a multivolume index of the personal papers of Tomás Garrido Canabal, which are housed in the Archivo General de la Nación. It promises to be an extraordinary research tool for Garrido scholars.

6. Alfonso Taracena, *Historia de la revolución en Tabasco* (Villahermosa: Ediciones del Gobierno de Tabasco, México, 1974), 360.

7. Múgica's unconventional (and unpopular) requirement that everyone traveling along the stretch between the capital and the outlying community of Atasta push a cartload of dirt found echo in the Road Law of 1925. On the Atasta road requirement and other Múgica reforms in Tabasco, see Taracena, *Historia de la revolución en Tabasco*, 343, 351–52, and 359.

8. According to Baltasar Dromundo's somewhat dramatic telling of it, the death of Obregón—the man to whom Garrido's political ambitions and fortunes were tied—prompted Garrido to dash off a telegram to Calles. According to Dromundo, Garrido's brief message to President Calles, which simply stated "I am at your orders," proved to be Garrido's "political salvation." Dromundo, *Tomás Garrido: Su vida y su leyenda*, 110.

9. "25,000 hombres darán la bienvenida a los Generales Plutarco Elías Calles y Lázaro Cárdenas en Villahermosa," *El Nacional*, Mar. 25, 1934.

10. Specifically, Avila Camacho accused Garrido of "not always abid[ing] by the law." Archivo Histórico y Fotográfico de Tabasco (hereafter AHFT), Abelardo Rodríguez Proyecto Tabasco (hereafter ARPT), rollo 4, "Situación Política," folio 18.

11. AHFT-ARPT, rollo 4, "Situación Política," folios 21–25.

12. Garrido himself is said to have once acknowledged that he lived "at the margin of the Constitution." Dromundo, *Tomás Garrido: Su vida y su leyenda*, 63.

13. An analysis of road building in revolutionary Mexico can be found in Wendy Waters, "Re-Mapping the Nation: Road Building as State Formation in Post-Revolutionary Mexico, 1925–1940" (Ph.D. diss., The University of Arizona, 1999).

14. "Ley Vial para el estado de Tabasco," *Periódico Oficial del Estado de Tabasco* (hereafter *POET*), May 7, 1925. Women were not required to work on roads; the leveling and opening of paths and roads was understood to be a masculine purview.

15. "Ley Vial para el estado de Tabasco." Not surprisingly, financially secure Tabascans frequently opted to pay $1.50 (Tabasco's minimum wage) to hire a replacement. A Garrido-era educator who had taken advantage of this provision explained the logic of it in an interview I conducted with him in 2001. "The man with work, [such as] a storekeeper, was not going to leave his shop, it was better to pay [for a substitute]." Interview with Jorge Ruiz Andrade conducted by Kristin Harper, Nov. 16, 2001, Macuspana, Tabasco.

16. Apart from Garridista Tabasco, I know of no other example in revolutionary Mexico where individuals were legally obligated to perform unremunerated roadwork. However, the long-standing custom of *faenas*, a rotating system of voluntary labor, was used for roadwork and other projects deemed of public interest elsewhere in Mexico during the revolutionary era. See Waters, "Re-Mapping the Nation," 98; and Keith Brewster, *Militarism, Ethnicity, and Politics in the Sierra Norte de Puebla, 1917–1930* (Tucson: University of Arizona Press, 2003), 137–38. My thanks to Mary Kay Vaughan for encouraging me to seek out examples of faena labor in revolutionary Mexico. The

1937 novel *El Indio* also makes reference to the practice of using unpaid laborers to open highways. See Gregorio López y Fuentes, *El Indio*, trans. Anita Brenner (New York: Continuum Publishing, 1999), 208–9, 218–19, and 221. Additionally, Christopher R. Boyer notes that when Lázaro Cárdenas was governor of Michoacán he ordered municipal authorities to recruit volunteers for road building. See *Becoming Campesinos: Politics, Identity, and Agrarian Struggle in Postrevolutionary Michoacán, 1920–1935* (Stanford, CA: Stanford University Press, 2003), 189.

17. AHFT, Dirección General de Gobierno (hereafter DGG), rollo 4, "Aviación," folios 5–14.

18. "Aviación," folios 5–14.

19. "Aviación," folios 29–45. The text of the 1898 addition to Article 5 can be found in Sergio Elías Gutiérrez S. and Roberto Rives S., *La Constitución Mexicana al final del siglo XX*, second edition (Mexico D.F.: Las Líneas del Mar, 1995), 137.

20. Casa de Cultura Jurídica del Estado de Tabasco, Series Juzgado Amparos, Civil, Penal, Amparos 1926, Leg. 1, exp.12.

21. José López C. and M. Jimenez to Tomás Garrido C., Apr. 18, 1926, Archivo General de la Nación (hereafter AGN), Tomás Garrido Canabal (hereafter TGC), Actividad Pública, Gobernador (hereafter AP-G), caja 11, exp. 5.

22. Luis Rivera et al. to Tomás Garrido C., Oct. 7, 1928, AGN-TGC, caja 118, exp. 27.

23. The repeal of the Road Law can be found in *POET*, Mar. 31, 1928, 4.

24. Geney Torruco Saravia, *Villahermosa, Nuestra Ciudad*, vol. 2 (Villahermosa, Tab.: H. Ayuntamiento Constitucional del Centro, 1988), 727.

25. AHFT-DGG, rollo 20, "Trabajos Forzados," folio 43. Quiroz thought the number of days local campesinos had to labor on roads was unjust, given that "these poor wretches need to work to maintain their families and to be able to provide their children with clothes and supplies to attend school."

26. AHFT-DGG, rollo 19, "Atropellos de Autoridades," folio 402.

27. AHFT-DGG, rollo 20, "Trabajos Forzados," folio 34.

28. Correspondence between Ovidio Ruiz and Tomás Garrido C., AGN-TGC-AP-G, caja 13, exp. 2. Emphasis in the original.

29. Interview with Luz Esperanza Marin Dehesa Viuda de Castro conducted by Kristin Harper, Aug. 14, 2001, Balancán, Tabasco.

30. Roads, in fact, did excite some people, even if they had to build them themselves and without pay. See Waters, "Re-Mapping the Nation," 91.

31. Certainly the existence of rudimentary or unfinished roads was not a problem unique to Tabasco. For Veracruz, see Waters, "Re-Mapping the Nation," 105. In flood-prone Tabasco, water was always a consideration. Whether or not it turned out to be practicable, the authors of the Road Law did include a provision that the roads had to be of such a height that not even when floodwaters were at their highest could roads be submerged. See "Ley Vial para el estado de Tabasco."

32. Dirección General de Estadística, *Quinto censo de población*, May 15, 1930.

33. Interview with Jorge Ruiz Andrade (emphasis mine).

34. Memorandum sent to Pascual Ortiz Rubio by Manuel López Garduno, May 29, 1931, AGN-TGC-AP-G, caja 22, exp. 25. The date suggests that López Garduno traveled to Tabasco during the dry season, which may account for the fact that he encountered no travel problems.

35. "Tomás Garrido Canabal," *Rumbo Nuevo*, Apr. 13, 1944, 3.

36. Enrique Canudas, *Trópico rojo: Historia política y social de Tabasco, los años garridistas 1919/1934*, vol. 2 (Villahermosa: Gobierno del Estado de Tabasco, 1989), 134–35.

37. From what I can gather, only a primary education was available in Nicolás Sánchez Pascual's community at that time.

38. Interview with Nicolás Sánchez Pascual conducted by Kristin Harper, Sept. 1, 2001, Macuspana, Tabasco.

39. Interestingly, the same community where young Nicolás Sánchez Pascual and his friend approached Garrido had recently been the site of a deadly anticlerical struggle between Garridista authorities and uncompromising Catholics. See Severo García, *El Indio Gabriel: La matanza de San Carlos* (Mexico D.F.: Editorial Jus, 1957). To this day, the grisly act of Garridista militants setting fire to a church with people inside is remembered as one of the most ignominious episodes of the Garrido era. See, for example, Rodolfo Uribe Iniesta and Bartola May May, *T'an I K'ajalin Yokot'an (Palabra y pensamiento Yokot'an)* (Cuernavaca: Universidad Nacional Autónoma de México, Centro de Investigaciones Regionales de México, 2000), 60–61.

40. Even though roadwork was required of all male inhabitants of the state irrespective of their socioeconomic status, it is reasonable to assume that the poor performed a disproportionate share of roadwork since wealthier residents could afford to pay for substitutes.

41. Interview with Francisco Sánchez Cruz conducted by Kristin Harper, Aug. 26, 2001, Villa Vicente Guerrero, Centla, Tabasco.

8

Marte R. Gómez of Tamaulipas

Governing Agrarian Revolution

Michael A. Ervin

> I believe that politics has been very well defined as "the art of the possible." . . . Some statesmen waste their moment and do nothing. They defraud their destiny. But nobody can do more than circumstances permit.[1]

Marte R. Gómez was born on July 4, 1896, in the border town of Reynosa, Tamaulipas. Although he returned to his home state in the 1920s and 1930s, first as head of the state's Agriculture Department and later as governor, Gómez spent his early years beyond Tamaulipas's borders. The son of Rodolfo, a soldier who saw duty in many cities, young Marte was educated on the move, from León and Aguascalientes to Tacubaya and Mexico City.[2] Upon his graduation from one of Porfirian Mexico's most coveted primary schools, Gómez earned entrance at age twelve to the National School of Agriculture (ENA) on the eve of the revolution.

Gómez's early revolutionary career was devoted to the study of Mexico's "agrarian problem" in order to discover its solutions. From 1909 to 1923, as an ENA agronomy student and later as a National Agrarian Commission (CNA) official in Yucatán and Morelos, the young agronomist's experiences provided three pillars of an agrarian ideology that informed all of his activities in the years ahead. First, his ENA education instilled in him a belief in the need to modernize and expand agricultural production. While productive small farmers had the right to constitutional protections, Gómez believed that unproductive haciendas and the "routines" of farmers that led to low yields had to be reformed in order to feed a hungry nation after a destructive civil war. Second, his encounters with rural Mexicans in Morelos and Yucatán committed him to providing *campesinos* with land, in the form of communally held *ejidos*, to ameliorate their impoverishment.[3] Gómez wrote how "the memory of those terrible days" among the Zapatistas, witnessing their sacrifices for the cause of land reform, had filled him with "the spirit of an ideal *agrarista*."[4]

The task of reconciling the seemingly contradictory goals of redistribution and expanded production led to the third pillar of his agrarian ideology: cooperativism. As a CNA official in Morelos, Gómez highlighted the successes of *ejidatarios*, who through cooperative work had purchased tractors for common use.[5] Only through cooperative organization, with the decided aid of the state, could campesinos obtain the machinery, credit, irrigation, and other resources necessary to make their ejidos productive and competitive in a capitalist marketplace. In October 1922, the young agronomist wrote Circular 51, the CNA's first attempt to promote ejido organization and production. Worried that "the evolution of agricultural technology tends to abolish small-scale agriculture" due to "an insurmountable incompatibility between [it] and mechanization," Gómez called upon agronomists to "organize cooperatives in all the population centers" and collect a fund, based on 15 percent of ejido harvests, to help modernize and expand production.[6] Gómez believed that through cooperativism the ejidos could become a principal pillar of Mexico's agricultural production.

In the years that followed, the young agronomist moved from Ciudad Victoria, Tamaulipas, to Mexico City and back again in an effort to enact his agrarian program. In 1925, he headed up the Agriculture Department under Tamaulipas governor Emilio Portes Gil, and he was largely responsible for the extraordinary expansion of agrarian reform there.[7] In 1926, Gómez helped establish the new National Bank of Agricultural Credit, which he devoted to the organization of credit cooperatives throughout Mexico. From 1928 to 1930, Gómez served as interim president Portes Gil's Minister of Agriculture following the assassination of Alvaro Obregón, and he expanded the agrarian-reform program to unprecedented levels.[8] After a brief exile in France during the Ortiz Rubio presidency from 1930 to 1932, Gómez returned to Mexico City as a federal senator, and then as acting minister of treasury under president Abelardo L. Rodríguez. In 1936, Gómez was elected governor of Tamaulipas and served from 1937 to 1940. His career of revolutionary public service climaxed with a second stint as minister of agriculture for president Manuel Avila Camacho from 1940 to 1946.

This chapter tells the story of Gómez's four-year governorship during the Cárdenas presidency. In 1937, Gómez encountered numerous obstacles to realizing his revolutionary program in Tamaulipas. Powerful regional interests stood in the way of land distribution. A bankrupt state treasury and poor educational facilities, transportation networks, and irrigation systems limited the productive capacities of Tamaulipans. Finally, the advent of collectivism in Cardenista Mexico seemed to spell the demise of cooperativism. In the end, Gómez's governorship must be viewed in light of the phrase "the art of the possible" quoted at the outset of this essay. Governor Gómez utilized all of the resources at his disposal in an effort to enact the agrarian program that he had devised as early as 1922.

OVERCOMING THE OBSTACLES TO AGRARIAN REVOLUTION IN TAMAULIPAS

When Marte Gómez assumed the governorship of Tamaulipas in February 1937, numerous obstacles stood in the way of implementing his program. First, the new governor encountered a patchwork of powerful interests in all corners of the state. In the north, the border zone dominated by the Río Bravo and the cities of Reynosa and Matamoros remained largely in the hands of ranching and cotton interests that had withstood the onslaught of agrarian reform in the 1920s.[9] In the south and east around Ciudad Madero and Tampico, rich petroleum reserves led to the development of an oil enclave that responded more to national and international forces than to the reforms of state governors. Further inland was the sugar-producing zone surrounding Ciudad Mante. There, large haciendas owned by revolutionary elites, especially former president Plutarco Elías Calles and his closest allies, dominated the landscape and local politics. Further west, but still in the south and bordering on the state of San Luis Potosí, was the Fourth District, where military colonists answered to General Francisco Carrera Torres, the caudillo based in Tamaulipas's neighboring state. Only in the Central District, home to the state capital of Ciudad Victoria, did the new governor find a region transformed by his predecessors' agrarianism, and thus friendly to Gómez and his program.

Gómez's link to one of those predecessors, former governor Emilio Portes Gil, provided a second obstacle to the fulfillment of the young governor's program. Scholars in general agree that the Gómez governorship represented a return to the dominance of Portesgilismo in the state, which remained in effect until 1947.[10] Portes Gil's opposition, especially the oil workers of Tampico, often reminded Tamaulipans that Gómez had come to office as a member of a "political faction" rather than as a candidate of popular appeal.[11] The governor went out of his way to distance himself, at least publicly, from his boss. Even before his election, Gómez claimed that "Portes Gil always sustained [the idea] that we did not aspire to build us a feudal estate in Tamaulipas, and on this occasion we should demonstrate that."[12] The young agronomist did not even consider a run for the governorship until the people of Tamaulipas had shown support for his candidacy.[13] Once in office, the governor committed himself to free and open elections to demonstrate his neutrality. In June 1937, Portes Gil's opponents pushed through José Cantú Estrada's candidacy for Northern District federal deputy to Gómez's dismay.[14] He did nothing to oppose it, however. In fact, the governor constantly reiterated a deep commitment to "municipal freedom" and "constitutional democracy," proclaiming that "those citizens who aspire to public posts will find impartiality and constitutional guarantees in the state of Tamaulipas."[15]

The case of Tampico stands out as the exception that proved the rule of Gómez's impartiality. From Portes Gil's administration onward, the oil workers of Tampico were always the state's most powerful social group, and the least receptive to the tutelage of Tamaulipas's governors. Upon taking office, Governor Gómez did what he could to reach out to all workers. He reestablished the state's Labor Department, which required all new businesses to certify the hiring of unionized workers. He raised the minimum wage between 30 and 40 percent. He decreed renter and utilities laws that supported worker interests. Most importantly, he sided with President Cárdenas during the tense days surrounding the oil industry's nationalization.[16] Such policies did not earn Gómez the support of Tampico's oil workers, whose association with Vicente Lombardo Toledano's national Confederation of Mexican Workers proved to be a constant thorn in the governor's side. As a result, Gómez openly challenged the oil workers' candidate for Tampico's municipal presidency in 1938. Rather than a fair and impartial election, the hotly contested mayoral race was ultimately decided by the Tamaulipas Congress, in favor of a close Gómez associate, and against the vociferous cries of imposition by Tampico workers.[17]

Beyond the Tampico elections, good reasons existed for Gómez to minimize his public association with Portesgilismo. Since the early 1930s, rural politics in the state had turned extremely violent due to the bitter battle between Portesgilistas and supporters of Rafael Villarreal, state governor from 1933 to 1935 who used his office to purge Portesgilistas from the Tamaulipas Agrarian League and use it as his own base of popular support. Portes Gil loyalists responded by forming their own Liga Legítima de Comunidades Agrarias, and conflict and violence ensued, making the work of agrarian reform impossible.[18] The struggle reached a crescendo in early 1935, when Villarrealistas murdered Portesgilista ejidatarios in multiple attacks. Eduardo Morillo, a loyal Gómez subordinate and by then federal deputy for Tamaulipas, reported feeling "responsible in large part" for the killing, for having pulled the ejidos into partisan political battles.[19]

Upon assuming office, Gómez thus sought to replace division and violence with unity and peace among rural Tamaulipans. In December 1937, he wrote to the leader of the ejido Estación Cruz, Luis Garza, about the need to "liquidate political hatreds and struggle to build a spirit of fraternity among all of the sons of Tamaulipas." The governor believed that labels like Villarrealista and even Portesgilista should disappear altogether. "In all ejidos," he said, "there is not, nor should there be, anyone other than 'ejidatarios.'" He added that "there can be no agrarismo" while "enemy campesino groups" existed.[20] Gómez boasted, in fact, that five years of "bad politics" had been overcome by an "apolitical" first year as governor.[21]

Gómez's first year in office was also devoted to dealing with another obstacle to the fulfillment of his program: a bankrupt state treasury. Early on, he claimed that a "tremendous irregularity" in state finances had led the Cárdenas administration to place a "Jewish embargo" upon his budget.[22] "My dreams as governor of Tamaulipas are, for the moment, simply nightmares," he complained, because his early work was "reduced to paying [the] debts" of his predecessor.[23] To do so, the new governor implemented reforms to raise funds and regularize Tamaulipas's financial books. First, Gómez updated the state's accounting practices, a process that continued throughout his governorship.[24] More significantly, Gómez completely overhauled the state's Land Registry, raising funds rapidly simply by recounting urban and rural properties that had escaped tax assessments for years. And while state officials had "to break much resistance" in the process, the governor's commitment to a reform "without exceptions, without singling anyone out, without *compadrazgos*" seemed to mollify many fears.[25] With such reforms well underway by the end of 1937, Gómez claimed that "next year is when I will come to be known" for social expenditures.[26]

Other tax measures, however, had already created a great deal of controversy during his first year in office. Both state residents and Mexico's Supreme Court rejected Gómez's annulment of certain tax exemptions instituted under previous administrations.[27] His 3 percent tax on lottery ticket sellers met similar resistance among the people.[28] Most explosive of all was the governor's "celibate tax" passed in November 1937. Referred to as the "single's tax" by its opponents, the law imposed a progressive tax, ranging from 5 to 20 percent of income, upon all single men without family obligations. In part, the celibate tax sought to encourage population expansion in Mexico's northern frontier. The law claimed that the state "is obliged to realize that we are only 395,000 Tamaulipans" and that "it is necessary to outline a demographic policy."[29] More than demographic, the law's purpose was clearly social in nature. All funds raised by the tax, in their totality, were used to provide health services to women. Gómez wanted the tax to force "those who don't want to maintain a family to help to maintain the great family of disinherited people that society continues to resist recognizing."[30]

Responses to the tax varied widely. Among the foreign community, the law fell "like a bomb," as assorted Chinese, Arab, Spanish, and American businessmen came out against its seemingly anti-foreigner nature, calling the law "fascist" and "unconstitutional" in the process.[31] Some worker groups, especially the Tampico oil workers, resisted the law through humor and political agitation. Some workers considered, only partly in jest, organizing a "single's union" to defend their interests.[32] At demonstrations, other workers sang songs asking Saint Anthony if Governor Gómez's first name wasn't Cupid, rather than Marte.[33] All joking aside, the workers of El Aguila Petroleum, led by Salomón Gutiérrez, took to the streets and courts against the measure, threatening work stoppages and strikes if the governor did not abolish the law.[34] Local and even national newspapers covered the issue. Gómez complained that Mexico City's *Excélsior* misrepresented facts by claiming that the tax was paying for his "agrarian slashing." *La Prensa* argued that the tax was funding Gómez's supposed presidential campaign. And while Gómez recognized that "the Celibate Tax has been a tinderbox," he had no intention of repealing it.[35] In the months ahead, the governor vigorously defended the law's purposes and practice.

Tax and other reforms were not the only weapons used by Gómez to improve his state's finances and expand its expenditures. Gómez also benefited from projects high on the agenda of president Lázaro Cárdenas, especially road construction and education. Between 1937 and 1940, over eleven million pesos were invested in Tamaulipas road construction alone, with six million coming from the state budget, and another five million from federal monies. Under Gómez, some crucial highways were either fully completed or well under construction, connecting the state's major hubs in a modern transportation network.[36] In educational expenditures, a similar pattern of federal-state cooperation emerged, especially after the 1938 federalization of Tamaulipas's schools. In 1937, Tamaulipas spent 2.1 million pesos on public education, with 1.2 million pesos from the state budget, and the rest coming from federal sources. By 1940, spending on education totaled nearly four million pesos split almost evenly between state and federal monies.

More than benefiting from federal projects over which he had little control, Gómez also tapped federal budgets by turning to people in positions of power for help. Over the course of two decades, as CNA official, ENA director, minister of agriculture, and minister of treasury, the governor had developed many friendships and political alliances that helped expand the state's capacity to pay for his programs. Through the Ministry of Treasury's Ignacio Sanabria, and especially the ministry's director of credit, Pascual Gutiérrez Roldán—a former ENA student—Gómez's administration received favorable federal financial treatment.[37] When Gómez complained of limited help from the treasury in 1938, Gutiérrez Roldán retorted that Tampaulipas had received "the most equitable and friendly treatment that any state could have received" during difficult budgetary times.[38] In 1940, when Gutiérrez Roldán informed the governor that the accustomed federal aid would not be as hearty as in the past (Gómez had to "sacrifice himself" in the words of Cárdenas), the governor griped that "I won't be sacrificing as much as Tamaulipas."[39] The federal government still came up with over two million pesos for Tamaulipas's budget that year, however.[40]

The result of Gómez's financial measures was a period of booming budgets throughout his governorship. From 3 million pesos in 1936, prior to his coming to office, the state budget climbed to 4 million in 1937, 4.1 million in 1938, 4.7 million in 1939, and a whopping 5.7 million in 1940.[41] Supporters and detractors alike could not deny that Gómez's financial wizardry had provided the state with its largest budgets ever, placing Tamaulipas "among the states with the largest budgets" in the nation.[42]

The budgetary problem behind him, Governor Gómez turned to enacting his agrarian program. He started with redistribution, which exploded in 1937 as a result of state and federal cooperation. Even before the year was out, after only ten months in office, Gómez had handed out ninety-six provisional possessions, affecting over 140,000 hectares and 4,200 ejidatarios. Gómez correctly called the effort "the most intense redistributive activity ever developed in Tamaulipas."[43] Redistribution expanded in the years ahead. In 1938, nearly 5,200 beneficiaries received over 172,000 hectares of land. Gómez claimed that, for the first time, campesinos' "hunger for lands" was declining, as new ejido requests were being outstripped by the government's resolution of outstanding land claims.[44] In the end, Gómez surpassed his own hopes for land distribution totals. After four years, the governor had distributed almost 650,000 hectares of land to over 18,600 beneficiaries (see table 8.1).

Just as important as the quantity of the land distributed was its location. From the beginning, Governor Gómez, in concert with President Cárdenas, tackled the problem of Tamaulipas's powerful regional interests. The first to fall was the Fourth District, under the influence of General Francisco Carrera Torres, close ally of minister of agriculture and former San Luis Potosí governor Saturnino Cedillo. In August 1937, Cárdenas forced Cedillo to resign his post and began to undermine the caudillo's power base. Gómez responded by redistributing Fourth District lands at "an accelerated

Table 8.1.   Tamaulipas Land Distribution under Governor Marte R. Gómez

Year	Beneficiaries	Land (Hectares)
1937	4,539	147,000
1938	5,164	172,800
1939	4,950	205,800
1940	3,987	123,865
Total	18,640	649,465

Source: "Sumamente fructífera," *El Mundo,* Jan. 2, 1939, 6; "La labor," *El Mundo,* Jan. 2, 1938, 6; "El gobierno del estado rindió al Congreso amplio informe de su gestión administrativa," *El Mundo,* Jan. 2, 1940, 8; "Fecunda como pocas," *El Mundo,* Jan. 3, 1941, 12.

rhythm."[45] When news of a possible Cedillista rebellion emerged, Governor Gómez negotiated Carrera Torres's neutrality and organized Fourth District ejidatarios and military colonists to ensure their loyalty to the government. At the end of January 1938, an attack by the forces of Nicolás Rodríguez alerted officials to the coming rebellion.[46] Once again, Gómez went to work. In February he traveled to Tula and Jaumave to make more provisional possessions of ejidos.[47] In May, he was back in Miquihana, handing out 11,500 hectares of land to two hundred beneficiaries.[48] In August, he returned to Tula and Ocampo to distribute 18,379 hectares of land to Fourth District ejidatarios.[49] So serious was the redistribution that private farmers complained that they would not "submit themselves to the slavery of agrarian leaders" as a result of the "wide reach that has been conceded to the agraristas of the region."[50] The reform succeeded in its goals, however. For one, the ejidatarios defended the government against the Cedillistas, as twenty-two Tamaulipan campesinos died fighting the rebellion.[51] Just as importantly for Gómez, the Fourth District had been opened to his agrarian program and the military colonists subdued. In March, General Carrera Torres was transferred to Oaxaca; by October, the colonists themselves had been completely disarmed.[52]

Next up on Gómez's effort to break powerful regional interests was the Northern District, especially around the city of Matamoros.[53] There, small and medium-sized cotton farmers and cattle ranchers had resisted agrarian reform since the days of the Portes Gil governorship. The first ejido grant in the region, El Ebanito, had been greeted with violence, provoking "an armed encounter," with "the precedent more or less repeated with subsequent cases, provoking the fear of the agrarian authorities and the state government, which preferred not touching such a thorny situation."[54] The stalemate ended in 1935, when a Matamoros flood ignited the government's interest in the region once again. In 1936, the Ministry of Communications (SCOP) dispatched Eduardo Chávez to oversee an irrigation project to protect residents along the Río Bravo and to irrigate lands to expand the region's cotton production. In January 1937, prior to taking office, Gómez met with Cárdenas, who informed the incoming governor that the irrigation project would move forward with full federal support.[55]

Immediately upon taking office, Gómez moved to make the project his own. Traveling constantly between Ciudad Victoria and Matamoros, Gómez incited federal and state employees to work. In March, the governor issued a detailed report to President Cárdenas regarding the project.[56] His plan described a broad reform that included the SCOP, the Agrarian Department, and the state government, working together to completely transform Tamaulipas's Northern District. For Gómez, a piecemeal irrigation system could not end the vicious battles between small farmers and ejidatarios, both of whom had rights to the region's land and water.[57] Instead, the government needed to redraw the region's map entirely, so that all parties could work together to create one of Mexico's most important cotton zones.

The Bajo Río Bravo project, as it was called, picked up pace in the years ahead. In February 1938, President Cárdenas called upon all government ministries to work together to solve the region's problems and dispatched Gómez's trusted colleague, Pascual Gutiérrez Roldán, to begin distributing credit to the region's now more numerous ejidatarios.[58] In July, the governor handed out nearly 9,000 hectares of land, including the symbolically loaded confirmation of Lucio Blanco's Los Borregos ejido, the first ejido granted in Mexico in 1913.[59] In 1939, two events magnified the importance and complexity of the Bajo Río Bravo project. In January, reports of the misery of Mexican residents in the United States led President Cárdenas to dispatch Ramón Beteta to Texas to determine which groups wanted to return to an agricultural life in Mexico.[60] Repatriated Mexicans were promptly incorporated into the Río Bravo project. And in March, news of nearby Nuevo León campesinos literally dying of hunger as a result of low water levels emerged from the Don Martín Irrigation District.[61] No expense was spared to carve out a space in the Bajo Río Bravo project for the drought victims.[62]

In April 1939, President Cárdenas toured Tamaulipas's Northern District with Governor Gómez and issued a decree whose measures mirrored those of Gómez's 1937 plan.[63] The greatest obstacle, according to the president, was the region's "anachronistic" land tenure system, which had to be transformed in order to make room for all social groups, from small farmers and ejidatarios to drought victims and repatriated communities. Each plot was to contain ten hectares of irrigated land, more than enough for the "sustenance of a campesino family." In all, the plan projected a zone of 30,000 hectares of irrigated land devoted to cotton production.

By 1940, Tamaulipas's Northern District looked nothing like it had in 1936 as a result of both the Bajo Río Bravo project in Matamoros, and a much broader agrarian program that included lands surrounding Reynosa to the west. In the Bajo Río Bravo zone, over 2,000 heads of household now produced primarily cotton on well over 16,000 hectares of cleared lands, with more clearing yet to do. Beyond Matamoros, ejido cotton production throughout the north expanded due to the combined efforts of ejidatarios, the federal Banco Ejidal, and Gómez's administration. In 1937, the Ejido Bank worked with cooperative societies to plant 5,864 hectares of land, resulting in 2.2 million kilograms of cotton worth nearly 780,000 pesos. In 1939, the ejidos produced 4.3 million kilos of cotton worth 1.7 million pesos on 10,772 hectares of land.[64] By 1940, ejido cooperatives accounted for one-third of the state's nearly 22 million kilograms of cotton.[65] Gómez's transformation of the North was well underway.

One final region remained in order to complete Gómez's agrarian revolution: El Mante. Perhaps no effort better reflected the governor's continued commitment to his agrarian program than that of El Mante, a 20,000-hectare irrigation district devoted to sugarcane production in south-central Tamaulipas. Since its creation in the 1920s, the El Mante district benefited not ejidatarios, but private landowners, many of them friends and relatives of former president Plutarco Elías Calles, the revolution's famed *jefe máximo*. By 1937, however, national events once again had worked in Gómez's favor, allowing him to move into El Mante soon after taking office. In June 1935, President Cárdenas began the purge of Callistas at the national level that culminated in April 1936 with the former president's expulsion from Mexico.[66]

With Calles removed, the governor's agrarian program in El Mante began with land distribution. Gómez immediately called upon the region's campesinos to request land from an agrarista government. On July 17, 1937, the ejido El Mante received the first grant of 542 hectares, including lands expropriated from the properties of Generals Pablo González, Gregorio Osuna, and Aarón Sáenz, among many other associates of Calles.[67] In all during that first year, seventeen ejidos received provisional possession of lands from Governor Gómez. In 1938, little land distribution occurred in El Mante, as federal and state officials jointly planned the region's complete restructuring in an effort to provide each ejidatario with six hectares of irrigated land. In January 1939, Gómez began the definitive distribution, with major expropriations of lands belonging to the Calles, Sáenz, and Osuna families, among others.[68] By November, thirty-two ejidos held nearly 17,000 hectares of the region's land, almost 10,000 of them irrigated.[69]

After redistribution, Gómez worked to expand ejido production. In this sense, the El Mante project was a work in progress "within the limits of the possible," according to Gómez.[70] In 1937, the governor obtained credit for the ejidatarios through friends at the Banco Ejidal. Although with funds short at the Ejido Bank, Gómez once again turned to the Ministry of Treasury's Pascual Gutiérrez Roldán, who provided resources for cooperative tractor purchases.[71] The El Mante ejidatarios received over 400,000 pesos to plant 300 hectares of land, with the average plot standing at a paltry 1.5 hectares per ejidatario. The next year, 1938, "was fecund for the work of organizing ejido cultivation" according to Gómez. By the 1938–1939 agricultural year, nearly 400,000 more pesos were invested into well over 600 hectares, with the average plot reaching three hectares per ejidatario. By 1939, Gómez boasted, the average plot size stood at 5.5 hectares per ejidatario, and the campesinos were making "their own well-being with the fruit of their own efforts and with the technical help of the Banco Ejidal."[72]

A complete solution to the El Mante problem involved much more than land distribution and ejido production, however. In 1938, the region's sugar mill, owned by the Compañía Azucarera del Río Mante—whose president was Aarón Sáenz—came under increasing attack as well. Worker strikes seriously disrupted the mill's operations in February.[73] In June, President Cárdenas called upon minister of agriculture José Parres to head up a commission to decide the region's future, and that of the mill, once and for all.[74] Starting in November, strikes and violence between rival worker groups brought the mill to a near standstill.[75] By then, national politicians were publicly demanding action against the sugar mill, which they claimed had cost the nation millions of pesos in order to benefit a few wealthy and powerful individuals.[76] In February 1939, President Cárdenas put an end to the uncertainty and nationalized the mill.[77]

The mill's expropriation did not end the uncertainty entirely, however. An important struggle emerged in the aftermath of nationalization regarding just what form El Mante production should take.[78] In the 1930s, many of Gómez's agronomy colleagues had rejected cooperativism and embraced collectivism as the solution to rural Mexico's problems. Under Cárdenas, the agronomists Manuel Mesa, Emilio López Zamora, and others organized the League of Socialist Agronomists to push the collectivist position.[79] By expropriating both factory and field, and uniting the two in a common endeavor, the collectivists believed that redistribution and higher production could be reconciled, and the future of the Mexican Revolution secured. The experiments in Laguna cotton, Yucatán henequen, and Michoacán rice production demonstrated the power of collectivist arguments in Cardenista Mexico.

The struggle over El Mante's future came to a head when López Zamora and Gómez presented their opinions to President Cárdenas following the mill's expropriation.[80] López Zamora complained about the continued existence of private farmers, both large and small, who undermined the efforts of El Mante workers and ejidatarios.[81] Hence, the only solution was complete expropriation of all lands and collective organization. Governor Gómez disagreed. He lashed out at both Mesa and López Zamora for their "campaign undertaken to obtain total expropriation," because many of the region's small properties were constitutionally protected and had to be respected.[82] Moreover, Gómez viewed the arguments in favor of El Mante collectivism as ploys of worker groups, especially those associated with the national Confederation of Mexican Workers, to gain control in the region.[83] As a result, the governor embraced a separation between factory and field in order to allow ejidatarios and small farmers to solve their own problems, free from the intervention of mill workers or other outside interests. He added that "the government of Tamaulipas . . . will be the first" to support total expropriation if the president so ordered, but he clearly hoped to sway Cárdenas to his cooperativist viewpoint.[84]

As part of his shift to more conservative policies in the last three years of his rule, Cárdenas ultimately sided with the governor, and by 1940, El Mante, like many other regions of Tamaulipas, little resembled itself in 1936. In the 1940–1941 sugar harvest, ejido cooperatives financed by the

Banco Ejidal dominated the region, producing 208 million of the coopera-tive's 315 million tons of sugarcane, which translated into 22 million of the mill's 33 million kilograms of finished sugar.[85] As elsewhere in the state, the foundations for Gómez's cooperative ejido revolution were solidly laid.

CONCLUSION

When Marte Gómez came to power as Tamaulipas governor in 1937, he had already worked for two decades to enact an agrarian program that could rec-oncile the seemingly contradictory goals of redistribution and expanded production. Upon assuming office, Governor Gómez began to extend that program systematically throughout the state. To do so, the governor certainly benefited from a sympathetic president whose interests coincided with his own. At the same time, Gómez also demonstrated an uncanny ability to uti-lize national politics to overcome the obstacles to revolution in Tamaulipas.

In the end, Gómez's two decades of service reflected a fundamental dif-ference between himself and the revolution's many other governors. Some chose agrarian reform as a platform from which to launch highly successful regional and national political careers. Others, like Marte R. Gómez, uti-lized political careers to foment an agrarian revolution. In this sense, Gómez truly lived his phrase, "the art of the possible."[86] For over two decades, Gómez marshaled all of the available resources in support of ful-filling the great agrarian promise of the revolution.

NOTES

1. Marte Gómez, quoted in James Wilkie and Edna Monzón de Wilkie, eds., *México visto en el siglo XX* (Mexico: Instituto Mexicano de Investigaciones Económicas, 1969), 119.

2. Marte Gómez, *Biografías de agrónomos* (Chapingo: Colegio de Postgraduados, 1976), 248.

3. An "ejido" was the unit of land distributed to "ejidatarios." The Spanish word "campesino" is used instead of its standard translation, "peasant."

4. An "agrarista" was a supporter of agrarian reform. Gómez to José Vasconcelos, Aug. 11, 1923, in Antonio Carrillo Flores, ed., *Vida política contemporánea: Cartas de Marte R. Gómez*, vol. 1 (Mexico: Fondo de Cultura Económica, 1978), 23.

5. Gómez, "Estudio . . . del Estado de Morelos y programa general para su re-construcción," Aug. 30, 1922, "Trabajos presentados al Segundo Congreso Nacional Agronómico," Colección Marte R. Gómez [CMRG], 19, 24–25.

6. Eyler Simpson, *The Ejido: Mexico's Way Out* (Chapel Hill: University of North Carolina Press, 1937), 318–21; Arnaldo Córdova, *La Revolución Mexicana: La ide-ología del nuevo régimen* (Mexico: Ediciones Era, 1973), 284.

7. Heather Fowler-Salamini, "Tamaulipas: Land Reform and the State," in *Provinces of the Revolution: Essays on Regional Mexican History, 1910–1929*, ed. Thomas Benjamin and Mark Wasserman (Albuquerque: University of New Mexico Press, 1990), 204–5.

8. For presidential land distribution totals, see James Wilkie, ed., *Society and Economy in Mexico* (Los Angeles: UCLA Latin American Center Publications, 1990).

9. On Tamaulipas's regional divisions and interests, see Arturo Alvarado Mendoza, *El portesgilismo en Tamaulipas: Estudio sobre la constitución de la autoridad pública en el México posrevolucionario* (Mexico: El Colegio de México, 1992).

10. Alvarado Mendoza, *El portesgilismo en Tamaulipas*; José Carlos Mora García, *Historia breve del gobierno de Tamaulipas en el período del Gobernador Marte R. Gómez, 1937–1941* (Ciudad Victoria: Cactus Ediciones, 2001).

11. "Los obreros hablan de derrocar al Ing. Gómez," *El Mundo*, Jan. 31, 1938, 1, 6.

12. Gómez to Eduardo Morillo, Oct. 25, 1935, Archivo Marte R. Gómez [AMRG], 1935 Cartas.

13. For more on Gómez's selection, see Morillo to Gómez, Aug. 29, 1935, AMRG, 1935 Cartas; and Portes Gil to Gómez, Dec. 4, 1935, in Carrillo Flores, *Cartas*, 1:451.

14. Gómez to José Cantú Estrada, Feb. 20, 1937, in Carrillo Flores, ed., *Cartas*, vol.1, 475–6.

15. "La labor del Gobno. del Estado fué de organización y de orden," *El Mundo*, Jan. 2, 1938, 1; Gómez to Ulises Irigoyen, Feb. 4, 1939, in Carrillo Flores, *Cartas*,1:546.

16. "Una junta de gobernadores en México para tratar lo del conflicto petrolero," *El Mundo*, Mar. 11, 1938, 3; Gómez to Jaime Torres Bodet, Mar. 2, 1938, and July 2, 1938, and Gómez/State Governors to Cárdenas, Mar. 24, 1938, in Carrillo Flores, *Cartas*, 1:510, 521–23, and 515–16.

17. Gómez's candidate, Jesús Fernández, had served the Portesgilista agrarian reform since the 1920s. For more on the outcry surrounding Fernández's election, see "Acusan al Gob. del Estado de hacer labor contra la unificación obrera," *El Mundo*, Nov. 20, 1938, 1, 5; and "Los tres ayuntamientos de Tampico hacen nombramientos," *El Mundo*, Jan. 2, 1939, 1, 5.

18. Estanislao Peña to Angel Posada, July 12, 1934, AMRG.

19. Morillo to Gómez, Apr. 11, 1935, AMRG, 1935 Cartas, 1.

20. Gómez to Luis E. C. Garza, Dec. 8, 1937, in Carrillo Flores, *Cartas*, 1:505.

21. "La labor," *El Mundo*, Jan. 2, 1938, 1–2.

22. Gómez to José Siurob, May 20, 1937, in Carrillo Flores, *Cartas*, 1:484; and Gómez to Pascual Gutiérrez Roldán, May 3, 1937, AMRG, 1937 Cartas.

23. Gómez to Irigoyen, Oct. 22, 1937, in Carrillo Flores, *Cartas*, 1:496.

24. "La labor," *El Mundo*, Jan. 2, 1938, 4, 6.

25. "Sumamente fructífera fué la labor del Gobierno del Edo.," *El Mundo*, Jan. 2, 1939, 4.

26. Gómez to Irigoyen, Oct. 22, 1937, in Carrillo Flores, *Cartas*, 1:496.

27. "Fallo de la Suprema Corte contra el Gobierno del Estado," *El Mundo*, Nov. 5, 1937, 1, 8.

28. "Los vendedores de billetes no van a cubrir impuestos," *El Mundo*, Nov. 8, 1937, 5.

29. "Un impuesto a los solteros se establece en Tamaulipas," *El Mundo*, Nov. 25, 1937, 1.

30. Gómez to Eduardo Bustamante, Sept. 17, 1937, in Carrillo Flores, *Cartas*, 1:492.

31. It was considered anti-foreigner because many businessmen traveled to Mexico alone. "El Proyecto del Impuesto a los solteros se comentó, vivamente en Tampico y C. Madero," *El Mundo*, Nov. 26, 1937, 1, 8.

32. "El Proyecto del Impuesto a los solteros," *El Mundo*, Nov. 26, 1937, 1.

33. "Los obreros hablan de derrocar . . . ," *El Mundo*, Jan. 31, 1938, 6.

34. "Los primeros amparos contra la Ley del Celibato, fueron interpuestos ayer," *El Mundo*, Jan. 6, 1938, 1, 5; "Verdadera lluvia de amparos contra la nva. Ley del Celibato," *El Mundo*, Jan. 16, 1938, 1–2; "Los obreros hablan de derrocar . . . ," *El Mundo*, Jan. 31, 1938, 6; "La Ley del Celibato se combatirá en todo el Edo.," *El Mundo*, Feb. 4, 1938, 1, 7.

35. Gómez to Torres Bodet, Mar. 2, 1938, in Carrillo Flores, *Cartas*, 1:509.

36. For more on road construction projects, see "Fecunda como pocas fué la labor desarrollada por el Ing. Marte R. Gómez en favor del Estado de Tamaulipas," *El Mundo*, Jan. 3, 1941, 6.

37. See, for example, Gómez to Gutiérrez Roldán, Oct. 28, 1937, AMRG, 1937 Cartas; Gutiérrez Roldán to Gómez, Feb. 3, 1940, AMRG, 1940 Cartas.

38. Gutiérrez Roldán to Gómez, Mar. 3, 1938, AMRG, 1938 Cartas, 2.

39. Gutiérrez Roldán to Gómez, Feb. 3, 1940, AMRG, 1940 Cartas.

40. "Fecunda como pocas," *El Mundo*, Jan. 3, 1941, 10.

41. "La labor," *El Mundo*, Jan. 2, 1938, 6; "Sumamente fructífera," *El Mundo*, Jan. 2, 1939, 6; "Fecunda como pocas," *El Mundo*, Jan. 3, 1941, 10.

42. "Fecunda como pocas," *El Mundo*, Jan. 3, 1941, 12.

43. Gómez, "Memorándum sobre la situación de los nuevos ejidos de Tamaulipas," Nov. 25, 1937, AMRG, 1937 Cartas, 1.

44. "Sumamente fructífera," *El Mundo*, Jan. 2, 1939, 6.

45. Mora García, *Historia breve*, 10.

46. "Los sangrientos sucesos registrados en Matamoros," *El Mundo*, Feb. 1, 1938, 1–2, 6; "La aflictiva situación que prevalece en Matamoros se remediará desde luego," *El Mundo*, Feb. 4, 1938, 1, 3.

47. "Nuevas dotaciones de tierras en el Municip. de Jaumave hizo el Gob.," *El Mundo*, Feb. 27, 1938, 4.

48. "Repartirá más tierras el Gobdor.," *El Mundo*, May 10, 1938, 6.

49. "Un gran reparto de tierras hizo el Gob. del Estado . . . ," *El Mundo*, Aug. 20, 1938, 4.

50. "Zafarrancho por cuestión de tierras," *El Mundo*, Nov. 3, 1938, 1.

51. "Sumamente fructífera," *El Mundo*, Jan. 2, 1938, 1.

52. "Carrera Torres se hará cargo de la 28a. Zona Militar," *El Mundo*, Mar. 14, 1938, 3; "Los ex-colonos militares en todo Edo. desarmados por orden superior," *El Mundo*, Oct. 7, 1938, 6; "Se consumó el desarme de colonos de Tula," *El Mundo*, Oct. 22, 1938, 1, 5.

53. For other Gómez projects in the north, see Salvador Aguilar Chávez, *Memoria del Distrito de Riego del Bajo Río San Juan, Nuevo León y Tamaulipas* (Mexico: CNI, 1941), CMRG.

54. Gómez to Cárdenas, Mar. 5, 1937, in Carrillo Flores, *Cartas*, 1:478.

55. Mora García, *Historia breve*, 6–7.

56. Gómez to Cárdenas, Mar. 5, 1937, in Carrillo Flores, *Cartas*, 1:478–80.

57. "El Gob. del Estado habla de la situación de la Z. de Matamoros," *El Mundo*, Feb. 6, 1938, 1, 8. For small farmers' continued resistance to the agrarian program, see "Tres mil agricultores piden garantías," *El Mundo*, Oct. 30, 1938, 1–2.

58. "La aflictiva situación," *El Mundo*, Feb. 4, 1938, 1, 3; "Refaccionarán en Matamoros a los ejidatarios," *El Mundo*, Feb. 13, 1938, 1, 4.

59. "La mayor dotación de tierras será hecha por el Gobernador en el Norte del Estado," *El Mundo*, July 30, 1938, 6.

60. "Los repatriados colonizarán el latifundio 'La Sauteña,' de Tam.," *El Mundo*, Jan. 7, 1939, 5; "Al fin van al socorro de los compatriotas que quieren venir de EE.UU.," *El Mundo*, Apr. 6, 1939, 5.

61. For more information, see Secretaría de Hacienda y Crédito Público (SHCP), "Informe rendido por el Ing. Luis Margain T. sobre las obras en el valle bajo del Río Bravo," CMRG, 34.

62. "Los colonos de Don Martín hállanse en grave situación," *El Mundo*, Mar. 11, 1939, 5; "Están muriendo de hambre los ejidatarios de C. Anáhuac, N. L.," *El Mundo*, Mar. 12, 1939, 1, 3.

63. "La zona baja del Río Bravo se convertirá en un gran vergel," *El Mundo*, Apr. 27, 1939, 1, 3–4.

64. The statistics come from SHCP, "Informe rendido por el Ing. Luis Margain T.," CMRG, 34–41.

65. Cristóbal Guevara Delmas, "Perfiles de la reforma agraria en Tamaulipas," tésis para obtener el título de licenciado en derecho (Mexico: UNAM, 1951), 118.

66. For one concise treatment of the Cárdenas/Calles split, see Hans Werner Tobler, *La Revolución Mexicana: Transformación social y cambio político, 1876–1940* (Mexico: Alianza Editorial, 1994), 617–22.

67. Mora García, *Historia breve*, 10.

68. "La finca de Calles en El Mante afectada por reparto agrario," *El Mundo*, Jan. 20, 1939, 1, 8; "Hizo nuevos repartos de tierras el Gob. de Estado Ing. Gómez," *El Mundo*, Jan. 21, 1939, 6.

69. Gómez, "Memorándum al Sr. Presidente de la República sobre la situación agrícola y agraria de 'El Mante,'" Nov. 18, 1939, CMRG, 6, 60.

70. Gómez, "Memorándum al Sr. Presidente," 5.

71. Gutiérrez Roldán to Gómez, Aug. 22 and Oct. 18, 1937, AMRG, 1937 Cartas.

72. Gómez, "Memorándum al Sr. Presidente," 5–8. For more information, see Jorge Barojas Armiño, "Situación agraria de El Mante, Tamaulipas. Memorándum al C. Ing. Marte R. Gómez, Gobernador Constitucional del Estado," Apr./May 1940, AMRG.

73. "Los agricultores de caña suspenden sus contratos . . . ," *El Mundo*, Feb. 4, 1938, 1, 5.

74. "El C. Secretario de Agricultura estuvo en ésta y fué a Tuxpam," *El Mundo*, June 21, 1938, 1, 6.

75. "La pugna de los trabajadores del Mante paralizó la zafra," *El Mundo*, Nov. 15, 1938, 1, 5; "Ola de sangre invade a El Mante," *El Mundo*, Dec. 14, 1938, 6; "Corrió la sangre en 'El Mante,'" *El Mundo*, Jan. 19, 1939, 1–2.

76. "Pide el Congreso el embargo y la expropiación del Ingenio," *El Mundo*, Dec. 11, 1938, 1, 6.

77. "Expropió El Mante el Pdte.," *El Mundo*, Feb. 19, 1939, 1, 8.

78. "Los trabajadores de El Mante quieren la entrega del Ingenio," *El Mundo*, Feb. 20, 1939, 1, 8; "La nueva organización en el Ingenio del Mante se está llevando a cabo," *El Mundo*, Mar. 31, 1939, 5; "Quieren administrar el ingenio del Mante quienes allí laboran," *El Mundo*, Apr. 6, 1939, 6.

79. The league published numerous tracts on the agrarian problem. See, for example, Marco Antonio Durán, *Los sofismas de la reforma agraria* (Mexico: Liga de Agrónomos Socialistas, 1939).

80. Emilio López Zamora, *La situación del Distrito de Riego de El Mante* (Mexico: Ed. Ramírez Alonso, 1939); Gómez, "Memorándum al Sr. Presidente."

81. On landowners' efforts to undermine the work, see "Es sumamente grave la situación en El Mante," *El Mundo*, Mar. 15, 1939, 1, 8.

82. "La Liga de Agrónomos pide la expropiación del I. del Mante," *El Mundo*, Dec. 13, 1938, 5.

83. On Gómez's wariness of the mill workers' intentions, see "Están divididas la Confederación Campesina de México y la CTM," *El Mundo*, Jan. 26, 1938, 3; and "No quiere el Gob. la hegemonía de la CTM en ésta," *El Mundo*, Oct. 15, 1938, 1. Adding to his fears, the League of Socialist Agronomists was linked to the CTM.

84. Gómez, "Memorándum al Sr. Presidente," 61, 66.

85. Sociedad Cooperativa de Ejidatarios y Obreros del Ingenio del Mante, "Informe del consejo de Administración . . . sobre el segundo ejercicio social" (Mexico, 1941), CMRG, 3–4.

86. See note 1.

9

Efraín Gutiérrez of Chiapas

The Revolutionary Bureaucrat

Stephen E. Lewis

On the face of it, Efraín A. Gutiérrez was one of Mexico's most important revolutionary governors. During his four-year term in Chiapas (1936–1940), Gutiérrez implemented the political, economic, and social agenda of his friend and benefactor, president Lázaro Cárdenas (1934–1940). He redistributed more land to more peasants in Chiapas than all of his predecessors combined. He organized the state's workers and peasants into federal unions that eventually constituted significant blocs of the official party. Despite fierce resistance, his administration implemented social policies on behalf of Chiapas's many indigenous peoples. As if this were not enough, Gutiérrez accomplished all of this in an impoverished frontier state where local ranchers and planters were legendary for their tenacious resistance to federal reforms and interventions.

In spite of these considerable achievements, history seems to have forgotten Governor Gutiérrez. The two most authoritative and exhaustive multi-tomed biographical encyclopedias, the *Diccionario histórico y biográfico de la Revolución Mexicana* and the *Diccionario Porrúa de historia, biografía y geografía de México* do not mention him.[1] Many of his accomplishments were short-lived or had unintended consequences, and he was unable to impose his will on vast regions of Chiapas. His relative anonymity is also explained by the fact that Cardenismo was in retreat during the second half of his four-year term. Without the determined support of an interventionist, actively mobilized federal government, Gutiérrez struggled—along with precious few allies—to implement federal agrarian, labor, and *indigenista* policies in Chiapas.

This chapter places Gutiérrez in the context of the state's idiosyncratic revolutionary trajectory, which not only lends added weight to Gutiérrez's achievements, but also helps explain their fleeting and easily distorted nature. The chapter takes a close look at Gutiérrez's record in the Chiapas highlands, where he struggled to implement the Cardenista blueprint. Lastly, it considers his work in Soconusco, where the former agronomist registered his most impressive victories against lowland planters in the land reform of 1939 and 1940.

CHIAPAS AND THE REVOLUTION

Although a handful of historians still claim that the revolution never arrived in Chiapas,[2] most agree that the state did in fact experience the "fiesta of bullets." That said, the revolution was imposed belatedly (in 1914) by troops loyal to first chief Venustiano Carranza and failed to generate popular sympathy and participation. To the contrary, the Carrancistas' actions and legislation sparked a determined resistance organized by ranchers and planters known as Mapaches, or raccoons, because they mobilized at night and devoured uncooked corn in the fields. With few exceptions, the state's indigenous peoples did not participate directly in the fighting, although all factions used Maya peasants as load-bearers, guides, and workers and brutally requisitioned the food supplies of communities that lived in "enemy" territory. In the end, the Carrancistas were unable to transform Chiapas through top-down reforms and lost their war of attrition to the tenacious Mapaches. Chiapas therefore entered the postrevolutionary period looking remarkably like it had in 1910.[3]

The state's first governor after 1920, Tiburcio Fernández Ruiz, had led the Mapache resistance. During his turbulent four-year term of office, he explicitly rejected federal intervention in state affairs. Federal labor and agrarian reform laws were consistently weakened, undermined, or not applied. His violent interventions in municipal and state elections left the state in almost constant turmoil, which tested the patience of president Alvaro Obregón (1920–1924) and his interior minister (and future president) Plutarco Elías Calles. In 1925, the Obregonista Carlos Vidal became governor. Though initially more cooperative than Fernández Ruiz, Vidal decided to back General Francisco Serrano in the upcoming presidential election (and not Obregón, whom Calles sought to impose for a second term), leading to his murder and the bloody purge of his closest collaborators in Chiapas. Raymundo Enríquez served as governor from 1928 to 1932. Neither he nor his predecessors were able or willing to fully implement the reforms that we associate with the revolution.[4]

Chiapas's next governor (and Gutierrez's direct predecessor) was Colonel Victórico Grajales (1932–1936). By the time Lázaro Cárdenas became president in December 1934, Grajales was midway through his four-year term as governor. A well-off *finquero*, his priorities had been made abundantly clear. He hijacked Chiapas's labor and agrarian organizations by placing ranchers and planters at the head of the Confederation of Peasants and Workers in Chiapas (Confederación Campesina y Obrera de Chiapas, or CCOC). His administration suffocated agrarian reform and threatened, beat, and sometimes killed *agraristas*. In many municipalities he refused to staff local labor boards (Juntas Municipales de Conciliación), which made it difficult for peasants to register their complaints.[5]

And there was much to complain about. Labor relations retained their Porfirian character as Tzotzil and Tzeltal Maya laborers were contracted in the state's central highlands and Tojolabal, Mam, and mestizo workers along the Guatemalan border. The planters' agents often used alcohol and various forms of coercion to come up with the necessary workforce. This notoriously abusive labor system, known as *enganche* (literally, "hooking"), thrived under the Grajales administration, even though state and federal law prohibited it. The infamous *tienda de raya* (company store) was also prohibited on paper, but one could be found on every major plantation in Chiapas. Workers were often paid in company scrip redeemable only at the overpriced tienda de raya. Even when workers were paid in cash, violations of the minimum wage had become institutionalized. Needless to say, extreme levels of violence were used to keep the state's campesinos, workers, and political opposition under control.[6]

A loyal Callista, Grajales diligently implemented the anticlerical agenda of the *jefe máximo*. Perhaps he felt obliged to Calles and his fledging political party, the National Revolutionary Party (PNR, or Partido Nacional Revolucionario). Perhaps he was personally inspired by Tomás Garrido Canabal, a fellow Callista who governed neighboring Tabasco directly or indirectly from 1922 to 1935. For Garrido, known as the "caudillo of the southeast" because his influence and his ambitions transcended Tabasco's boundaries, anticlericalism was a means of amassing personal power and forging a modern, docile citizenry. Grajales may have had similar aims. In the words of a presidential adviser, he "subordinated his social agenda to Garrido Canabal, burning saints in public plazas and creating a guard of red-shirts; he decreed democracy among the dead; and he raised seeds, pigs and goats to the status of icons."[7] Shortly after taking office, Grajales and the state government limited the number of practicing religious ministers in the state to four. In 1934, the Grajales administration ruled that all religious place-names in the state be eliminated: San Cristóbal de Las Casas became Ciudad Las Casas, San Bartolomé de los Llanos became Venustiano Carranza, San Pedro Chenalhó became Chenalhó, and so on.[8] That fall, PNR activists and state and federal teachers organized saint-burnings in the plazas of the state's principal towns. Grajales also expelled Bishop Gerardo Anaya and all the priests from the state except one who renounced Catholicism in a public ceremony in December of that year. While such demagoguery won Grajales the praise of the Callista congress and the official press corps in Mexico City, this highly unpopular campaign made him vulnerable to public opinion locally.[9]

In time, Grajales's close identification with Calles became a liability. After President Cárdenas asserted his independence from the jefe máximo in June 1935, he purged his cabinet of Callistas and forced fourteen Callista governors out of power by nullifying elections, granting mandatory leaves, or closing state legislatures. In seven other states Cárdenas used regularly scheduled elections to purge Callistas. He was willing to allow Governor Grajales to serve out his term, due to expire on November 30, 1936, even though the governor's policies and priorities were antithetical to his own. Grajales lasted so long in part because President Cárdenas could find few suitable replacements. His ideal candidate would be a Chiapanecan with no ties to the Mapaches and Callistas who ran the state in the 1920s and early 1930s. This candidate would be strong enough to face down Grajalistas, but pliant enough to accept direction from Mexico City. Cárdenas's advisors made it clear that few men, if any, fit the bill.[10]

Cárdenas eventually settled on the young agronomist Efraín Gutiérrez. During the revolution, Gutiérrez had interrupted his studies at the National Agricultural College to fight with Emiliano Zapata in Morelos. He later worked for the state government of Michoacán from 1928 to 1932, when Cárdenas was governor. During the first two years of the Cárdenas presidency Gutiérrez directed the National Bank of Agrarian Credit and served as general secretary of the Agrarian Department, for which he received mixed reviews. He used these posts to make contacts with high functionaries and employees in the immigration, agricultural, forestry, finance, and education ministries.[11]

For Cárdenas, Gutiérrez was the best choice among many undesirable options. He would be loyal, and his links to several federal ministries appealed to the Cardenista project of strengthening the hand of federal government in renegade states. Though born in Chiapas, Gutiérrez had been absent from the state for twenty-four years when he returned to initiate his campaign. His time away from Chiapas meant that he was indebted to none of the major factions that had controlled the state since 1920. It also meant that Gutiérrez had few allies in Chiapas. He would need the full support of the president to defeat the handpicked successor(s) of outgoing governor Grajales.

THE CARDENISTA IMPOSITION

The imposition of Gutiérrez first involved an extremely controversial purge of the state branch of the PNR. Once that was accomplished, Gutiérrez had to win the PNR party plebiscite. Grajales did whatever he could to impose his own candidate, Samuel León Brindis, claiming with justification that Gutiérrez was an imposed outsider, the candidate of the meddlesome federation. Gutiérrez, for his part, promised to bring Cardenismo to Chiapas and hinted that he would nullify Grajales's anticlerical decrees. Although Gutiérrez was declared the winner of the April 5 party plebiscite, the political situation in the state remained tense because none of the other candidates recognized his victory. Nevertheless, the imposition moved forward as planned; on July 12 federal employees of the agrarian reform, education, forestry, and agriculture ministries helped Gutiérrez prevail in the general election over Grajales's new candidate. One night after his victory, Gutiérrez survived an assassination attempt by two dozen gunmen. Grajales then swore that he would never turn his office over to Gutiérrez. On September 22, 1936, Cárdenas acted on the threat and asked the national Senate to depose Grajales. Two days later the federal army closed down and occupied state government offices in Tuxtla. Amador Coutiño was named interim governor until Gutiérrez took office on December 15, 1936.[12]

Gutiérrez, in his first address to the state legislature, recognized that the year's election cycle had been "one of the most contentious in the history of Chiapas" and called on all citizens to set aside the "passions and rancor born in the heat of the battle."[13] Gutiérrez then took the opportunity to announce his agenda as governor. He promised to more than triple the budget of the state's agrarian commission. He would hire an additional thirty agronomists and resolve claims pending from prior administrations. Gutiérrez also promised to unify worker and peasant associations in the state, in keeping with the wishes of President Cárdenas. He closed his address by declaring that he "detested political camarillas" and would not allow any of his collaborators to use their position in his government for personal gain.[14]

THE STRUGGLE FOR THE HIGHLANDS

The Cardenista agenda quickly confronted trouble in Chiapas. Though Gutiérrez was technically the governor of the entire state, he struggled to impose his will on the state's central, eastern, and northern municipalities. In part, the challenge to his authority was endemic to Chiapas and its miserable transportation and communication infrastructure. The northern municipalities were so poorly connected to Tuxtla Gutiérrez, the state capital, that the federal government in the 1930s considered placing them under the jurisdiction of the neighboring state of Tabasco. The main eastern municipalities were not linked to the state capital by a paved highway until the 1970s. In the central highlands, the challenge was of a political nature.

Ciudad Las Casas was the de facto political and economic capital of the central highlands. It exercised direct and indirect control over the nearby indigenous municipalities of Chamula, Zinacantán, Larráinzar, Zapotal, Huistán, and Tenejapa and had routinely blocked the reforms and social campaigns emanating from Mexico City. Nothing threatened Las Casas like Cardenista *indigenismo* (state policies designed for indigenous peoples by non-Indians). In order to neutralize the Cardenista offensive, the town's leaders turned to Alberto Pineda, the general who twenty years earlier had led the defense of the highlands against a different type of federal intrusion—the top-down Carrancista "revolution" of 1914–1920. Pineda took advantage of the fragility of the Cardenista transition just days after Grajales was thrown out of office. Aware that the state PNR would try to impose its own candidate in Las Casas's upcoming municipal elections, on September 30 Pineda, the local police, and armed supporters broke into the local offices of the PNR, disarmed general secretary Wistano Molina, and threw him in jail while Pineda registered himself as a candidate. Interim governor Coutiño was unable to prevent Pineda's election on November 15. Because Las Casas controlled directly or indirectly all of the neighboring municipalities in its district and named the municipal presidents, secretaries, and agents, Pineda was perfectly situated to obstruct Cardenismo in the highlands.[15]

Shortly after taking office, Pineda decided to use the religious issue to challenge Gutiérrez's authority. On January 24, 1937, he allowed exiled bishop Gerardo Anaya to make a triumphant return to Ciudad Las Casas. Five days later the state government—not yet prepared to reverse existing anticlerical legislation—sent the bishop back into exile.[16] Over the next few months, tensions simmered between Governor Gutiérrez and the renegade municipal president. Pineda continued the age-old practice of using unremunerated indigenous labor for public works projects in Las Casas and blocked agrarian reform in the municipality. He refused to cooperate with the federal anti-alcohol campaign. Federal teachers (especially women) were harassed in the surrounding indigenous communities.[17] When state and federal indigenistas planned a May Day parade through Ciudad Las Casas, Pineda and his supporters broke it up with insults and violence. Some even rumored that Pineda was stashing arms in preparation for a major armed rebellion in the name of religious freedom.[18]

On July 9, 1937, Pineda undertook his most audacious move yet. With the support of the town's economic and social elite and its underground Catholic hierarchy, Pineda ordered his supporters—including members of the town council and the municipal police—to storm fifteen of the town's churches that had been closed three years earlier by Grajales. He handed over keys to eight of the churches and urged his mob to bust down the doors of the other seven. Several federal soldiers guarding the churches were wounded in the attacks.[19]

Governor Gutiérrez responded quickly to the provocation. Citing Pineda's "anti-revolutionary activities," "financial irregularities," and violations of the state's Religion Law (Ley de Culto) and Articles 5 and 130 of the federal Constitution, Governor Gutiérrez asked the state Congress to withdraw official recognition of the entire town government of Ciudad Las Casas.[20] On July 20, 1937, the federal garrison forced Pineda out of office. One day later the state government named Cardenista legislator Isidro Rabasa to head a new town government.

CARDENISTA INDIGENISMO IN CHIAPAS

Finally, Cardenistas controlled the highlands. The next several months passed in a blur of indigenista activity. Gutiérrez's director of the Department of Indigenous Social Action, Culture, and Protection (Departamento de Acción Social, Cultura y Protección Indígena) was Erasto Urbina, a former immigration official who used his fluency in Tzeltal and Tzotzil to coordinate the vote of highland indigenous communities during the contentious, violent elections of 1936. Urbina's "election committee" members became municipal secretaries in the most important indigenous municipalities, replacing mestizos. Urbina also replaced traditional, monolingual *escribanos* (scribes) with bilingual, literate young native men willing to do his bidding. He then created the Indigenous Workers' Union (Sindicato de Trabajadores Indígenas, or STI), which soon claimed nearly 25,000 members. The STI took over the Free Placement Agencies (Agencias Gratuítas de Colocaciones) that had been previously managed by the Department. All debt labor contracting was to take place in one of the STI's offices rather than at fiestas, liquor establishments, or jails. Thanks largely to Urbina's STI, working and living conditions for highland indigenous migrants improved considerably.

When Governor Gutiérrez addressed the state legislature after his first year in office, he could point to several successes. Apart from implementing an indigenista agenda in the highlands, two large labor confederations had been created in the state. The confederation of workers consisted of 288 unions of banana workers, coffee pickers, masons, shoe-shiners, and others. Under Gutiérrez's direction, the state's labor board generally ruled in favor of striking workers and helped broker collective bargaining agreements on all of the coffee plantations in the regions of Soconusco and Mariscal. The minimum wage for work on banana plantations rose considerably, and the daily workload on coffee plantations was reduced slightly. Gutiérrez also boasted that he had respected municipal autonomy—only in Las Casas had he been forced to intervene and change local government.[21]

The Gutiérrez administration also reformed the state's laws in several important ways, including adopting a law that called for the creation of a tribunal for minors and the handicapped. Falling under the rubric of "handicapped" were Indians who, in determined cases, were considered incapable of committing a crime due to their "primitive nature" and their "ignorance."[22] This reform was first studied by Gutiérrez's advisors in fall 1936 and underscored the often paternalistic dimension of Cardenista indigenismo. Its proponents argued that Indians should not be judged by the same standards as individuals of "average culture." According to Amador Coutiño, who served as interim governor in fall 1936, Indians had been misled as much by their pre-conquest "fanaticism" as by the "false doctrines of religious catechists" after the conquest. As a result, Indians possessed "a rudimentary mind and a complete and utter mental backwardness [*atraso mental*] that prevents them from understanding the illegality of the infractions that they commit." For this reason, "acts that seem monstrous to a moderately civilized man seem absolutely normal to them." Interim Governor Coutiño justified the creation of a separate court for Indians by arguing that modern penology included laws for *incapacitados*.[23] Although the Gutiérrez administration adopted this reform, it appears that it was never put into actual practice. Not only did it recall the colonial period, when the Spanish crown "protected" Indians by granting them their own court system, it also treated Indians as a separate category. This violated the sprit of Cardenista indigenismo, which sought above all to incorporate Mexico's many indigenous ethnic groups into a unified rural proletariat.

PINEDA'S "WATERLOO" AND
GUTIÉRREZ'S DEFEAT IN THE HIGHLANDS

In March 1938, Governor Gutiérrez was shocked to learn that his nemesis, Alberto Pineda, would return as municipal president of Las Casas. Mexico's Supreme Court had ruled that the Gutiérrez administration violated Article 115 of the Constitution, which guarantees the "free municipality," when it withdrew official recognition of Pineda's municipal government. This was a huge setback for Governor Gutiérrez, who expected (and indeed, needed) more support from federal authorities. Neither he nor the interim municipal president in Las Casas, Isidro Rabasa, was initially prepared to hand over power to Pineda, who returned to Las Casas by plane on April 22. Rabasa and his supporters prepared to defend themselves by force. That night, as Pineda and his supporters attempted to seize the municipal palace, a shootout ensued in which three municipal policemen were wounded.[24]

Rabasa and his supporters held on to the municipality for another two and a half weeks, if barely. May Day 1938 provided Cardenistas with one last opportunity to rally support in the highlands. With Governor Gutiérrez in attendance, Urbina led a parade of more than 15,000 predominantly indigenous peasants through the streets of Las Casas. According to partial eyewitnesses, the paraders "deliriously" manifested their support for Rabasa and shouted constant "vivas" in the name of Governor Gutiérrez.[25] In Las Casas's central plaza, local educators installed blackboards and organized an academic competition for local indigenous students. In the words of Governor Gutiérrez, "the humble Chamulan child, converted into a disciple of the Revolution's new school, demonstrated that the government's efforts to redeem him from his state of backwardness have not been useless." Alongside this "moving spectacle," the children's parents "paid tribute to the fatherland by donating their savings . . . to help pay the national debt" which was contracted when President Cárdenas expropriated the U.S.- and British-held oilfields in March of that year.[26]

This indigenista display did little to sway the state's courts, which ruled that the Supreme Court's decision be respected. On May 8, Gutiérrez relented and sent agents to negotiate Pineda's return. Later that day Pineda once again took office and called an extraordinary session of his reconstituted municipal government. He crowed about his victory and invoked the long-standing grievances that residents of Las Casas held against outsiders, especially lowland governors like Gutiérrez.[27]

Immediately after the celebration came the counterrevolution. Days after Governor Gutiérrez withdrew the state police force from Las Casas, Cárdenas began receiving telegrams from peasant organizations claiming Pineda's allies were attacking them. Pineda spent the rest of May reversing previous indigenista legislation, tying up pending agrarian reform requests, and purging Urbina's muchachos from their positions of local authority.[28] In early June Pineda decided to take action against Urbina himself, who not only directed the Department of Indigenous Social Action, Culture, and Protection, but had also become head of the municipal PNR and was running for a seat in the state legislature. On the night of June 11, as Urbina rode his horse across the central plaza in Las Casas, he was shot and wounded. Hired guns from Tabasco may have been involved; Urbina attributed the attack to *enganchadores*, alcohol merchants, and Catholic "fanatics."[29]

The attack on Urbina sealed Pineda's fate, but apparently the matter was not the governor's to resolve. Four days later, the national senate asked Pineda to come to Mexico City and granted the state government the right to name a local government as it saw fit. Las Casas was placed under martial law by federal forces under Urbina's command.[30] Three men would serve as municipal president of Ciudad Las Casas before the end of the year, none as bold as Rabasa. Arguably, Gutiérrez won the battle with Pineda but lost the war in the highlands. His opponents had managed to blunt the Cardenista offensive. Furthermore, at the national level, the Cárdenas administration assumed a more moderate course and may have lost the will to fight losing battles in places like highland Chiapas. By 1939, the governor's enemies sensed his weakness and began attacking Cardenista municipal governments throughout the state.

MEASURED SUCCESS IN SOCONUSCO

Even in the best of times, Governor Gutiérrez's grip on the highlands was tenuous. He was much more popular along the Pacific Coast and especially in Soconusco, a fertile zone of export agriculture just north of the Guatemalan border. Large banana and especially foreign-owned coffee plantations dominated the landscape. During his election campaign and his clash with Pineda, Gutiérrez received much-needed support from banana and coffee workers and federal teachers in Soconusco. In December 1938, all of the labor unions unified earlier by Gutiérrez joined the Confederation of Mexican Workers (Confederación de Trabajadores de México, or CTM). The CTM was one of the four pillars of the newly reconstituted (and renamed) official government party, the Party of the Mexican Revolution (Partido de la Revolución Mexicana, or PRM). Gutiérrez further increased the budget of the state's agrarian commission, hired additional agronomists and engineers, and prepared the terrain for the dramatic land expropriation of March 1939.

The *reparto agrario* in Chiapas coincided with shifting foreign and domestic winds that made planters of ethnic German descent suddenly vulnerable. In the mid-1930s, broad sectors of the Mexican population sympathized with European fascism, including many planters and merchants with German, Italian, and Spanish ties in Chiapas. Tapachula's Club Alemán (German Club), which featured a Nazi flag and an enormous portrait of Hitler, threw boisterous parties every April 20 to commemorate the Führer's birthday. These parties were celebrated openly and received local press coverage.[31] President Cárdenas, however, despised fascism and committed Mexico to the defense of the Spanish Republic during the Spanish Civil War (1936–1939). In March 1937, Mexico became the only Western country to sell arms to the Spanish Republic in its attempt to suppress the military revolt of Catholic nationalist Francisco Franco and his allies: the Spanish Falange, Benito Mussolini, and Adolf Hitler.[32]

As the Cárdenas administration and its allies in labor, education, and the political left attempted to forge a "popular front" against fascism, local conditions conspired against ethnic Germans. In Chiapas, the deplorable state of the coffee industry in the late 1930s forced many Mexican planters to sink into debt with German creditors. In May 1938, Mexico City's colony of

Chiapanecos warned that Soconusco was "controlled by German and Spanish latifundistas and capitalists, by Nazis and the Spanish Falange, who either own the land directly or loan money at usurious rates."[33] Nationalism, envy, and charges of unfair and exclusionary business practices had many Chiapaneco politicians calling for the internment of Germans even before Mexico entered World War II.[34]

Land reform finally came to Soconusco in March 1939. Governor Gutiérrez chose the region's most important planter of German descent as his principal target: Enrique Braun. Cardenistas correctly identified Braun with the state's Callista faction and with the murders of several strikers and union leaders on his plantations. Nearly half of the 7,988 hectares expropriated in March came from Braun's property and was used to create six *ejidos*.[35] What made this expropriation exceptional was not the quantity of land, which was quite modest, but the fact that Braun's plantations were among the most productive in Mexico.

When Governor Gutiérrez reported to the state legislature in November 1939, he claimed that seventeen months of intense labor had paid off. "With the efficient collaboration of the Federal Agrarian Delegation and the enthusiastic work of the engineers of the state office of Agrarian Affairs, we revindicated the peasants of Soconusco with lands that had always been considered untouchable." Gutiérrez made it clear that he deserved credit for the reparto, claiming that President Cárdenas had given him "the exclusive responsibility for resolving the agrarian problem in Soconusco."[36] Later in 1940, Gutiérrez and President Cárdenas seized the moment and expropriated land from most remaining large coffee plantations in Soconusco and Mariscal.

Unfortunately, the victory of Soconusco's *ejidatarios* was short-lived. Most of the processing plants remained in the hands of wealthy families, and Cardenista institutions like *ejidal* banks, marketing agencies, and cooperative societies were soon transformed from tools of emancipation into mechanisms of control. By 1942 Soconusco's ejidatarios were literally at war with officials of the Ejidal Bank in Tapachula. They complained that they were still alienated from the fruits of their labors; those who formerly controlled production had been replaced by a new owner, "which calls itself the bank."[37] Anyone who questioned the bank's appropriation of ejido funds was "accused of being a reactionary and an agitator, etc.; his loan was suspended, they took away his work and chased him from the ejido."[38] Workers in Cacahoatán complained that they were still "slaves of capital" and not "free citizens," because the true beneficiaries of the Ejidal Bank were people "favored by the bank, who benefit from the sweat and sacrifice of others."[39] Although it would be unfair to blame Governor Gutiérrez for the way that ejido institutions were manipulated after his term of office had expired, it is important to realize that the reparto in Soconusco ultimately implied new forms of controlling restless coffee workers.

Other accomplishments of Gutiérrez's tenure were also double-edged. In the highlands, Erasto Urbina's highly touted STI became a paper tiger within months of its formation, and its Free Placement Agencies merely replicated the function once performed by the despised enganchadores (and often employed them). It prevented genuine indigenous participation in its collective bargaining agreements with planters and never once called a strike. Cardenista agrarian reform in the highlands was also problematic. Urbina and his mounted agents controlled the pace and nature of the reform by keeping radical federal agraristas out of the highlands. When he and his men hurriedly (and often violently) created dozens of ejidos in the highlands in 1939 and 1940, conflicts typically ensued within and between communities over competing claims.[40] Ultimately, Cardenista indigenismo in Chiapas spawned a new form of *caciquismo* (bossism), for Urbina's bilingual indigenous scribes would come to dominate highland communities politically and economically in the ensuing decades.[41] In the end, indigenismo in Chiapas was more about political and economic control than social emancipation.

CONCLUSION

The ambivalent outcome of Cardenismo in Chiapas explains in part why some journalists and historians have overlooked the achievements of Governor Gutiérrez. Others, like Chiapanecan journalist and chronicler José Casahonda Castillo, credit the land reform of 1939 and 1940 to President Cárdenas and the social ferment in Chiapas during this period to the Marxist head of the CTM, Vicente Lombardo Toledo. Casahonda describes Gutiérrez as a good, loyal worker, "a career bureaucrat who did not know how to lead. He left matters in the hands of others."[42] Did he ever—Gutiérrez was the consummate absentee governor. In 1937, shortly after besting outgoing governor Grajales in a bruising election in which many lives were lost, Gutiérrez was absent from the state 136 days, appointing his close collaborators (including his brother) as interim governors. In 1938, when Alberto Pineda was still challenging his control over the highlands, Gutiérrez missed 137 days. In 1939, the year of maximum agrarista activity in Chiapas, he was out of the state 129 days. During the eleven remaining months of his term in 1940, he was absent an incredible 178 days.[43] Some historians speculate that Gutiérrez may have had health problems that could only be treated in Mexico City. But Gutiérrez was only forty years old when he took office, and the consistency of his absences over his four-year term points to other reasons.

Gutiérrez may have become disheartened by the degree of resistance posed by Pineda and others in the state. But surely he knew what he was getting into when he and the Cardenista coalition took on Victórico Grajales. It does appear that, over time, many of his staunch allies in the state abandoned him. In October 1938 Gutiérrez wrote to President Cárdenas defending himself from attacks made by his close associates, including state representatives Salvador Coutiño, Amet Cristiani, and—most surprising of all—Isidro Rabasa, whom Gutiérrez had just named to head Chiapas's branch of the newly reconstituted official party, the PRM. According to Gutiérrez—who "detested" *camarillas*—these men were angry because he had blocked their nepotism and their quest for favors, monopoly rights, and tax concessions. Perhaps his former partners expected paybacks after two years of loyal struggle.[44] As Casahonda writes, many joined Gutiérrez's gubernatorial campaign in 1936 because he represented hope, renovation, and a new style of government. When he failed to meet expectations, these allies abandoned him.

There may be one other compelling reason why Governor Gutiérrez took so many extended absences from his home state. According to members of his extended family, his urbane, sophisticated wife was never happy about living in Tuxtla. Her dislike of the state capital hardened early in his term after a shoe-shopping excursion downtown. When she got home she opened one of the shoeboxes and found a scorpion hiding alongside her recent purchase. With that, Mrs. Gutiérrez made it known that she would henceforth reside in Mexico City. Although the governor himself was comfortable in Chiapas, he was alone when he was in Tuxtla, without his wife and, by late 1938, without allies.[45]

It is therefore easy to overlook the accomplishments of governor Efraín Gutiérrez, even though no other governor in the history of twentieth-century Chiapas expropriated more high-quality land, and none did more to improve working conditions in the state. Gutiérrez also brought an end to the state's anticlerical conflict; by late 1937, his administration was allowing parishioners to reopen their churches, and priests and eventually the bishop returned from exile or emerged from hiding.[46] José Casahonda, who claims that Gutiérrez was a poor leader, still admits that "during his regime the peasant and the worker gained a great deal. It was quite simply the Revolution."[47] Perhaps Casahonda does not contradict himself with this statement. After all, the "institutional revolution" that Calles announced in 1929 was designed to be precisely that—a revolution of institutions. Gutiérrez introduced and strengthened federal labor and agrarian institutions in the state, then implemented as best he could the reforms enshrined in the Constitution of 1917. He may not have been particularly flashy or memorable, but an "institutional revolution" calls for loyal bureaucrats willing to implement official policy, not charismatic, pistol-toting caudillos with agendas of their own. In this regard, Governor Gutiérrez might be considered a prototype of post-1940 Mexican politicians, who

152 *Stephen E. Lewis*

tended to be relatively colorless managers and overseers. In an era when regional strongmen elsewhere still challenged the authority of the central government, governor Efraín Gutiérrez, the revolutionary bureaucrat, may simply have been ahead of his time.

NOTES

1. *Diccionario histórico y biográfico de la Revolución Mexicana,* vol. 2, Chiapas, Chihuahua, Distrito Federal, Durango (Mexico, D.F.: Instituto Nacional de Estudios Históricos de la Revolución Mexicana, 1991); *Diccionario Porrúa de historia, biografía y geografía de México,* 6th ed. (Mexico: Editorial Porrúa, S.A., 1995 [1964]).

2. The most recent historian to make this claim is Jan De Vos, "El indígena chiapaneco idealizado: Tres aplicaciones al procedimiento lascasiano," *Mesoamérica* 46 (Jan. 2004): 218.

3. Thomas Benjamin, *A Rich Land, a Poor People* (Albuquerque: University of New Mexico Press, 1996 [1989]), 95–143; Jan Rus, "Revoluciones contenidas: Los indígenas y la lucha por los Altos de Chiapas, 1910–1925," *Mesoamérica* 46 (Jan. 2004): 57–85.

4. Benjamin, *Rich Land,* 149–86.

5. Archivo General de la Nación (hereafter AGN), Cárdenas, Atropellos autoridades civiles, 542.1/20, from Liga Central de Comunidades Agrarias del Estado de Chiapas adherida a la Confederación Campesina Mexicana, México, D.F., Dec. 11, 1934.

6. AGN, Cárdenas, Atropellos autoridades civiles, various documents, including "Memorandum: Resumen de los cargos que organizaciones campesinas, elementos obreros y políticos hacen al gobernador del estado de Chiapas, Coronel Victórico Grajales," México, D.F., Dec. 13, 1934.

7. AGN, Cárdenas, Elecciones Chiapas, 544.2/6, from M. E. Guzmán to Secretario Particular Luis I. Rodríguez, México, D.F., Aug. 28, 1935, 8.

8. *Periódico Oficial del Gobierno del Estado de Chiapas,* Tuxtla Gutiérrez, Decreto número 132, 2–3.

9. See Stephen E. Lewis, *The Ambivalent Revolution: Forging State and Nation in Chiapas, 1910–1945* (Albuquerque: University of New Mexico Press, 2005), 71–80; Julio Ríos Figueroa, *Siglo XX: Muerte y resurrección de la Iglesia Católica en Chiapas* (Mexico: PROIMMSE/UNAM, 2002), 75–104.

10. AGN, Cárdenas, Elecciones gobernador, Chiapas, 544.2/6, from M. E. Guzmán to Secretario Particular Luis I. Rodríguez, Mexico, D.F., Aug. 28, 1935, 1–8; Luis Javier Garrido, *El partido de la revolución institucionalizada* (Mexico: Siglo XXI Editores, 1991 [1982]), 186–200.

11. AGN, Cárdenas, Efraín Gutiérrez, 565.1/60, from J. O. Gutiérrez to Pres. de la República, Mexico, D.F., Nov. 2, 1935; Cárdenas, Elecciones gobernador, Chiapas, 544.2/6, leg. 7; Benjamin, *Rich Land,* 193.

12. AGN, Cárdenas, Elecciones gobernador, Chiapas, 544.2/6, from Dip. Mario E. Balboa to Pres. de la República, Mexico City, June 2, 1936; Benjamin, *Rich Land,* 193–94.

13. *Mensaje dirigido al pueblo chiapaneco, por el C. Ing. Efraín A. Gutiérrez, al otorgar la protesta de ley, como gobernador constitucional, ante el H. Congreso del Estado, el día 15 de diciembre de 1936* (Tuxtla Gutiérrez: TLE, 1936), 12.

14. *Mensaje dirigido al pueblo chiapaneco,* 5–7, 14.

15. AGN, Cárdenas, Elecciones Chiapas, Municipales, 544.5/496, from María M. de Molina to Presidente de la República, Las Casas, Sept. 30, 1936; Archivo Histórico del Municipio de San Cristóbal de Las Casas (hereafter AHMSCLC), 1936–1937, from Wistano Molina to Juez de Distrito, Tuxtla Gutiérrez, Las Casas, Oct. 1. 1936.

16. AGN, Cárdenas, Ley de Cultos, 547.4/496, telegram from Josefa Aguilar V. de Cortés to Cárdenas, Las Casas, Jan. 29, 1937; also see Cárdenas, Templos, 547.2/2, telegram from Estela Jiménez, Comisario de Ac. Social, Frente Único Revolucionario de Chiapas to Cárdenas, Las Casas, Jan. 29, 1937.

17. AHMSCLC, 1937/3, from Inspector Manuel Castellanos to Pres. Muni. Gral. Alberto Pineda O., Ciudad Las Casas, June 30, 1937; also 1937/6, from Pres. Muni. Sub. Dip. Isidro Rabasa and Secretario Fidel Molina B. to Oficial de Acuerdos de la Sria. Gral de Gobierno in Tuxtla José Palacios Ochoa, Las Casas, Sept. 3, 1937.

18. AGN, Cárdenas, Elecciones Chiapas, Municipales, 544.5/496, from Gobernador Gutiérrez to Cárdenas, Tuxtla, July 19, 1937.

19. AGN, Cárdenas, Elecciones Chiapas, Municipales, 544.5/496, telegram from General Comandante 31/a. Zona Militar to Presidente, Tuxtla Gutiérrez, July 9, 1937.

20. *Periódico Oficial,* July 20, 1937. For a full discussion of the clash over Ciudad Las Casas, see Stephen E. Lewis, " El choque del siglo: Los coletos y el cardenismo, 1936–1940," in *Chiapas: De la independencia a la revolución,* eds. Mercedes Olivera y María Dolores Palomo (Mexico: Centro de Investigaciones y Estudios Superiores en Antropología Social, Consejo de Ciencia y Tecnología del Estado de Chiapas, 2005), 73–95.

21. *Informe Rendido por el C. Gobernador Constitutional del Estado de Chiapas Ing. Efraín A. Gutiérrez, ante la XXXVI Legislatura Constitucional de esta entidad federativa, de las labores desarrolladas durante su ejercicio ejecutivo, comprendido entre el 15 de diciembre de mil novecientos treinta y seis y el treinta y uno de octubre de mil novecientos treinta y siete* (Tuxtla Gutiérrez: TLE, 1937), 10–11.

22. *Informe Rendido por el C. Gobernador Constitutional del Estado de Chiapas Ing. Efraín A. Gutiérrez,* 16.

23. *Informe que rinde el C. Lic. Amador Coutiño C., Gobernador Provisional del Estado, ante la H. XXXVI Legislatura Local, en la sesión de apertura de trabajos del primer año de su ejercicio legal* (Tuxtla: Imprenta del Gobierno del Estado, 1936), 10–11.

24. AHMSCLC, 1938/1, from Subteniente and Comandante de la Partida y de la Policía José A. Borges to Pres. Muni. Subs. Dip. Isidro Rabasa, Ciudad Las Casas, Apr. 22, 1938; 1938/2, minutes of extraordinary session of H. Ayuntamiento Constitucional de Ciudad de Las Casas, Ciudad de Las Casas, May 8, 1938, 1–3; AGN, Cárdenas, Elecciones Chiapas, Municipales, 544.5/496, various, including telegram from Comandante de la Zona Antonio Ríos Zertuche to Presidente, Las Casas, Apr. 24, 1938.

25. AGN, Cárdenas, Conflictos obreros, 432.2/253-2-4, from Lic. Roberto Villa, Venancio Corzo and Joaquín Salgado, Ciudad Las Casas, May 1, 1938; also see AGN, Cárdenas, Elecciones Chiapas, Municipales, 544.5/496, telegram from Srio.

Generales of Confed. Obrera Chiapas and others to Cárdenas, Tuxtla Gutiérrez, May 5, 1938.

26. *Informe rendido por el C. Gobernador Constitucional del Estado de Chiapas Ing. Efraín A. Gutiérrez, ante la H. XXXVII Legislatura Constitucional de esta entidad federativa, de las labores desarrolladas durante su ejercicio ejecutivo, comprendido entre el primero de noviembre de mil novecientos treinta y siete al treinta y uno de octubre de mil novecientos treinta y ocho* (Tuxtla Gutiérrez: TLE, 1938), 18.

27. AHMSCLC, 1938/2, minutes of extraordinary session of H. Ayuntamiento, Constitucional de Ciudad de Las Casas, Ciudad de Las Casas, May 8, 1938, 4.

28. AHMSCLC, 1938/1, from Sub. Tte. Policía del Estado, Comandante de la Partida José A. Borger to Pres. Muni. Alberto Pineda, Ciudad de Las Casas, May 9, 1938; AGN, Cárdenas, Elecciones Chiapas, Municipales, 544.5/496, various; and Universidad de Ciencias y Artes de Chiapas, Departamento de Acervos Especiales y Archivo Histórico (hereafter UNICACH/DAEAH), 1938, from Srio. Gen. Lucas López and Srio. de Organización of the Liga de Comunidades Agrarias del Estado de Chiapas Nicolás Espinosa to Pres. del Comité del Estado del P. R. M., Tuxtla, Las Casas, May 20, 1938.

29. AGN, Cárdenas, Elecciones Chiapas, Municipales, 544.5/496, from Erasto Urbina to Cárdenas, Las Casas, June 12, 1938; Antonio García de León, *Resistencia y utopía: Memorial de agravios y crónica de revueltas y profecías acaecidas en la provincia de Chiapas durante los últimos quinientos años de su historia*, 2 vols. (Mexico: Ediciones Era, 1985) 2:209–10.

30. AGN, Cárdenas, Elecciones Chiapas, Municipales, 544.5/496, various from Sen. Dr. Gustavo Marín to Cárdenas.

31. Gustavo Montiel, *Recordando el Soconusco y su perla* (Mexico: B. Costa-Amic, 1979), 110; "Aniversario del Natalicio del Fuehrer Hitler," *El Sur de México*, Tapachula, Apr. 21, 1938, 1.

32. Friedrich E. Schuler, *Mexico between Hitler and Roosevelt: Mexican Foreign Relations in the Age of Lázaro Cárdenas* (Albuquerque: University of New Mexico Press, 1998), 55–59.

33. *Colonia Chiapaneca*, Revista Anual de sus Actividades, México, D.F., May 1938, 21.

34. "Alemanes y Japoneses en Chiapas serán concentrados a Perote, Ver.," *El Sur de México*, Tapachula, May 11, 1942, 1.

35. "Cómo fue hecha la repartición de tierras en el Soconusco" in *Chiapas Nuevo*, Tuxtla, Mar. 23, 1939, 4.

36. *Informe rendido por el C. Gobernador Constitucional del Estado de Chiapas Ing. Efraín A. Gutiérrez, ante la H. XXXVII Legislatura Constitucional de esta Entidad Federativa, de las labores desarrolladas durante su ejercicio ejecutivo, comprendido entre el 1 de noviembre de mil novecientos treinta y ocho y el treinta y uno de octubre de mil novecientos treinta y nueve* (Tuxtla: TLE, 1939), 8–9.

37. AGN, Avila Camacho, Ejidos, Exp. 703.4/238, from Liga Central de Comunidades Agrarias de la República, México, D.F., to Presidente, México, D.F., Apr. 8, 1942.

38. AGN, Avila Camacho, Ejidos, Exp. 703.4/238, from Comité de Defensa de los Intereses de los Trabajadores Cafeteros del Soconusco and Comité Central Ejecutivo

del Sindicato de Trabajadores de la Industria del Café del Soconusco to Presidente, Tapachula, July 5, 1942.

39. AGN, Avila Camacho, Ejidos, Exp. 703.4/238, from Rosendo Morales and others to Presidente, Cacahoatán, July 15, 1942.

40. Benjamin, *Rich Land*, 229; George Collier, "Peasant Politics and the Mexican State: Indigenous Compliance in Highland Chiapas," *Mexican Studies/Estudios Mexicanos* 3, no. 1 (Winter 1987): 82; María Eugenia Reyes Ramos, *El reparto de tierras y la política agraria en Chiapas, 1914–1988* (Mexico: UNAM, 1992), 62; and Jan Rus, "The 'Comunidad Revolucionaria Institucional': The Subversion of Native Government in Highland Chiapas, 1936–1968," in *Everyday Forms of State Formation: Revolution and the Negotiation of Rule in Modern Mexico*, eds. Gilbert M. Joseph and Daniel Nugent (Durham: Duke University Press, 1994), 259–60.

41. Rus, "The 'Comunidad Revolucionaria Institucional,'" 275–77.

42. José Casahonda Castillo, *Cincuenta años de revolución en Chiapas* (Tuxtla Gutiérrez: Instituto de Ciencias y Artes de Chiapas, 1963), 75.

43. Casahonda, *Cincuenta años de revolución en Chiapas*, 164–66.

44. AGN, Cárdenas, Atropellos autoridades civiles, Chiapas, 542.1/20, from Gutiérrez to Cárdenas, Tuxtla, Oct. 12, 1938.

45. Personal communication with Chiapas historian (and distant relative of Don Efraín) Sergio Nicolás Gutiérrez, Aug. 31, 2004.

46. AHMSCLC, 1937/6, from Pres. Muni. Subs. Dip. Isidro Rabasa to Jefe de la Oficina Federal de Hacienda, Ciudad Las Casas, Dec. 8, 1937; Ríos, Siglo XX, 106.

47. Casahonda, *Cincuenta años de Revolución en Chiapas*, 119.

10

Maximino Avila Camacho of Puebla

Timothy Henderson and David LaFrance

It is certainly true that many Mexican revolutionaries fought for the noblest of ends. Yet the protagonists in the literature spawned by that great social movement tend to be colorful, larger-than-life, utterly corrupt opportunists, and the tone of such works inclines toward cynicism and despair. Maximino Avila Camacho has the dubious distinction of being the actual model for one such fictional character—the brutal and corrupt General Andrés Ascencio in Angeles Mastretta's bestselling *Arráncame la vida*[1]—and he could be easily have been the prototype for many of the characters that populate the rich fiction of great Mexican authors like Mariano Azuela, Juan Rulfo, Rosario Castellanos, and Carlos Fuentes. It would require a fair degree of literary art to render plausible his near-superhuman greed, ruthlessness, lasciviousness, improbity, sycophancy, and hypocrisy, and to explain how these traits helped pave the way for such an impressive political ascent. Maximino Avila Camacho not only served as governor of the important state of Puebla, but he founded a political dynasty that would come to include the six subsequent state governors (including Maximino's brother, Rafael) as well as numerous state and union officials who dominated Puebla's political scene into the 1970s. Maximino's younger brother, Manuel, was president of Mexico from 1940 to 1946, and one of his protégés, Gustavo Díaz Ordaz, was president from 1964 to 1970. Maximino was often mentioned as a potential presidential candidate in his own right. Until recently, his named adorned one of Puebla City's principal streets, a clear indication of the esteem in which he was officially held.

He was born on August 23, 1891, in Teziutlán, Puebla, the son of Manuel Avila and Efrocina Camacho. The town of about 12,000 is located in what locals call the *tierra fría* (cold country) of Puebla's northern sierra region, nestled among high slopes eroded by frequent tropical rains and often misted by clouds. Maximino's father was a rancher and driver of mule-trains—typical trades for the region—and the family was far from affluent.

At the age of twelve, before finishing his primary studies, Maximino quit school to help support his family. He parlayed his clerical skills into jobs as an office worker on haciendas, a notary's assistant, and a sales agent for the Singer Sewing Machine Company.[2] With the outbreak of the revolution, as his family's fortunes declined, Maximino sought a clerical job with the federal government. In 1912, he wrote to president Francisco I. Madero boasting of his clerical skills and his willingness to take any job, "even a dangerous one."[3] The president replied, but he offered only to help the young man enter the military academy, the Colegio Militar. As fate would have it, the start of his studies coincided with a violent coup that overthrew the revolution's leader, Francisco I. Madero. Archconservative Generals Félix Díaz and Victoriano Huerta spearheaded these so-called Ten Tragic Days, and Huerta soon established a dictatorial regime renowned for its ruthlessness. A history of support for Huerta's coup was a major political liability in later days, so it was understandable that Maximino always vehemently denied allegations of his participation, claiming he had not yet entered the academy when the coup took place. One witness claimed that during 1914, Maximino fought on Huerta's behalf in northern sierra of Puebla, and that he later falsified papers to get himself accepted (with a rank higher than the one he had earned) by the victorious faction, the followers of the self-styled "First Chief of the Revolution," Venustiano Carranza.[4] Already, Maximino's career was beginning to display a pattern, namely that his rise in rank and responsibility was more often achieved through chicanery than through skill and courage. On several occasions, only strategic alliances with more powerful men and the fortuitous outbreak of antigovernment rebellions saved him.

Between 1914 and 1920, Maximino developed useful contacts with a number of high-ranking generals, among them Alvaro Obregón, supreme commander of the Carrancista forces. Obregón made a bid for the presidency of Mexico in 1920, and Maximino quit the army to work on his campaign. In 1920, when Obregón's political campaign gave way to a successful armed rebellion, Maximino alighted on the winning side.[5]

Late 1920 found Maximino serving on the staff of the secretary of war, General Benjamín G. Hill. When General Hill died suddenly, apparently from poisoning, Maximino's military career was imperiled. The Obregón government seized the occasion to reduce the army's budget and manpower, and the best Maximino could get were minor postings in the state of Michoacán and in the Ministry of the Interior (Gobernación) in Mexico City. During this time, however, he began to nurture another of the strategic alliances that would later pay big dividends for his political career, serving as a personal aide to General Lázaro Cárdenas, future president of Mexico.[6]

In late 1923, his career got a fresh boost from another antigovernment rebellion, this one fronted by former interim president and finance minister Adolfo de la Huerta. This time, Maximino remained loyal to the government. He and his brother Manuel were assigned to defend the city of Morelia, the capital of Michoacán. Although they lost the battle, the brothers fought bravely and were rewarded with promotions. Maximino was promoted to brigadier general, only two steps down from the army's highest rank. Perhaps more importantly, the Avila Camacho brothers' bravery impressed General Cárdenas, further developing perhaps the key alliance of their careers.[7]

Over the next several years, Maximino occupied a series of zone commands (*jefe de operaciones militares*). His first such posting was to the distant southern state of Chiapas, where he meddled in local politics and fell into the bad graces of local strongman Carlos Vidal.[8] In order to keep the peace, the government transferred him to the opposite geographical extreme, the northern border state of Coahuila. Maximino resented his reassignment, and in an unguarded moment, he wrote a private letter in which he spoke of overthrowing the government of then-president Plutarco Elías Calles and of assassinating the undersecretary of war, General Joaquín Amaro. As it turned out, the threatening letter ended up in Amaro's hands, resulting in Maximino's being ordered to the national capital, where he was placed in the category of *"disponible"*—a kind of military purgatory, without command and awaiting assignment. Maximino was at pains to patch things up with Amaro, sending him gifts including a valuable horse and pistol, and later naming Amaro godfather to his oldest son, Maximino, Jr.[9]

Maximino was rescued from this purgatory by yet another rebellion, this time the Cristero revolt, an uprising of Catholics against the anticlerical measures of the Calles government. In mid-1926, the Mexican government, desperate for experienced officers, sent Maximino to Guanajuato and then to southern Zacatecas, where he held sway over an area that included northern Jalisco, the heart of the rebels' territory. By most accounts, his conduct in this episode was a far cry from his supposed bravery in the defense of Morelia two years earlier. To be sure, few prominent figures in the revolution managed to avoid being tarred by political foes. Even so, the stories related about Maximino's behavior during the Cristero War stand out for the extremes of corruption and cruelty they depict. While only desultorily pursuing the rebels, so the stories go, Maximino enriched himself by selling government arms to the insurgents, creating a regional monopoly on the slaughter and distribution of meat from stolen cattle, confiscating property from anyone even rumored to be associated with the Cristero rebels, and killing anyone who questioned his actions, including an outraged father who accused Maximino of abducting and raping his daughter. On one occasion, he is said to have ransomed a pair of priests caught contravening the anti-church laws, pocketing some 5,000 pesos. And, as in Chiapas, Maximino ran afoul of local authorities who accused him of interfering in state affairs: Governor Francisco Bañuelos claimed that Maximino had arrested local officials and used his troops to protect haciendas from the government's agrarian reform program. One school of thought holds that the Cristero War was motivated more by the abuses of the federal army than by religious grievances.[10]

Maximino seems to have shared some of his ill-gotten booty with his soldiers, as well as with local *agraristas* (radical land reformers) and regional allies. He also apparently sent some of it to President Calles and his erstwhile antagonist, Joaquín Amaro. In the wake of the conflict, Calles remarked that he had had to turn back whole freight cars full of goods from the war zone, much of it sent to him by the brothers Avila Camacho (Manuel, too, was fighting in western Mexico). Maximino's efforts seem to have paid off: Amaro ordered a rather toothless investigation of the charges against Maximino and subsequently elevated him to the army's second-highest rank, brigade general, in September 1929.[11]

Mexico's revolutionary politics experienced several of their tensest and bloodiest moments as the 1920s drew to a close. The powerful General Alvaro Obregón campaigned for reelection to the presidency, giving rise to an abortive military rebellion in 1927. On July 17, 1928, Obregón was murdered while attending a banquet celebrating his reelection. Although the assassin was apparently motivated by religious extremism, rumors of conspiracy were rife. Amid this tense situation, President Calles declared his intention to end the era of strongmen (*caudillos*) and to replace the perpetual skirmishing of ambitious *políticos* with enduring institutions and laws. He began by creating a new, "official" political party, the National Revolutionary Party (PNR). No sooner had the PNR begun its work than another armed rebellion broke out (March 1929), while at the same time, José Vasconcelos—former education minister and one of Mexico's most distinguished intellectuals—launched a presidential campaign in opposition to the new government party. It soon became clear that the government had no intention of allowing opposition politics to prosper, and few were surprised when the government declared an overwhelming victory for its man, Pascual Ortiz Rubio. After the inauguration, harassment of Vasconcelos and his embittered supporters increased. Maximino Avila Camacho most likely played a role in the most notorious instance of political terror. Scores of Vasconcelistas were arrested and held at the Hacienda de Narvarte near Mexico City, which served as headquarters for the Fifty-first Cavalry Regiment under Maximino's command. After being interrogated, some sixty prisoners were loaded into trucks and transported at night to a hill near the

town of Topilejo, where they were forced to dig their own graves before being hanged and haphazardly buried. The secret slaughter was exposed a few
weeks later when a hungry dog unearthed decomposed body parts. The degree of Maximino's culpability in the massacre is not known, but his overall history suggests that he regarded terror and mass murder as perfectly acceptable political tools.[12]

By the early 1930s, Maximino's days of semi-poverty in the mountains of
Puebla were a fading memory. As recently as 1923 he had lacked the relatively paltry five hundred pesos needed to pay for his military uniforms and
was obliged to appeal to President Obregón for assistance. Over the ensuing years, on his modest general's salary he had managed to accumulate at
least two houses in Mexico City and one in Guadalajara, three ranches with
many cattle and horses, and several cars. It was around this time that he di-
vorced his first wife and married a young and attractive Italian woman, Margarita Richardi (Richardi was the inspiration for Angeles Mastretta's novel,
Arráncame la vida). He also managed to father many children—so many
that sources tend to be vague on the issue. "I don't remember how many
there were," wrote one visitor, "but if they didn't quite amount to a dozen,
they were pretty close." And although Maximino had only one legitimate
wife at a time, he cheerfully confessed that his children were "flowers from
different flowerpots."[13]

Not surprisingly, Maximino began to harbor political ambitions. In particular, he began to covet the governorship of his native state of Puebla, and
he thought his alliance with President Ortiz Rubio would make him a shoo-
in for the nomination. When Jefe Máximo Calles forced Ortiz Rubio to resign in 1932, Maximino's hopes dimmed, but only briefly.[14] In late 1934,
General Lázaro Cárdenas was elected president, and he chose Manuel Avila
Camacho as his sub-secretary of defense. He also named Maximino zone
commander of Puebla.

Disregarding complaints from those who viewed him as an interloper—
he had, after all, been absent from his native state for nearly two decades—
Maximino blatantly exploited his post as military zone commander of
Puebla to prepare the ground for his run for the governorship. Between
January and September 1935, he reconfigured and expanded the military
zone under his command so that it came to include the entire state. Previously, the northern sierra had pertained to a different district. He also ensured that loyal officers were named to subordinate positions; he appointed his minions to head up local paramilitary units; he struck deals
with workers and peasants; he curried favor with landed, commercial, and
business interests, including the entrepreneur William O. Jenkins, a native
of Shelbyville, Tennessee, who was well on his way to becoming the rich-
est man in Mexico; he cemented ties with local and state politicians; and
he maintained close connections with Cárdenas and brother Manuel in

Mexico City. It was fast becoming clear that Maximino had a formidable talent for hardball politics, Mexican style.[15]

The gubernatorial campaign began in earnest in late September 1935 when he resigned from the army. The vote was slated for November 1936.[16] Maximino's main rival for the PNR nomination—which was tantamount to election—was Gilberto Bosques, a former schoolteacher who had served as both a state and federal deputy. Bosques, a left-leaning populist, enjoyed much support from organized workers and peasants, as well as from the state's principal daily, *La Opinión*. Maximino campaigned energetically in the countryside, although his appeals were less populist than practical. He carefully cultivated the influential network of the official party, which was formidable at the municipal level where its local committees acted as virtual shadow governments. Maximino also had the support of the army, the state branch of the official party (his brother headed the PNR state committee), the outgoing governor, and the authorities in Mexico City. Moreover, his conservative rhetoric appealed to the urban middle and upper classes dismayed by Puebla's recent history of political and social instability and put off by the leftist rhetoric of Bosques, which seemed to promise only continued turmoil.[17]

The PNR primary election, which was held in April 1936, was marred by considerable fraud and violence, including an attempt on Bosques's life. The PNR debated the merits of the two candidates for more than a month before finally declaring Maximino the victor.[18] Bosques supporters, led by the Regional Federation of Workers and Peasants (FROC), the local affiliate of the Vicente Lombardo Toledano–led Mexican Workers Confederation (CTM), protested the outcome in Mexico City. Perhaps as many as thirty thousand workers traveled in bus and train caravans to the national capital to pressure Cárdenas to withdraw his support of Maximino and to back Bosques. The president, however, avoided the demonstrators and ignored their demands.[19]

Lázaro Cárdenas is generally regarded as the most progressive and populist president in Mexico's history, so his apparent endorsement of Maximino Avila Camacho is puzzling. Maximino represented nearly everything Cárdenas is supposed to have abhorred: cynicism, cruelty, corruption, conservatism, indifference toward the poor, and amorality. The most plausible explanation for this holds, quite simply, that Cárdenas was not as radical as he has traditionally been portrayed. He was, rather, cautious and pragmatic. He tolerated other conservative governors during his presidency, including Miguel Alemán in Veracruz and Román Yocupicio in Sonora. Regardless of his own ideological disposition, a bit of Machiavellian wheeling and dealing was essential for political survival. This was especially true during the 1934–1936 period, when Cárdenas needed to stave off the challenge to his national and party leadership from former president and Jefe Máximo

Calles. Eventually, with the backing of people like Maximino, Cárdenas was able to force Calles into exile in the United States. In short, Cárdenas was willing to soft-pedal some of his leftist proclivities in exchange for maintaining order and security in key regions, and so long as Maximino refrained from frontal confrontation, he was a useful asset. Indeed, some have charged that Cárdenas's efforts to cultivate the support of workers and peasants were merely a ploy to shore up his political position against the many challenges to it. Also helping account for this apparent anomaly is the fact that Cárdenas was a longtime acquaintance and even friend of the Avila Camacho brothers, and Manuel was secretary of war in his cabinet.

The general election was held in July 1936, and Maximino won easily. The vote had originally been scheduled for November 1936, but party officials advanced the date a bit in order to cut short the campaign period and reduce the opposition's ability to mobilize against the official candidate.

Maximino Avila Camacho, then forty-five years old, became chief executive of the state of Puebla on February 1, 1937. It was immediately apparent that his regime would not be "revolutionary." It was clearly not designed to impart greater justice to those at the bottom of the social ladder, or to assert Mexican nationalism against often overbearing foreign powers—key demands of the revolutionaries of 1910. There was nothing in Maximino's personality or policies to indicate he had any interest in such ideals. He was vain, corrupt, and authoritarian, with a considerable taste for employing violence of all sorts, up to and including murder, in order to get his way. As a politician, he was conservative, anticommunist and antisocialist, acquisitive, and eager to curry favor with the rich. Nevertheless, Maximino proved to be an adept politician who served Cárdenas and the official party well. He not only stabilized the theretofore highly fractious state but also established a so-called *cacicazgo* (an authoritarian system of government based on clientelist relationships headed by a local strongman) that would continue long after his death.

Many of Maximino's methods were predictable enough. He used nepotism and cronyism to ensure control: brother Rafael took the powerful post as head of the state chapter of the official party, while brother Gabriel became police chief of Puebla City. He also used the tried and true method of constantly rotating officials so as to foil challenges to his executive power, and he took care to tarnish the reputation of his predecessor, José Mijares Palencia, by ordering a close inspection of state finances.[20]

At the institutional level, Maximino effectively used the official party apparatus—by now, a well-oiled machine—to reward supporters and ensure the selection of his preferred candidates for both state and federal congress. Not surprisingly, he was thus able to persuade Puebla's chamber of deputies to grant him extraordinary powers to make laws and undertake initiatives free of parliamentary meddling.

Maximino worked to get his political tentacles down to the very local level, mostly by exploiting the municipal committees of the PNR. He also dispatched officials known as *visitadores de administración* (administration inspectors)—men who bore considerable resemblance to the *jefes políticos* (political bosses) of Porfirian days—to keep close tabs on happenings at the local level. Maximino did not hesitate to annul town government elections and replace town councilmen with his own appointees, thereby violating another of the revolution's vaunted ideals: local autonomy (*municipio libre*). Maximino was especially zealous when asserting his authority at the community level, since it was here that that the votes were counted for all government elections.

Maximino made good use of his military connections—the fruit of his own long military career and the fact that his brother, Manuel, was secretary of war. He had much say in deciding who was appointed military commander in his state. This arrangement ruptured a longtime practice whereby the central government appointed zone commanders who were independent of state governors in order to ensure the proper checks and balances.

Maximino cast a wide net in his search for allies, seeking out like-minded leaders in hopes of forming a sort of mafia of right-wing governors. Given his clout with the central government and his own state's great economic importance, Maximino was the natural godfather for such a group. The conservative governors of Mexico State, Morelos, Hidalgo, Tlaxcala, and Sonora played key roles in helping to check radical mass organizations and their leaders at the national level. Also, after Cárdenas took the dramatic step of expropriating foreign oil companies in 1938, Maximino was able to exploit the anger of national and international business—and the economic downturn that resulted from it—in order to nudge Cárdenas in a more conservative direction.[21]

While none of the methods mentioned so far departed greatly from the standard operating procedures for postrevolutionary governors, Maximino was in some respects an innovator. His methods moved beyond the established governmental institutions to include key individuals and groups, all of whom came in one way or another to recognize the advantages of collaborating with—or at least not openly opposing—the regime. That is to say, he was able to enhance his own power by cozying up to many powerful people and institutions who had come to regard themselves as the revolution's big losers—conservative businessmen and industrialists, landowners, the Catholic clergy. He needed only remind them of all they had lost and of all they stood to gain by a judicious alliance with a skilled operator such as himself.

Indeed, Maximino understood well how wealthy conservatives perceived Puebla's recent history. During the revolution and its aftermath, Puebla numbered among Mexico's most violent and volatile states. Strategically located along the vital Mexico City–Veracruz axis, it was one of the country's most highly industrialized states, boasting several important textile mills. In the countryside, grain haciendas and sugarcane plantations used the labor of peasants in nearly medieval fashion. Discontent among workers and peasants exploded during the revolution, and such profound discontent meant that politics were bound to be unstable. During the 1920s, some fourteen men occupied Puebla's governorship, not one of them completing a full term in office. President Calles did his best to stabilize the situation, using the Regional Confederation of Mexican Workers (CROM) in an effort to suppress dissident labor organizations and agrarian leaders. Violence in Puebla's factory towns and rural areas was endemic throughout the 1920s. The capitalist class of Puebla—owners of factories and haciendas—was dominated by conservative Spanish Catholics, men who longed for a labor force that was docile in the face of harsh conditions and little pay. Failing that, they would settle for a government that was strong enough to restrain popular demands and create the appearance of such a labor force.

Maximino's goals as governor were simple enough. "The philosophy of our social movement," he said in a speech to Puebla's chamber of commerce, "is to collaborate with those who own capital and with those who help to maintain and to increase it, on the basis of understanding, equity and social justice. . . . We Mexican revolutionaries have learned the need to organize the government in such a way that the State always acts as the guardian of the masses."[22] He aimed, in other words, to channel social movements and demands into clientelist networks dominated by the state—music to the ears of conservative capitalists. Obviously, Maximino used the epithet "revolutionary" with considerable license, but otherwise he can hardly be accused of dissembling.

From the outset, Maximino understood the importance of spinning the story in his favor. Unfortunately for him, Puebla's most influential newspaper, *La Opinión*, was openly hostile. As he would do in nearly every other field, Maximino was able to find a collaborator—in this case, a *La Opinión* employee named Julian Cacho, who offered to found a new daily on state-owned premises. That paper, *El Diario de Puebla*, was of course firmly in the Avila Camacho camp. Cacho went on to become a state and federal representative and the president of the official government party in the state of Puebla. The editors of *La Opinión*, by contrast, were soon forced to flee the state. One journalist, José Trinidad Mata, editor of a weekly magazine called *Avante*, was assassinated in 1939, and it was widely assumed that Maximino had ordered the killing. Maximino later founded several national newspapers and magazines, including the newspaper chain that began publishing *El Sol de Puebla* in 1945. *El Sol* remains Puebla's leading daily.[23]

Dominating Puebla's fractious labor movement was a matter of immediate concern. Mexico's leading labor organization, CROM, had fallen on hard times by the mid-1930s, mostly because of its association with strong-man Calles, whose power was being frontally challenged. Much of the rank and file had come to view the CROM's leadership as corrupt and inept, and a schism was practically inevitable. In 1932, Marxist labor leader Vicente Lombardo Toledano—a childhood friend of the Avila Camacho brothers—bolted from the CROM to found the Mexican Workers Confederation (CTM), which became the principal vehicle through which Lázaro Cárdenas wrested power from Calles. In Puebla, the CROM split into two factions. The more radical faction linked itself to the CTM and styled itself the Regional Federation of Workers and Peasants (FROC). The rivalry quickly became violent and intense, especially in the key textile manufacturing city of Atlixco. When the FROC called for a general strike in early 1935, the CROM asked for government support and protection against FROC violence. Maximino, at the time chief of military operations for Puebla, was happy to oblige. His brutal repression of the FROC strike helped to cement his alliance with the local CROM, which ironically experienced something of a renaissance in Puebla even while growing moribund elsewhere in the republic. The Puebla CROM, in fact, became one of the principal pillars propping up Maximino's power.[24]

The FROC managed to win the municipal elections in the city of Puebla and to remain in office for 1936–1937, but its days were numbered. The union dug itself deeper into Maximino's bad graces when it campaigned against him in the race for governor. As governor, Maximino took every opportunity to harass and crush the FROC. He removed its representatives from the Conciliation and Arbitration Board, which was set up to decide labor-management disputes. He appointed a well-known foe of radical labor, Gustavo Díaz Ordaz, to the board (Díaz Ordaz would go on to become president of Mexico). The government took to declaring an increasing number of labor actions "illegal." Maximino also cleverly cultivated the allegiance of a handful of opportunists within the FROC's ranks, especially an ambitious young man named Blas Chumacero. Chumacero was willing to break ranks with his union in order to form a politically fruitful alliance with Maximino, one that would enable him to emerge as Puebla's most prominent labor leader for many years.[25] Maximino supplemented such political strategies with a campaign of terror and intimidation against the FROC. Several prominent FROC leaders found themselves arrested on trumped-up charges, and there were many incidents involving more lethal instruments—knives, machetes, clubs, and pistols. From early 1938 to mid-1940, union members were being killed at the rate of one per month.[26]

The final blow to the FROC came with the presidential election of 1940, which pitted General Juan Andreu Almazán against Maximino's younger brother, Manuel Avila Camacho. Maximino became one of Manuel's most determined and ruthless backers. The FROC, ironically, supported the relatively conservative Almazán. Blas Chumacero and other FROC leaders quit their union to form the Workers' Federation of Puebla (FTP), which supported Manuel Avila Camacho's campaign. Maximino sent federal troops to help the FTP evict the FROC from its Puebla headquarters. From that point onward, the FROC was effectively finished, and Puebla's once fractious labor movement could fairly be described as a full-fledged client of the Avilacamachista state apparatus.

Maximino took a similar approach to agrarian issues. His goal was to transform a chaotic and factionalized peasantry into an obedient clientele. To that end, Maximino first used the military to attack bandits and freelancing *caciques*. He then worked to bring the more obsequious caciques into his government—a strategy that, in some cases, paid handsome political dividends to those compliant caciques. And finally, he worked to promote a single peasant organization—at first, the Emiliano Zapata Peasant Federation (CCEZ), which was superseded in 1938 by the League of Agrarian Communities and Peasant Unions of Puebla (LCA)—at the expense of all competitors. Although he was hardly a radical champion of the cause of peasants, Maximino's strategy was in fact perfectly in accord with the one promoted by Lázaro Cárdenas at the national level—that is, to unify peasants and workers within organizations that could be incorporated into the machinery of the official party. The LCA, like many local peasant organizations throughout Mexico, eventually merged with the National Peasant Confederation, and accordingly became part of the Mexican government's increasingly complex single-party state.[27]

Maximino was, of course, indifferent toward the matter of providing real justice to the rural poor. That was evident in his most celebrated maneuver in the agrarian field, his intervention on behalf of his friend and ally, the rich North American entrepreneur William O. Jenkins. During the 1910s and 1920s, Jenkins had used all manner of chicanery to amass one of the largest landholdings in central Mexico, the enormous sugarcane complex at Atencingo in southern Puebla. Peasants linked to the revolutionary agrarian movement of Emiliano Zapata, led by the tenacious Dolores Campos, a.k.a. "Doña Lola," managed to have nearly 90 percent of Jenkins's lands expropriated by the mid-1930s, despite a campaign of terror and intimidation unleashed by the landowner. Even so, Jenkins retained the highest quality lands and irrigation works, as well as the central cane-processing mill. Jenkins further improved his situation by recruiting the ever-obliging FROC leader Blas Chumacero over to his side, thus undercutting the local peasants' union. He then took advantage of a 1934 law allowing hacienda employees (*peones*) to petition for land under the agrarian reform (previously, only free villagers were eligible to make such petitions, on the assumption that hacienda employees had no need for land). Under this scheme, the peones petitioned for the land, and the land was delivered to them as a single giant "ejido"—theoretically, a large collective farm. On paper, this appeared as a very impressive instance of agrarian reform, wherein a large chunk of real estate was transferred from a great sugar baron to his impoverished workers. In actual practice, however, Jenkins and his assistants were able to ensure that only compliant peones received land, and these people continued to work under the close supervision of Jenkins and his managers, prodded by gun-toting mill hands on horseback. Jenkins kept a staff of *pistoleros* (gunmen) on hand to deal with troublemakers. Actual ownership of the land was thus reduced to a meaningless formality.[28]

In the areas of religion and education—which were intertwined during the 1930s owing to the government's efforts to implement anticlerical "socialist education" in public schools, igniting fierce opposition from conservatives and Catholics—Maximino lined up squarely with the conservative forces. He did little to protect federal schoolteachers who ventured into hostile territory with their socialist doctrines. Several teachers were killed, mutilated, or raped, especially in the northern sierra, Maximino's home region. An especially notorious episode took place in the fall of 1935, when religious extremists near Maximino's hometown of Teziutlán murdered three schoolteachers, nearly severing the head of one. Three schools were sacked and burned. Nothing was done to punish the perpetrators, who according to rumor were acting on orders from Maximino's mother, Efrocina.[29]

Maximino had little interest in the area of social welfare and was content to leave such matters to his wife, who headed the state agency that oversaw the hospitals, orphanages, and mental institutions. State funding for such institutions obeyed a Darwinian logic, and accordingly the governor's wife was obliged to beg the federal government for funds to provide an operating room and clothing for patients. And yet, when one of Maximino's favorite horses died—he was a great aficionado of *charro*, or cowboy, culture—he ordered that an autopsy be performed on the animal, something available to only the most privileged of human corpses.[30]

Maximino gladly accepted the support of conservative and religious organizations. He made a point of salting his speeches and newspaper advertisements with conservative, anti-radical, and anticommunist buzzwords, clearly a calculated appeal to conservative sentiments. Implicit in this was the scapegoating of workers and peasants for the instability of recent decades. Workers and peasants, it seemed, were slated to act only as stage props in the new drama of unity, cooperation, peace, and progress Maximino envisioned. Some of the organizations Maximino allied with had unsavory overtones of fascism. These included the United Front of the Middle Class, which saw the governor as a bastion against the "exotic doctrines that [the government] wants to impose in our midst" (this included such radical notions as coeducation of the sexes); and Mexican Revolutionary Action (ARM), better known as the "gold shirts," an organization which was clearly modeled after the Blackshirts and Brownshirts of fascist Italy and Germany. ARM's legal advisor, Manuel Márquez, was Maximino's first choice for the position of rector of the state university—a choice that was met with such strident protests from students that he was quickly replaced.[31]

The removal of an unpopular university rector was a victory for progressive forces, but such victories were rare and fleeting. By the end of Maximino's term the latitude within which dissident movements operated was severely circumscribed, and the tenor of public life in Puebla seemed to have reverted to the nineteenth century. Schools taught docility and patriotism, urging young people to respect authority and to be content with their place in the social hierarchy. Religious schools re-opened, and religious ceremonies were held on public streets, despite constitutional prohibitions. The poor remained poor, while the propertied classes enjoyed a security they had not known since the dictatorship of Porfirio Díaz. Also harking back to the darkest days of the dictatorship was a pall of fear, for few were unaware of their leader's willingness to use bribes, threats, and murder to gain his ends, and to sanction a variety of criminal activities on the part of friends and allies. By the end of Maximino's term, the Mexican Revolution, with all its vaunted ideals, was a distant memory indeed.

Of course, Maximino never intended for the governorship of Puebla to be the pinnacle of his political career. Had he had his way, he would have been tapped instead of his younger brother as the official party's candidate. When told that President Cárdenas had selected his mild-mannered sibling, he exploded in a rage. "It can't be! . . . It should be me! . . . Manuel is a beefsteak with eyes!" Maximino's friends managed to calm him down by assuring him that Manuel was a good compromise, for Cárdenas was rumored to be considering his left-leaning friend, General Francisco Múgica, as official candidate. Conservatives rallied around Manuel Avila Camacho precisely because his personality was so colorless. A colorful character like Maximino would surely have ruffled many feathers.[32]

For the time being, Maximino hoped for, and expected, the position of minister of communication and public works (a post he coveted, perhaps owing to its tremendous potential for graft). He felt entitled to the post as a reward for his hard work on behalf of his brother's presidential campaign. Maximino was enraged when Manuel chose Jesús de la Garza for that post, a man Maximino regarded as a left-leaning mediocrity. He charged that Lázaro Cárdenas—the unquestioned leader of Mexico's "official left" and now Maximino's bitter enemy—was behind the choice, and he lambasted his brother for allowing himself to be so dominated. He threatened to issue a "manifesto" denouncing his brother's government, but once again cooler heads counseled patience.

As it happened, political trends were moving in ways quite amenable for a man of right-wing sympathies like Maximino. The crisis of World War II allowed the government to insist on greater control over labor unions, and dominating labor unions was something of a specialty for Maximino. Even communist labor leader Vicente Lombardo Toledano—a childhood friend of the Avila Camachos, but now a sworn enemy to Maximino—argued that the defeat of fascism required the suppression of labor's demands, at least for the time being. In the lower house of Congress, several Avila Camacho allies who styled themselves the "Renovación" group were working to neutralize the left and to push their conservative agenda. One of their number, Enrique Carrola Atuna, launched an anticommunist crusade in June 1941 when he denounced three known left-wingers in the president's cabinet, a group that included Secretary of Communication de la Garza. In September, de la Garza was dismissed from the cabinet, and Maximino was tapped to replace him.

Maximino was determined to let his little brother know that he would not be a toady even if his little brother was president of the republic. Without notifying the president, he showed up at the office of the Ministry of Communication with an escort of some fifty automobiles and several motorcycles. Armed with Thompson machine guns, Maximino and several of his closest collaborators rode the escalator up to the secretary's office, marching in military fashion, while many more of his supporters stormed the stairways. "I'm just exercising my rights," he insisted. "I don't owe anything to anyone!"[33] His inauguration ceremony, which took place on October 2, 1941, was attended by more distinguished guests than could fit into the building. Speeches congratulating the new minister lasted for two solid hours.

Maximino's real achievements as secretary of communication were unimpressive, although some progress was made in the communications field— a railroad bridge over the Suchiate River dividing Mexico and Guatemala, a handful of new roads, and the completion of the important highway connecting the cities of Puebla and Oaxaca. Avila Camacho's home state of Puebla, and in particular his home region, the northern sierra, appear to have benefited disproportionately.[34]

In fact, Maximino devoted his tenure as communication minister principally to his greatest passions: politics and self-enrichment. Even though one avowed Cardenista—labor minister Ignacio García Téllez—remained in the president's cabinet, Maximino found ways to usurp some of his functions. He zealously swore to promote "harmony between capital and labor" and to "use all legal means to impede professional agitators from slowing the normal and growing progress of national production."[35] His trespassing into areas outside that of his legitimate competence made clear that he regarded his post as eminently political, and that he recognized few limits on his power. His aim was nothing less than to do away once and for all with the influence of the official left, which was spearheaded by Cárdenas and

Lombardo Toledano, and to sell himself to the Mexican public as the principal bulwark against their nefarious aims.

Although Maximino was one of the best-known political figures of his day, there was little beyond his own colossal ego to indicate that he ever had a serious chance of realizing his presidential ambitions. There was, to begin with, the problem of the appearance of nepotism. The 1940 presidential election had been marred by blatant fraud and violence, and the regime—while it had no intention of permitting truly free and fair elections in 1946—was at least sensitive enough about appearances to nix any dynastic intentions. Maximino's presidential ambitions were also impeded by his general notoriety. Such was his fame as a womanizer that when the salty *ranchera* singer Lucha Reyes—a woman who was said to sprinkle gunpowder on her eggs each morning and to sleep with her pistol by her side—committed suicide in 1944, the rumor mills immediately speculated that Maximino must have played a role in the melodrama.[36] Further clouding Maximino's presidential hopes were his pro-fascist sympathies. His principal business associate during the 1940s was the wealthy Swedish industrialist Axel Wenner-Gren, who was known to be cozy with the likes of Hermann Goering and Benito Mussolini—associations that landed him a place of honor on the U.S. blacklist during World War II. Maximino himself was rumored to keep a portrait of Benito Mussolini in the bedroom of his home in Puebla. When the United States tried to place anti-Axis propaganda in Mexican cinemas, it was shut out of the many movie houses owned by Avila Camacho confederate William O. Jenkins. Some charged that this was at Maximino's urging.[37]

As if this weren't enough to doom Maximino's potential candidacy, his corruption was the stuff of legends. His fondness for kickbacks earned him the nickname "Mr. 15 percent." Greatly fond of luxury, he owned more than two hundred silk suits and two hundred pairs of shoes, preferring to choose outfits that matched the color of whatever car he was riding in on a given day. He boasted of owning some twenty houses in the posh Mexican neighborhood of Lomas de Chapultepec, twenty automobiles, and a half-million pesos' worth of pure-blooded Arabian horses. He was suspected of increasing his fortune by taking advantage of wartime shortages to manipulate the prices of rice, corn, and meat, accepting bribes freely, and scalping tickets to popular attractions.[38]

Although Maximino publicly insisted that the size of his fortune was vastly exaggerated—it amounted, he claimed, to be worth only about three million pesos—a U.S. diplomat estimated that his fortune increased by about that amount each week. Such charges were given credence less than a year after his death when his widow, the still young and attractive Margarita Richardi, tried to remarry, thereby jeopardizing the inheritance of Maximino's relations. On the eve of the wedding, Margarita's betrothed—a movie actor named Jorge

Vélez—was shot and wounded. Vélez was attacked again in the hospital as he tried to recover. The couple managed to marry in the hospital, but soon thereafter they were machine-gunned en route to the Mexico City airport. They survived the attack unscathed, although Margarita's sister was wounded. One of Maximino's sons was arrested, and a warrant was issued for his brother Gabriel, who was suspected of being the "intellectual author" of the crimes. Maximino's widow and her fiancé, however, left the country so they would not have to testify at trial, and the government hushed up the potentially embarrassing case.[39]

Clearly, Maximino's extremist political proclivities and his general notoriety made him an unlikely choice as president. And indeed, Maximino publicly renounced any pretensions to the national presidency in an interview with journalist José Valadés in mid-1943.[40] According to his friend Gonzalo N. Santos, however, in reality his hopes remained stubbornly alive, despite his obviously failing health. Toward the end of Manuel Avila Camacho's presidential term, there was much speculation that the next official candidate would be Miguel Alemán, a man for whom Maximino had no use. Maximino discussed the matter with Santos, and Santos recorded their dialogue as follows:

> "Are you going to head up my campaign?" Maximino asked Santos.
> "No," Santos replied. "For a simple reason."
> "Which is?"
> "For the simple reason that you're not going to have any campaign," Santos replied. "Your friends, your true friends, will not allow it."
> "Very well," said Maximino. "I'm no idiot. Your firmness in this matter leads me to understand that this thing with Alemán is a done deal, but I will tell you one thing: you're going to tell my brother Manuel . . . that Miguel Alemán will not become president of the Republic, because I swear on the milk of our mother doña Eufrocina that as soon as they launch the official candidacy of that bastard, I, personally, am going to leave his corpse at Manuel's feet."[41]

Santos noted that Maximino was "mortally pale and trembling" as he said this.

On the morning of February 17, 1945, Maximino went to the city of Atlixco to celebrate an "act of solidarity and fraternity between the textile workers of the CROM and of the CTM." He delivered a speech in one of the city's factories and then inaugurated a clinic and school for the workers.[42] After that, he presided over a banquet in the city of Puebla attended by more than 5,000 people, all of whom drank toasts to Maximino and swore fidelity. Maximino then returned to his home, where he suffered a massive and fatal heart attack.[43]

Maximino's death, like his life, spawned its share of rumors. There was much speculation that his enemies had slipped something into his food, though precisely which enemies it might be was unclear. *Time* magazine published the intriguing legend that the political fortunes of Miguel Alemán—who did indeed become Mexico's next president—had several times been "helped by death." He had been *diputado propietario*—a sort of understudy—to the representative from Veracruz when the titular representative died. He later became governor of Veracruz when the governor-elect was assassinated. And now, it seemed, his route to the presidency was cleared by the sudden demise of Maximino Avila Camacho.[44] Others supposed that perhaps Maximino had simply become too great an annoyance and embarrassment to the regime. Of course, there is always the most likely explanation: Maximino died of perfectly natural causes. He suffered from diabetes, had long been in poor health, and had a notorious penchant for riotous living.

Maximino Avila Camacho, for all his corruption and egotism, was a prototypical figure in modern Mexican history. He navigated the revolutionary upheaval with no discernible ideology, but with a list of powerful contacts that he could exploit to his political and economic advantage. As his fortunes improved, he was quick to discover the advantages of propitious alliances with the battered, but still rich and powerful, elites. Like Benito Mussolini—by some accounts, one of his idols—Maximino found that by becoming a competent enforcer of powerful and traditional elites, a bulwark against what they perceived as a threat to civilization from below, he could greatly enhance his own power. And indeed, he was eminently competent—even ingenious—in carrying out the task he set for himself. As historian Gregory Crider puts it, "Maximino's political brilliance was that he was able to step into a confused and tumultuous political scene and take advantage of existing conflicts, eliminating opponents and incorporating supporters into an expanding patronage network."[45] The government of Mexico, from 1940 onward, would successfully replicate his accomplishment at the national level.

For all his brilliance, however, Maximino was notably unsuccessful in burnishing his own image into one that was palatable to the Mexican public. As governor, he was nicknamed "The Mad Czar of Puebla," and his hopes of achieving the highest office in the land were doomed by the fact that most Mexicans saw him as crude, corrupt, violent, unprincipled, and intellectually dull. Perhaps understanding something important about his legacy, Maximino had Puebla's historical archives sold to paper factories. Historians may never know either the extent of his brilliance or the depths of his venality.[46]

NOTES

1. *Arráncame la vida* (Mexico: Ediciones Oceano, 1985) has twice been translated into English, first as *Mexican Bolero*, trans. Ann Wright (New York: Viking, 1989) and

then as *Tear This Heart Out*, trans. by Margaret Sayers Peden (New York: Riverhead Books, 1997).

2. Gustavo Abel Hernández Enríquez and Armando Rojas Trujillo, *Manuel Avila Camacho: Biografía de un revolutionario con historia*, vol. 1 (Puebla: Gobierno del Estado, 1986), 21–56; Sergio Valencia Castrejón, *Poder regional y política nacional en México: El gobierno de Maximino Avila Camacho en Puebla, 1937–1941* (Mexico City: Instituto Nacional de Estudios Históricos de la Revolución Mexicana, 1996), 17–19.

3. Alan Knight, *The Mexican Revolution*, vol. 1, *Porfirians, Liberals and Peasants* (Cambridge: Cambridge University Press, 1986), 266; Enrique Krauze, *Mexico: Biography of Power*, trans. Hank Heifetz (New York: Harper Collins, 1997), 493. For general coverage of Maximino's military career, see: Jorge Efren Arrazola Cermeño, "La oscura sombra del cardenismo en Puebla" (Doctoral thesis, Universidad Nacional Autónoma de México, 2002), 51–95; and Valencia Castrejón, *Poder regional y política nacional en México*, 19–41. Mexico City, Archivo General de la Nación, Ramo Revolución (hereafter AGN-RR), Avila Camacho to Madero, Nov. 27, 1912, box 1, file 29, document 350; AGN-RR, Madero to Avila Camacho, Nov. 30, 1912, box 1, file 29, document 350.

4. Mexico City, El Colegio de México, Archivo de la Defensa Nacional, microfilm, Medina to Carranza, Oct. 30, 1914, roll 7115/2; Mexico City, Fideicomiso Plutaro Elías Calles-Fernando Torreblanca, Archivo de Joaquín Amaro (hereafter CT-JA), Robles L. to Amaro, Feb. 20, 1925, series 03-01, file José Hurtado 1/4, document 44; CT-JA, Avila Camacho to Amaro, Mar. 31, 1925, series 03-02, file 1/7, document 413.

5. Austin, University of Texas, Archivo de Pablo González, microfilm, Commander Army of the East to Private Secretary of González, May 11, 1916, roll 4; Mexico City, Fideicomiso Plutarco Elías Calles-Fernando Torreblanca, Archivo de Álvaro Obregón, Nov. 12, 1918, Avila Camacho to Obregón, file 341/30, document 1; CT-JA, Avila Camacho to Amaro, Mar. 31, 1925, series 03-02, file 1/7, document 413.

6. Mexico City, Archivo General de la Nación, Archivo Obregón-Calles (hereafter AGN-OC), Torreblanca to Avila Camacho, July 5, 1922, file, 809-A-176; AGN-OC, Obregón to Sec. Gobernación, Sept. 29, 1922, file 809-A-176; AGN-OC, Private Secretary of President, internal memorandum, Nov. 1922, file 813-C-162.

7. CT-JA, Cárdenas to Amaro, Jan. 21, 1925, series 03-01, file Lázaro Cárdenas 1/4, document 24.

8. CT-JA, Avila Camacho to Amaro, May 25, June 5, 1925, series 03-02, file 1/7, documents 420, 430; CT-JA, Avila Camacho to Vidal, May 28, 1925, series 03-02, file 1/7, document 424; CT-JA, Cárdenas to Amaro, Dec. 23, 1924, Jan. 21, 1925, series 03-01, file Lázaro Cárdenas 1/4, documents 7, 24; CT-JA, Amaro to Hurtado, Feb. 27, 1925, series 03-01, file José Hurtado 1/4, document 45.

9. The threat reads, "No sabes cuantos males me ha causado el puto de Amaro que ya mero le mando pegar un tiro para que se le quite lo cabrón pero la venganza es dulce y muy pronto." CT-JA, Avila Camacho to Arellano, July 15, 1925, series 03-02, file 1/7, document 439; CT-JA, Avila Camacho to Amaro, Sept. 2, Oct. 22, 1925, series 03-02, file 1/7, documents 441, 444; Avila Camacho to Amaro, Sept. 26, 1926, series 03-02, file 1/8, document 485.

10. Fideicomiso Plucarco Elías Calles-Fernando Torreblanca, Archivo Plutarco Elías Calles (hereafter CT-PEC), Reynoso and Estrada to Calles, May 15, 1929, file

191, document 8; CT-JA, Avila Camacho to Amaro, Jan. 17, 1927, series 03-02, file 1/8, document 492; CT-JA, Anonymous to Amaro, series 03-01, file Andrés Figueroa 14/18, document 811; CT-JA, García to Amaro, May 20, 1928, series 03-11, file 5/69, no document number; CT-JA, Juaregui Mejía to Calles, July 30, 1928, series 03-02, file 1/8, document 516; AGN-OC, Bañuelos to Calles, July 7, 1928, file 707-V-17; CT-JA, Meza to Amaro, Oct. 17, 1929, series 03-11, file 5/122, no document number; "Memorias de Juan Andreu Almazán," *El Universal* (Mexico City), Aug. 21, 1958.

    11. CT-JA, Avila Camacho to Amaro, Nov. 21, 1926, series 03-02, file 1/8, document 490; CT-JA, Gómez to Amaro, Sept. 5, 1930, series 03-11, file 5/76, no document number; CT-JA, Amaro to Figueroa, June 5, 1928, series 03-01, file Andrés Figueroa 14/18, document 811; "Memorias de Juan Andreu Almazán," *El Universal,* Aug. 21, 1958.

    12. John W. F. Dulles, *Yesterday in Mexico: A Chronicle of the Revolution, 1919–1936* (Austin: University of Texas Press, 1961), 487–88.

    13. Gonzalo N. Santos, *Memorias: Una vida azarosa, novelesca y tormentosa* (Mexico: Grijalbo, 1986), 680.

    14. Mexico City, Archivo General de la Nación, Archivo Pascual Ortiz Rubio, Avila Camacho to Ortiz Rubio, Apr. 16, 1931, file 1883-A, Aug. 25, 1931, file 4765-A; CT-JA, Avila Camacho to Amaro, Aug. 3, 1931, series 03-02, file 1/10, document 635.

    15. AGN-LC, Avila Camacho to Cárdenas, Jan. 23, 1935, file 556.7/7; AGN-LC, Bermejo and Burgos to Cárdenas, May 30, 1935, file 556.7/7; AGN-LC, Ortiz Villa et al. to Sec. War, Jan. 19, 1936, file 555.1/103; *Excélsior,* May 31, 1935; *La Opinión,* Jan. 29, May 31, Aug. 23, 24, 1935; *El Universal,* May 30, 1935.

    16. For coverage of the election campaign, see Arrazola Cermeño, "La oscura sombra del cardenismo en Puebla," 100–27; Valencia Castréjon, *Poder regional y política nacional en México,* 41–64; and *La Opinión,* Sept. 1935 to Jan. 1937.

    17. Miguel Angel Peral, *Diccionario de historia, biografía y geografía del Estado de Puebla* (Mexico City: Peral, 1971), 106.

    18. José Alarcón Hernández, *Las normas del poder: Puebla, un espejo de la nación* (Mexico City: Porrúa, 1993), 84.

    19. Washington, D.C., National Archives, Records of the Department of State Relating to the Internal Affairs of Mexico, 1930–39, Record Group 59, microfilm, Daniels to Sec. State, May 15, 1936, roll 5, document 175–77; Washington, D.C., National Archives, United States Military Intelligence Reports, microfilm, May 19, 1936, Marshburn—G-2 report #7154, roll 2, documents 36–38; interview with Vicente Lombardo Toledano in James W. Wilkie and Edna Monzón de Wilkie, *México visto en el siglo XX: Entrevistas de historia oral* (Mexico City: Instituto Mexicano de Investigaciones Económicas, 1969), 352.

    20. Wil Pansters, *Politics and Power in Puebla: The Political History of a Mexican State, 1937–1987* (Amsterdam: CEDLA, 1990), 51–52.

    21. Adrian A. Bantjes, *As if Jesus Walked on Earth: Cardenismo, Sonora, and the Mexican Revolution* (Wilmington, DE: SR Books, 1998), 78, 184–85.

    22. Pansters, *Politics and Power in Puebla,* 72–73.

    23. Pansters, *Politics and Power in Puebla,* 64.

    24. Gregory S. Crider, "Material Struggles: Workers' Strategies during the 'Institutionalization of the Revolution' in Atlixco, Puebla, Mexico, 1930–1942" (Ph.D. diss., University of Wisconsin–Madison, 1996), 227–29.

25. Pansters, *Politics and Power in Puebla*, 58; Crider, "Material Struggles," 279.

26. Crider, "Material Struggles," 292.

27. Pansters, *Politics and Power in Puebla*, 60.

28. David Ronfeldt, *Atencingo: The Politics of Agrarian Struggle in a Mexican Ejido* (Stanford, CA: Stanford University Press, 1973), 14–42.

29. Mary Kay Vaughan, *Cultural Politics in Revolution: Teachers, Peasants, and Schools in Mexico, 1930–1940* (Tucson: University of Arizona Press, 1997), 122–23.

30. AGN-LC, R. de Avila Camacho and Villar to Cárdenas, Apr. 15, 1939, file 462.3/204; AGN-LC, Avila Camacho to Cárdenas, Mar. 18, 1940, file 101/137.

31. Jesús Márquez, "Oposición contrarrevolucionaria de derecha en Puebla, 1932–1940," in *Religión, política y sociedad: El sinarquismo y la iglesia en México*, ed. Rubén Aguilar V. and Guillermo Zermeño (Mexico: Universidad Iberoamericana, 1992), 40–46.

32. Santos, *Memorias*, 647–48.

33. Santos, *Memorias*, 745–47; 753–55.

34. Gustavo Casasola, *Historia gráfica de la Revolución Mexicana: 1900–1970* (Mexico: Editorial Trillas, 1992), 7:2548–49.

35. Luis Medina, *Historia de la Revolución Mexicana*, vol. 18, *1940–1952: Del cardenismo al avilacamachismo* (Mexico: El Colegio de México, 1978), 155–56.

36. José Agustín, *Tragicomedia mexicana 1: La vida en México de 1940–1970* (Mexico: Planeta, 1990), 30.

37. Stephen R. Niblo, *Mexico in the 1940s: Modernity, Politics, and Corruption* (Wilmington, DE: Scholarly Resources, 1999), 326.

38. Niblo, *Mexico in the 1940s*, 283–86.

39. Niblo, *Mexico in the 1940s*, 287–88.

40. Luis Medina, *Historia de la Revolución Mexicana*, vol. 20, *1940–1952: Civilismo y modernización del autoritarismo* (Mexico: El Colegio de México, 1979), 16.

41. Santos, *Memorias*, 833.

42. Casasola, *Historia gráfica de la Revolución Mexicana*, 7:2560.

43. Santos, *Memorias*, 836.

44. Medina, *Civilismo y modernización*, 81, 85ff.

45. Crider, "Material Struggles," 302.

46. David LaFrance interview with Pilar Pacheco, Director, State Archive, Puebla, July 11, 1995.

11

Baltasar Leyva Mancilla of Guerrero

Learning Hegemony

Paul Gillingham

Governors tend to disappear in the cracks between different readings of the postrevolutionary Mexican state. For political scientists who believed in a powerful center running a well-oiled corporatist machine, governors became fundamentally uninfluential once the real, mechanically efficient Partido Revolucionario Institucional (PRI, the Institutional Revolutionary Party) government emerged. Governors, in the analyses of Brandenburg and González Casanova, were harried men, continually reminded of their status as disposable creatures of the president by the multiple checks of federal agencies, monies, and military zone commanders.[1] As Roderic Camp concluded, governors held "fluctuating and often ineffective" positions; Tuohy and Ronfeldt described them as "middle-level elites" in the revolutionary state.[2] Peter Smith's sampling of governors' origins reinforced this image of regional sovereignty in decline: only 4 percent of governors between 1946 and 1971 moved up from positions in state politics to the federal level (compared to 23 percent of the 1911–1946 cohort), while the most common origin lay in the subservient ranks of the rubber-stamp Senate.[3] That governors came under increasing everyday control from the 1940s onward is further evidenced by the steady decline in the numbers dismissed: while Calles (as *jefe máximo*) toppled twenty-one and Cárdenas seventeen, Díaz Ordaz only found it necessary to fire one governor.[4] Even radically opposed interpretations concur on gubernatorial impotence: thus governors similarly failed to dominate Jeffrey Rubin's "decentered" Isthmus, where regional boss Heliodoro Charis enjoyed greater political longevity and autonomy than his nominal superiors in Oaxaca.[5] Given that cities and even certain market towns have frequently been run by presidential rather than gubernatorial appointees, only unremarkable *municipios*—admittedly the main points of contact for Mexicans with formal politics—remain as the unchallenged preserves of gubernatorial authority for most of the twentieth century.

This understated consensus on the unimportance of governors is in itself highly significant. It was not so in the 1920s, when Gruening's list of governors could double as a catalogue of regional *caciques*—Carrillo Puerto, Cedillo, Garrido, Portes Gil, Tejeda, and Zuno, to mention some examples—all characterized by their considerable independence from a tottery national government.[6] Something of that independence and national significance (and totteriness) returned from the late 1980s onward as PRIista electoral control crumbled; Caroline Beer's analysis of the 1970–1998 cohort of governors reveals a clear correlation between increasingly competitive elections and rising numbers of "locally oriented" candidates.[7] The development, retreat, and resurgence of gubernatorial autonomy suggest a clear transition to a "golden age" of central power followed by its eventual decline.[8] That such a transition did not take place in the Cárdenas *sexenio* is a staple of recent historiography.[9] The study of governorship in the 1940s may, consequently, cut to the core of basic questions surrounding state formation in modern Mexico, enabling the autonomies of regional politicians and their constituents to be measured against the expanding capabilities of central government.

General Baltasar Leyva Mancilla seemingly agreed with scholars on the questionable benefits of being governor; when offered a run at the governorship of Guerrero, his first reaction was to refuse. His would-be kingmaker was state union boss Alfredo Córdoba Lara, whose distinctive gunman panache had taken him from childhood as a Chilpancingo bootblack to a central position in Guerrerense politics.[10] In 1944, he drove from Guerrero to Leyva Mancilla's barracks in Chihuahua to convince the general to take the job. Leyva Mancilla was reluctant, explaining that long absence from Guerrero had left him without local knowledge or networks.[11] He had, admittedly, been out of the state since his prerevolutionary days in a Chilpancingo primary school. A year in the Colegio Militar had prepared him for a rapid rise through the ranks of the Constitutionalist Army; the instability of the 1920s and 1930s combined with his knack for choosing the winning side to ensure continuing promotions. His family's backing for Obregón in Iguala during the Agua Prieta revolt in 1920 landed him an adjutant's job on the General Staff; the de la Huerta revolt saw him promoted to colonel; campaigns against Cristero and Cedillista rebels landed him a general's rank. By 1944 he had been General Antonio Guerrero's chief of staff in various military zones for sixteen years, and there, as a comparatively young, upwardly mobile, and administratively gifted officer, he was content to stay.[12]

That this long absence was as much a tactical excuse as a genuine reason for turning down the candidacy is clear from Leyva Mancilla's family history. His father Pablo was finance secretary in the 1890s, while his wife Fermina was one of the Neri clan, a leading Porfirian family that dominated state politics between 1921 and 1928.[13] Ex-governor Rodolfo still led the state Supreme Court in the 1940s.[14] His brothers were all soldier-politicians. Manuel, Efrén, and Rafael had been local deputies; his half-brother, Pablo Leyva, owned a sizeable hacienda near Chilpancingo and had been Gobernación secretary to governor Adrián Castrejón (1928–1932), a job later held by Rafael.[15] The women of the family contracted strategic alliances among the new regional elites. Leyva Mancilla's sister had married into the Carreto family, the *éminences grises* of the Berber governorship; his niece was married to Córdoba Lara, making him a *sobrino político*.[16] Leyva Mancilla was cousin to the Martínez Adames, an influential family with a long record in both federal and state politics; Arturo Martínez Adame was at the time Guerrero's senator.[17] He had numerous *compadrazgos* with emerging Guerrerense politicians such as Nicolás Wences García and Caritino Maldonado.[18] Such dense, politically charged kin networks were tantamount to a prefabricated campaign team.[19] He was, moreover, backed from the beginning by the Guerrerense diaspora, including heavyweights such as foreign minister Ezequiel Padilla, and by ex-governors Castrejón and Gabriel Guevara.[20] The key argument, however, was made by his patron General Guerrero. As Leyva Mancilla repeatedly stressed his lack of support, Guerrero telephoned the presidency. The assurance of Avila Camacho's backing was too much to refuse, and Leyva Mancilla agreed to run.[21]

There were several pragmatic reasons for his reluctance. Guerrero had been close to ungovernable since the revolution, which had left an armed society divided between landed elites and frustrated land reformers. Neither side had suffered enough losses to prevent enduring conflict after 1920. The next twenty-five years were marked by a struggle for land and power between *agraristas* and shifting coalitions of landowners, *licenciados*, violent entrepreneurs, and the (generally despised) "professional politicians," men who rose through unions, the bureaucracy, elected office, and federal contacts. The result was, as one traveller had it, "a permanent state of insurrection"; or as a Gobernación agent entitled his report, "a state [. . .] of anarchy," marked by six rebellions in the 1920s, and by rural counterinsurgency, streetfighting, and serial political assassination in the 1930s and 1940s.[22] In such Hobbesian conditions governors enjoyed few of the resources of a functioning state: tax revenues were the lowest in Mexico, the tiny state police force was ineffectual, and the courts were both venal and politicized.[23] The federal military zone commanders regularly ignored or overrode the governor's decisions; the reserves who served as police in most of the state replicated the zone commander's autonomy at the village level. Establishing alliances with the military and caciques could bring some measure of influence for the governor; it also, inevitably, gave his opponents material for protests to Mexico City. Governors were short-lived in this faction-filled, violent world: at the start of the 1944 campaign, no elected governor had finished his term since before the revolution, and no governor had progressed into a desirable national job. Finally—if such careerist considerations were not enough—Leyva Mancilla was well aware of the high personal cost of Guerrerense politics. Three of his brothers had been killed in state politics, at least one of them, Rafael, by the state government itself.[24]

He would, moreover, face a pent-up political demand for the governorship from the state's agraristas. One of the few constants amid the endemic uncertainty of political life was an unsatisfied agrarista claim to the governorship. Peasants formed an overwhelming majority of the population and the Liga de Comunidades Agrarias repeatedly reminded Mexico City of that fact in negotiating their quota of elected positions, alleging control of over 80 percent of the state's votes.[25] Guerrero's agrarista leader, Senator Nabor Ojeda, had played a key role in both overthrowing Governor Berber and installing his unknown successor, Rafael Catalán Calvo.[26] Ojeda, from the coast, had moved from the 1920s between elected positions and the agrarian bureaucracy; he had been one of the first secretaries-general of the Liga in Guerrero and a member of the national directive of the Confederación Campesina Mexicana under Cárdenas.[27] He was clearly marked as the agrarista contender for the next governorship from the early 1940s, and before campaigning even began he was in a powerful position.[28] The *ejidatarios* were unified behind his candidacy; the Federación de Organizaciones Populares, a numerous faction of the divided Confederación de Trabajadores Mexicanos (CTM), and even the state leadership of the Partido de la Revolución Mexicana (PRM) were all initially favorable. In the spring of 1944, Ojeda controlled the key PRM municipal committees on both coasts and in the central Bravo district; across the state he counted on a majority of *presidentes municipales*.[29] Were the election to be fair—as President Avila Camacho had promised—the agraristas were the evident favorites to take the governorship; local authorities, party representatives, and Gobernación agents all concurred that Nabor Ojeda was the popular candidate.[30]

Leyva Mancilla, however, became governor after an exhaustively prepared election. The decisive moment was not the constitutional, but rather the party primary election of November 1944. Both sectoral and regional conventions were rigged. Córdoba Lara's Confederación de Trabajadores Mexicanos held their convention without publicity and used apocryphal unions to declare Leyva Mancilla the workers' candidate; the Ojedistas were barred by state police from entering the Sector Popular's meeting; the Confederación Nacional Campesina (CNC) obeyed presidential instructions and never even convened to decide.[31] Bureaucratic maneuvering was paralleled by systematic physical intimidation. Ejidatarios in the Chilapa region were threatened with losing schools and land if they did not sign *adhesiones*; northern Ojedista miners met with refusals to process their paperwork; Chilpancingo agricultural workers were told to vote for Leyva Mancilla or lose their jobs.[32] The threatened violence sometimes materialized: Telésforo Guerrero, the PRM delegate in Cuautepec, was shot dead for refusing to sign blank electoral forms for the Leyva campaign; two out of three of the Las Cruces ejido's directors were executed by one of Castrejón's aides for supporting Ojeda.[33] When Leyva Mancilla won the primary, Nabor Ojeda called for the governor to be deposed and threatened to disobey the party before finally cancelling his candidacy.[34] His followers abstained in the constitutional election of January 15, which Leyva Mancilla won unopposed, albeit with "a very low number of voters"; the Liga delayed three weeks before professing loyalty to the regime.[35]

Guerrero's agraristas had reasons to be alienated beyond Ojeda's loss. The gubernatorial elections coincided with the municipal and legislative elections of December 1944, which at a stroke reversed virtually all the electoral gains that peasants had made since the 1920s. All the incoming local deputies were Leyvistas; only three of the seventy-two *ayuntamientos* were controlled by agraristas.[36] At a village level, moreover, the new political shift was formed by men thoroughly antithetical to the agraristas. In Coyuca de Catalán the new presidente municipal was Luis Brugada, a well-entrenched and hard-line landowner; in Cuetzala, Malaquías Rabadán, one of an extensive family of caciques accused of agrarista deaths; in Coyuca de Benítez, Luis Otero, a pistolero and cattle-rustler; in strongly Zapatista Igualapa, Higinio Morga, one of the Ometepec landowners.[37] Some outgoing ayuntamientos such as those of Teloloapan and Ciudad Altamirano tried to hand over power to the dissidents they recognized as winners, only to have Leyvista slates imposed by the military and the governor.[38] The new men, faces of a successful landowner restoration, were widely criticized as PANistas and Sinarquistas; the governor, even as he installed them, privately agreed.[39] The results caused protests in 49 percent of cases and outbreaks of violence in 17 percent of Guerrero's municipios.[40] By the summer of 1945, Leyva Mancilla and the new state legislature were in office, and all three remaining agrarista ayuntamientos had been toppled. It was a clean sweep of peasant representatives from every level of the political hierarchy.

This rancorous campaign and its heavy-handed *carro completo* result left Baltasar Leyva Mancilla a legacy of conflict, which his supporters then exacerbated through the jailings, job losses, political exclusion, and exile they inflicted on the losing agraristas.[41] Guerrero could be ruled (albeit with difficulty) against concerted peasant opposition; it was, however, impossible to survive in office against determined presidential opposition.

Leyva Mancilla was unfortunate in that the mismatch of state and federal electoral cycles left him with five years to serve under a president who had not appointed him. He had, furthermore, compromisingly close political ties to three of Miguel Alemán's national opponents. He sympathized with General Henríquez Guzmán in the jockeying for position that preceded the campaign season.[42] One of the governor's key supporters and his new military zone commander, General Adrián Castrejón, led the national Frente Zapatista in fierce opposition to the Alemán candidacy; another, Ezequiel Padilla, was Alemán's rival for first the party nomination and later the presidency.[43] There were, finally, credible reports of an assassination plot targeting Alemán during his campaign in Guerrero.[44] Nabor Ojeda, in contrast, declared astutely and early for Alemán, and was an important campaign organizer in the peasant leagues of both Guerrero and Veracruz.[45] When Alemán took office Leyva Mancilla consequently found himself enfiladed, caught between a militant popular opposition at home and a suspicious—if not downright hostile—president.

There was no honeymoon. Leyva Mancilla tried conciliation in the December 1946 municipal elections, promoting compromise slates that mixed his supporters with agraristas; Gobernación, however, was more interested in the Padillista rising than in his political scene shifting.[46] The revolt was relatively minor, involving some five hundred mustered and disarmed rural militiamen in Padilla's heartlands of northern Guerrero. When the governor requested that an additional regiment be sent to the region and maestros and peasants asked for arms to defend the revolution, the tentative rebels registered the absence of national rebellion and disbanded.[47] The ease with which they were allowed to melt away, however, led to agrarista accusations that Leyva Mancilla and Castrejón had been involved in the plot.[48] The same regions of the north and northwest were then hard hit by the outbreak of foot-and-mouth disease in 1947; the government's decision to shoot infected cattle triggered renewed mobilization. By August, two armed groups were being hunted by federal troops in the sierra; by mid-September they had formed a threatening cross-class alliance that brought together ejidatarios, cattlemen, and Padillistas.[49] In the early morning of September 22, one such group attacked and disarmed the Rio Balsas garrison and seized the train. Some hundred rebels then came down from the mountains, sending foot soldiers ahead on the train to attack the next town, Cocula, and leaving horsemen to demand money and arms from local merchants. The attack on Cocula failed: a platoon of federal soldiers and another of agraristas held out until peasant militias arrived to reinforce the town. The rebels retreated to the sierra, pursued by cavalry, infantry, and planes, and by September 26 they had dispersed.[50] The Balsas rebellion was hardly Leyva Mancilla's fault; it was only one of many violent reactions to the foot-and-mouth campaign. It came three weeks after the jacquerie at

Senguio, Michoacán, and at the same time as reports reached Mexico City of arms dumps in the Sierra de Puebla and revolutionary pamphlets in Morelos.[51] But two rebellions inside a year was a notably poor record; a clear breach of the first rule of regional governance—that subordinates must not demonstrably lose control—and fuel for the agraristas' attempt to topple Leyva Mancilla.

Such an attempt was entirely predictable, for constant repetition had by now ritualized the mechanics of overthrowing governors in Guerrero, where constitutional succession was the exception rather than the norm. Political actors since the 1850s had made traditional a highly patterned sequence of moves designed to forcibly change a state government. The real or invented misdemeanors of the incumbent—spectacular corruption, repressive violence, downright incompetence—were represented to the center as an unacceptable rupture of the political moral economy. That such charges were beyond mere opportunism was then signified by a potentially costly (but in reality often choreographed) symbolic act of violence by the dissidents. Simulacra of rural revolts, in which revolutionary manifestoes were printed, armed men mustered, and conflict with state forces avoided, were one option; marches and minor shootouts another; intimidating but usually bloodless crowd seizures of town halls a third. When effective, such action was a form of collective bargaining by riot which ended in a negotiated replacement of the offending governor amid renewed protestations of loyalty from the opposition. Yet even when it failed, the sporadic state violence such maneuvers provoked could work in the dissidents' favor. Repression could, in a variation of the guerrilla stratagem of "compromising the village," turn previous neutrals against the governor; it could also provide the final argument and convince Mexico City to abandon the state administration.

There were strong incentives, in short, for opposition movements in Guerrero to both dramatize and act out metropolitan expectations of an unruly frontier society. In May 1948, three years of agrarista complaints paid off when Alemán commissioned a statewide investigation by Gobernación's intelligence service.[52] Such investigations were barely encoded warnings; they had preceded the dismissals of governors López, Guevara, and Berber.[53] Yet the essentialization of Guerrero as an inherently violent state could also be useful to state elites. It cast elite violence as justified and reactive rather than aggressive; it further enabled the regional leaders to claim indispensability in mediating between a troublesome population and a distant national leadership. The central stereotype of *Guerrero bronco* may well have lent Leyva Mancilla a feeling of relative autonomy. When the Gobernación reports turned out to be critical but far from fatal—providing a catalogue of corruption and political violence, but failing to establish Leyva Mancilla's personal responsibility—he took the offensive.[54] In the

1948 municipal elections, critical for their influence over the gubernatorial succession, he excluded both peasant politicians and state powerbrokers and stacked local government with his own men.[55] His decision split the PRI, driving the agraristas to form an independent party, and required a significant degree of violence to enforce at the polling booths.[56] Thirty-six percent of the results were protested; when the ayuntamientos were handed over on January 1, the Ojedistas formed parallel, "legitimate" ayuntamientos in about a quarter of Guerrero's municipios, heavily concentrated in the north of the state.[57]

Leyva Mancilla was by now in trouble: he knew, as did most Mexicans, that the governors of Guanajuato and Chiapas had been deposed for postelectoral massacres. So he ordered his incoming ayuntamientos to proceed with "extreme tact and serenity" and asked that Gobernación inspectors be dispatched to settle the disputes in the municipios with the greatest tensions.[58] It was a clear political defeat; Nabor Ojeda called for a federal investigation and the governor's arrest.[59] More significant was Gobernación's opinion that the PRI was greatly divided, the opposition well-placed to prosper and the government "much weakened."[60] Finally, in a desperate attempt to improve his standing, Leyva Mancilla appropriated 100,000 pesos from the budget to prepare Guerrero for a presidential tour of inspection in February 1949. The tour was, however, a disaster. Days before Alemán's arrival, union leader Elpidio Rosales died when his car went into a gulley near Acapulco. The other passengers escaped unhurt, and Rosales's only significant injury was his crushed skull; the Acapulco *agente del ministerio público* thought it was a murder case and said so. The investigation was rapidly stopped, however, as the culprit in the opinion of both the public and the Rosales family was Leyva Mancilla's main backer and federal candidate for Acapulco, Alfredo Córdoba Lara.[61] When Alemán visited Acapulco, Rosales's widow cornered him and accused Córdoba Lara of murder, and when the president toured the coast, his motorcade was besieged by peasants who accused both governor and zone commander of violent repression. As a protest march of peasants left for Mexico City, the agent of the Dirección Federal de Seguridad (DFS) in Chilpancingo was simultaneously filing hostile reports on the governor.[62] By the end of March, press reports indicated that Leyva Mancilla would soon ask for indefinite leave, the gubernatorial euphemism for being fired.[63]

The press was wrong, however: Baltasar Leyva Mancilla survived another two years and became one of a handful of Guerrerense governors to complete their terms and leave office with some credit. A precise answer to the question of how he scrambled back from the brink would require more candid evidence than is likely to become available. He was admittedly favored by circumstances beyond his choosing, namely the presidential weakness of late 1948 and early 1949 and the absence of any clear and centrally acceptable replacement.[64] He also did much to save himself; and while weighing the relative significance of his efforts is difficult, it is evident that Leyva Mancilla's political survival owed much to a combination of his development of the state administration and economy, tactical political reforms, the opportunities for graft offered by Acapulco and—finally and perhaps critically—an adept self-association with Mexican nationalism.

Leyva Mancilla had not been an Alemanista, yet he was in many ways a model of that breed. His reproduction of the discourse of progress and modernization, the terminology and inflections of "the constructive revolutionary movement," was word-perfect. So, on the other hand, was that of most contemporaries. Acapulco's *El Trópico* could find little difference between the manifesto promises of Leyva Mancilla and those of his competitors in 1944; the problem, their columnist noted cynically, was that "when it comes to delivering there appear the mishaps, the delays, the lines like 'the budget won't stretch to it.'[65] This last problem was almost universal; the first priority of the more technocratic contemporary governors, such as Isidro Fabela in the Estado de México and Adolfo Ruiz Cortines in Veracruz, was to fill empty treasuries.[66] Administrative poverty was a particularly rehearsed excuse in Guerrero, where nonpayment of (already low) taxes was an ancient practice. The state coffers had historically held little more than the salaries of the state administration, and sometimes not even those.[67] Leyva Mancilla identified the significance of tax reform in his first report: "the transformation of the idea of the State, the astonishing growth in its functions and the unlimited panorama of public services" were, he said, unrealizable without a functioning treasury.[68] He went on to prove that his modernizing ambitions were more than rhetorical by centralizing tax collection, commissioning a new urban cadastral survey, periodically harassing the unusually ineffective rural tax collectors and passing sometimes drastic tax increases, particularly on alcohol production and sales.[69] The net effect, despite considerable resistance, was to increase the budget in real terms by 240 percent, outperforming even the rapidly expanding federal budget.[70]

Some of this increased revenue funded a bigger governmental machine. The state bureaucracy grew, particularly in the branches of the treasury, judiciary, education, and policing. The seven groups of mounted police which Leyva Mancilla inherited had grown to eleven by 1951. The state government also acquired new tools, such as a modern printworks, an official newspaper, and bulldozers for the road department. Moisés de la Peña was contracted for an economic survey of the state, and Alejandro Wladimir Paucic was asked for an adequate map. By 1948, 22 percent of the budget was assigned to public works and economic development.[71] Communications improved rapidly under Leyva Mancilla: some 1.5 million pesos were spent on the Iguala-Ciudad Altamirano highway, over 1,200 kilometers of feeder roads were built, and bush strips were cleared across the state for air services. The telephone system, erratic and unevenly distributed since the Porfiriato, expanded: in 1950 alone, the government installed 344 kilometers of lines in the remote regions of the Costa Chica and Tierra Caliente. Electricity replaced gas lighting in the major cities as the Colotlipa hydroelectric plant, conceived under Catalán Calvo, finally began service. Two million pesos of irrigation systems were constructed, principally on the Costa Grande, creating over 10,000 hectares of newly irrigated lands. The state contributed to building hospitals in Acapulco, Chilapa, Chilpancingo, Ometepec, and Tlapa.[72] The state government and the Dirección de Cooperación Interamericana de Salubridad Pública cooperated in a campaign to destroy mosquitoes, the vectors for malaria, a disease that was one of the main causes of death.[73] Education funding was sharply increased, doubling the number of state schools, tripling the number of maestros, and helping reverse over a decade's chaotic decline.[74] Particularly by prior norms of government in Guerrero, that was a significant catalogue of modernizing achievement.

Leyva Mancilla also implemented some political reform. He oversaw the rewriting of the state constitution and electoral law, eliminating some of the more striking anomalies.[75] On the informal side of politics, he was rarely personally implicated in political violence (although he did cover up for his family when, for example, his son Francisco was accused of killing the prominent PANista lawyer Ricardo Sámano, and for his close allies, such as Córdoba Lara).[76] His favored approach to federal interference was denial and stonewalling, but when under serious pressure, he was notably more adaptable than his predecessors. For example, he fired his much-loathed treasurer Jesús Martínez and sent him to prison for defrauding the state administration.[77] More critical, and revealing, was his surrender of influence over the 1949 congressional elections. Such contests were barometers of the clout of governors, as seats were bartered between state and federal governments in a revealing weighing-up of their relative influence and interest. Alemán, warned in no uncertain terms of the governor's unpopularity, ordered particular care in the selection of uncontroversial candidates. Many of the leading members of Leyva Mancilla's *camarilla* were seeking congressional seats; next to none of them were nominated. The deputyships went, instead, to a collection of veteran politicians, evident safe hands.[78] Against the background of a profoundly divided state PRI and a disliked and narrow governing group, this was self-evidently good politics. Yet good politics and Guerrerense government had not always gone hand in hand, and there were assorted precedents for governors to ignore pacificatory, hegemonic federal appointments and to sustain instead their own candidates against all comers. Leyva Mancilla, however, chose to beat a tactical retreat in 1949: in PRI-speak, "he got in line."

Perhaps more significant than any of the above, although certainly far murkier, were the profits that rapid development channeled to the private enterprises of local and national elites. The Leyva Mancilla sexenio was a good one for big business, and the overlap between the political classes and the new economic elite was sufficiently pronounced to qualify much of that business as graft. Adrián Castrejón, for example, owned the construction company that picked up the 1.5 million peso irrigation project in San Luis San Pedro.[79] The greatest opportunities lay in the newborn tourist industry centered on Acapulco, which reveled in the immediate postwar influx of visitors. By 1947, there were 75,000 tourists a year lodged in over seventy hotels, whose capitalization was estimated at over 200 million pesos.[80] From the outset of the Acapulco boom politicians had behaved like Porfirian *jefes políticos* reborn, grasping for land and control of local politics by all means possible. Maximino Avila Camacho had transferred the entire island of Caleta from national to his own private property. Governor Catalán Calvo and much of his cabinet were accused of planning the expropriation of two *ejidos* and their subsequent sale, far below market price, in return for bribes.[81] Such transactions are predictably ill-documented; yet in considering crony capitalism there can be, as Lawrence Whitehead has suggested, too much unease over absent evidence.[82] A combination of rumors and results can tell at least some of the story. In the case of Acapulco, rumors of corruption at the highest levels of state and national government were everyday fare. Political influence and business success were inseparable. Thus, the CTM convention was, in 1948 at least, composed in the main of "workers' representatives" who were in fact hotel owners, while new hotels went up on the lands expropriated in 1947 from fourteen bay area ejidos.[83] The results of such activity were eloquent. At the state level, Córdoba Lara and Leyva Mancilla both became important businessmen and real estate owners in Acapulco. At the national level, the winners were some of the president's closest associates, such as Manuel Suárez, and the Alemán family itself. Alemán in some ways micromanaged the expansion of Acapulco from the presidency; by the 1950s he and relatives such as his uncle General Juan Valdés owned some of the most valuable real estate in Acapulco.[84] In constructing this central portion of his commercial empire, Alemán had a self-evidently profitable relationship with the governor which provided a further reason for Leyva Mancilla's survival in office.

The governor did not choose to list such deals amongst his achievements in office. When pushed to summarize his sexenio he instead invoked his contribution to nationalism as the principal legacy of his time in office.[85] Leyva Mancilla had been told in early 1949 of a series of documents and an oral tradition that traced the grave of Cuauhtémoc, the last Mexica emperor, to the parish church of Ixcateopan. Bullying his way to a quick excavation, he was able to stand reverentially before the alleged remains of Cuauhtémoc—now recast as a Guerrerense.[86] From the tabloid press to the pages of Octavio Paz, the discovery of the tomb was conceived as a landmark in national history.[87] The state legislature struck a gold medal and awarded it to the governor, claiming that without his "more than usual patriotism" and "unlimited aid" the tomb would have remained undiscovered.[88] That was actually true. The Instituto Nacional de Antropología e Historia (INAH) had been disinterested from the start; the documents were clearly forged, and the recasting of history to make Cuauhtémoc a native of Ixcateopan was improbable.[89] Leyva Mancilla had found state funding, the right archaeologist—a doctrinaire *indigenista* named Eulalia Guzmán—and the relevant permits.[90] When the tomb was opened he obtained national prominence. When INAH declared it fraudulent, he banked yet more political capital as a vociferous public defender of the bones' authenticity. At home, he ordered ceremonies, produced commemorative books, and commissioned murals; in Mexico City, he interviewed politicians and sent vituperative letters to the national press.[91] Nationalist ritual enabled Leyva Mancilla to both play statesman and cultivate a domestic popularity that he had hitherto lacked. By March 1950, Gobernación reported, the "popular masses . . . wish [the new governor] might have the qualities of the departing governor, whose work they recognize as meritorious."[92]

This was a sea change from the opinions of early 1949. By June 1950 there were multiple signals of Leyva Mancilla's successful rehabilitation. While Alemán invited him to accompany the presidential tour of the southeast, rumors spread amongst the state bureaucracy that he would be reelected or invited to join the cabinet.[93] On leaving office, he was promoted and made official mayor of the Defense Ministry.[94] The lasting regional influence of Leyva Mancilla was a further testimony to his success in redeeming his governorship. His successor was Alejandro Gómez Maganda, his former private secretary; another private secretary, Leopoldo Castro García, was installed as head of the state's PRI despite the two men's poor relationship.[95] The Gómez Maganda cabinet was heavily stacked with Leyva Mancilla clients, who took, amongst other posts, Gobernación, the Treasury, and the attorney's office. By 1954 Leyva Mancilla was being accused, in a letter to the president, of establishing a traditional Guerrerense *cacicazgo*: "he will," the letter prophesied, "turn the state of Guerrero into a private political estate, become owner, boss and lord; he is arming his devoted followers, pulling strings in the principal places of the state, that he might continue to rule in a very hushed way."[96] This was overstatement, if for no other reason than its exclusion of rivals such as the Figueroa and Alemán families. Leyva Mancilla did, however, return to front-stage politics in the 1960s.

He headed the state PRI, represented Guerrero as senator, and saw a key member of his camarilla, Caritino Maldonado, installed as governor. Backstage, he remained influential, and he became, as one tribute put it, "the true patriarch of Guerrerense politicians."[97] Yet Leyva Mancilla was a patriarch who had learnt the necessity of being at times a satrap: a governor who in the final analysis obeyed Mexico City and provided at least some modernizing results to flesh out that distant overseer's discourse.

Baltasar Leyva Mancilla was not the only Guerrerense to learn where the boundaries of the possible lay in the art of 1940s politics. Adrián Castrejón's removal as zone commander was symptomatic of a broader process of extinction, that of revolutionary generals who set up fiefs in their own *patrias chicas*. The military would continue to be essential to rural systems of domination, but its political autonomy was in unmistakable decline. Most important of all, a once-radical peasantry was convincingly demobilized and absorbed into an unrepresentative and unresponsive system. Nabor Ojeda's 1944 campaign was the last agrarista claim to the governorship, and his majority was overcome by a numerically slight but broad elite coalition backed by the president. There were no peasant politicians in the 1950 election, and while campesinos detested the winner they barely protested the new political reality.[98] The unnecessarily high costs of completely excluding peasants had been, however, clearly demonstrated in the first four turbulent years of Leyva Mancilla's governorship, and the 1949 and 1952 federal elections would redistribute some appeasing congressional seats. The political history of the 1940s in Guerrero had handed out lessons, albeit unevenly, in hegemony: while powerbrokers had been reminded of the value of consent, peasants had been shown the effects of force and the inevitability of at least formal subordination.[99] The ensuing dynamic equilibrium of coercion and cooptation underpinned a clear transition. Leyva Mancilla presided over the creation of an expanded state whose politics were more formally patterned and centrally controlled (and somewhat less bloody) than those of its predecessors. Yet the fragility of that transition was equally clear: renewed and large-scale violence in the 1960s, 1970s, and 1990s would betray its lack of significant consensus.

NOTES

1. Frank R. Brandenburg, *The Making of Modern Mexico* (Princeton, NJ: Princeton University Press, 1959), 150–53; Pablo González Casanova, *Democracy in Mexico* (Oxford: Oxford University Press, 1970), 24.

2. Roderic A. Camp, "Mexican Governors since Cárdenas: Education and Career Contacts," *Journal of Interamerican Studies and World Affairs* 16, no. 4 (1974): 457, 479.

3. Peter H. Smith, *Labyrinths of Power: Political Recruitment in Twentieth-Century Mexico* (Princeton, NJ: Princeton University Press, 1979), 142–43, 150–51.

4. Carlos Moncada, *¡Cayeron! 67 Gobernadores derrocados (1929–1979)* (Mexico City: n.p., 1979), 389–92.

5. Jeffrey W. Rubin, *Decentering the Regime: Ethnicity, Radicalism, and Democracy in Juchitán, Mexico* (Durham, NC: Duke University Press, 1997), 51–62.

6. Ernest Gruening, *Mexico and Its Heritage* (New York: D. Appleton, 1940).

7. Caroline C. Beer, *Electoral Competition and Institutional Change in Mexico* (Notre Dame, IN: University of Notre Dame Press, 2003), 95–117.

8. Rubin, *Decentering the Regime*, 60–62; David Skerritt, "Peasant Organisation in Veracruz: 1920 to the Present" (D.Phil. thesis, Oxford, 1996), 4–5. That such a period existed but was both shorter and less monolithic than previously suggested is Arthur Schmidt's sensible conclusion in his "Making It Real Compared to What? Reconceptualizing Mexican History since 1940," in *Fragments of a Golden Age: The Politics of Culture in Mexico since 1940*, ed. Gilbert M. Joseph, Anne Rubenstein, and Eric Zolov (Durham, NC: Duke University Press, 2001), 39.

9. Alan Knight, "Cardenismo: Juggernaut or Jalopy?" *Journal of Latin American Studies* 26 (1994), 73–107; Mary Kay Vaughan, *Cultural Politics in Revolution: Teachers, Peasants, and Schools in Mexico, 1930–1940* (Tucson: University of Arizona Press, 1997), introduction; John Gledhill, *Casi Nada: A Study of Agrarian Reform in the Homeland of Cardenismo* (Austin: University of Texas Press, 1991), chs. 2 and 4; Ben Fallaw, *Cárdenas Compromised: The Failure of Reform in Postrevolutionary Yucatán* (Durham, NC: Duke University Press, 2001), 163–64; Adrian Bantjes, *As if Jesus Walked on Earth: Cardenismo, Sonora and the Mexican Revolution* (Wilmington, DE: SR Books, 1998), 219–24.

10. Alba Calderón to Gobernación, Jan. 4, 1949, Archivo General de la Nación, Fondo Dirección General de Investigaciones Políticas y Sociales (AGN/DGIPS)-103/EAC.

11. Author's interview, Juan Pablo Leyva, Chilpancingo, June 21, 2002.

12. I am grateful to Baltasar Leyva Ventura for generously providing me with a collection of family papers. B. Leyva Mancilla, "Datos biográficos" (unpublished undated manuscript), 1–2, "Hoja de servicio militar."

13. *Así somos* 3, 49 (Sept. 30, 1993); "Political situation in Guerrero," Mar. 8, 1926, AGN/DGIPS-136/310(7.1)1.

14. Leyva Mancilla report 1946.

15. I thank Ben Fallaw for providing some of the following references: Anselmo Aguilera et al. to Gobernación, Nov. 22, 1926, Archivo General de la Nación, Fondo Dirección General de Gobierno (AGN/DGG)-2.382/15/12; Elena Mora vda. de Contreras to Gobernación, Nov. 24, 1931, AGN/DGG-2.384/10/1; T. Bustamante, "Periodo 1934–1940," in *Historia de la cuestión agraria Mexicana: Estado de Guerrero, 1867–1940*, Jaime Salazar Adame et al. (Chilpancingo: Gobierno del Estado de Guerrero, 1987), 445; author's interview, Juan Pablo Leyva, Chilpancingo, June 21, 2002; Liga to Cárdenas, Feb. 21, 1940, AGN/DGG-2/012.2(9)/19/31.

16. Francisco Carreto profile, AGN/DGIPS-809/2-1/51/524; Alba Calderón to Gobernación, Jan. 4, 1949, AGN/DGIPS-103/EAC.

17. Alfredo Vázquez, *Excélsior*, to Leyva Mancilla, July 7, 1945, AHEG ramo ejecutivo-52/17.

18. Comisariados ejidales Coyuca de Catalán to Alemán, Feb. 20, 1948, AGN/ DGIPS-799/2-1/48/431; Caccia Bernal to Gobernación, Feb. 2, 1949, AGN/DGIPS-800/ 2-1/49/444.

19. PS-42 to Gobernación, Apr. 28, 1944, AGN/DGIPS-782/2-1/44/274.

20. PS-6 to Gobernación, Nov. 21, 1944, AGN/DGIPS-782/2-1/44/274; Ojeda to Alemán, Aug. 4, 1948, AGN/MAV-544.2/11; PS-42 to Gobernación, Apr. 30, 1944, AGN/DGIPS-782/2-1/44/274; Saavedra to Gobernación, Nov. 22, 1944, AGN/ DGIPS-88.

21. Author's interview, Juan Pablo Leyva, Chilpancingo, June 21, 2002.

22. Mario Appelius, *El águila de Chapultepec* (Barcelona: Maucci, 1931), 257; "Political situation Guerrero," Mar. 8, 1926, AGN/DGIPS-136/310(7.1)1.

23. Moisés T. de la Peña, *Guerrero económico* (Mexico City: n.p., 1949), 2:599–601.

24. F. J. López Romero, "Adios señor general Leyva Mancilla" (undated clipping, Leyva Mancilla papers); PS-10 to Gobernación, Feb. 9, 1940, AGN/DGIPS-140/14.

25. Liga de Comunidades Agrarias to Cárdenas, Nov. 7, 1937, AGN/LCR-543.1/37: Ojeda to Alemán, Nov. 11, 1944, AGN/DGG-2/311G(9)/239/2, vol. 2.

26. Assorted telegrams to Avila Camacho, Dec. 1940, AGN/MAC-544.2/11-3; *Ultimas Noticias*, Dec. 6, 1940; José Ortiz to presidency, Jan. 19, 1945, AGN/MAC-544.2/11-1; Marcial Rodríguez Saldaña, *La desaparición de poderes en el estado de Guerrero* (Chilpancingo: Universidad Autónoma de Guerrero, 1992), 116.

27. Miguel Angel Gutiérrez Avila, *Nabor Ojeda Caballero, el batallador del Sur* (Mexico City: Centro de Estudios Históricos del Agrarismo en México, 1991), 27–56; CCM to Cárdenas, Sept. 7, 1937, AGN/LCR-404.1/6292.

28. Ojeda to Avila Camacho, Nov. 12, 1942, Nogueda Radilla to Avila Camacho, June 16, 1943, AGN/MAC-542.1/9.

29. PS-87 to Gobernación, June 19, 1944, PS-42 to Gobernación, April 28 and 30, 1944, AGN/DGIPS-782/2-1/44/274.

30. Pérez Aldama to Gobernación, Aug. 28, 1944, AGN/DGIPS-88; Loreto Orozco to Gobernación, June 1, 1944, AGN/DGIPS-782/2-1/131/779; PS-42 to Gobernacion, May 16, 1944, AGN/DGIPS-782/2-1/44/274.

31. Ojeda to Alemán, June 5, 1944, Moisés Reyes Parra to Alemán, June 5, 1944, Comisariado ejidal de Los Arenales to Alemán, June 10, 1944, AGN/DGG-2/ 311G(9)/241/2, vol. 4; Liga to Avila Camacho, June 21, 1941, AGN/DGG-2/ 012.2(9)/19/31; PS-12 to Gobernación, July 10, 1944, AGN/DGIPS-782/2-1/ 44/274; Ojeda to Avila Camacho, Aug. 31, 1944, AGN/DGG-2/311G(9)/241/2, vol. 4; Ojeda to Avila Camacho, Nov. 22, 1944, AGN/DGG-2/311G(9)/239/2.

32. Comité Regional Campesino Chilapa to SEP, Oct. 15, 1944, AGN/DGG-2/ 311G(9)/239/2; Sindicato Minero Nacional to Avila Camacho, Nov. 8, 1944, AGN/ DGG-2/311G(9)/241/2, vol. 6; Villegas to Delegado General PRM, Oct. 26, 1944, AGN/DGG-2/311G(9)/239/2, vol. 2.

33. Orozco Aldaco to Avila Camacho, Nov. 9, 1944, AGN/DGG-2/ 311G(9)/239/2, vol. 2; Comisariado ejidal Las Cruces to Alemán, Sept. 1, 1944, AGN/DGG-2/311G(9)/241/2, vol. 4.

34. Ojeda to Avila Camacho, Nov. 22, 1944, AGN/DGG-2/311G(9)/239/2; Ojeda to Alemán, Nov. 27, 1944, AGN/DGG-2/311G(9)/241/2, vol. 6; Ojeda to Avila Camacho, Jan. 3, 1945, AGN/DGG-2/311G(9)/239/2, vol. 1.

35. Córdoba Lara to Avila Camacho, Jan. 15, 1945, AGN/DGG-2/311G(9)/241/2, vol. 6; Caracas Cruz to Gobernación, Jan. 15, 1945, AGN/DGIPS-788/2-1/45/347.

36. PS-6 to Gobernación, Nov. 21, 1944, AGN/DGIPS-782/2-1/44/274; Liga to Avila Camacho, Dec. 20, 1944, AGN/DGG-2/311M(9)/80; Catalán Calvo to Gobernación, Jan. 2, 1945, AGN/DGG-2.311M(9)/5B/75.

37. Catalán Calvo to Gobernación, Jan. 2, 1945, AGN/DGG-2.311M(9)/5B/75; Pedro Palacios to Procurador General de Justicia, DF, May 1, 1945, AGN/DGG-2/012.2(9)/19/18; PS-33 to Gobernación, July 23,1945, AGN/DGIPS-788/2-1/45/347; press clipping, Dec. 8, 1952, AP189/394.2DEL.

38. F. Martínez to Gobernación, Jan. 2, 1945, AGN/DGG-2.311M(9)/4B/24; Ojedista planilla Cd Altamirano to Gobernación, Jan. 2, 1945, AGN/DGG-2.311M(9)/4B/40.

39. See, for example, President comité municipal PRM to Chilpancingo, Dec. 6, 1944, AGN/DGG-2.311M(9)/4B/12; Catalán Calvo to President comité ejecutivo PRM, AGN/DGG-2.311M(9)/5B/75.

40. Author's analysis of electoral reports from 72 municipios in Guerrero, AGN/DGG-2.311M(9) series; Paul Gillingham, "Force and Consent in Mexican Provincial Politics: Guerrero and Veracruz, 1945–1953" (D.Phil. thesis, Oxford, 2005), 191.

41. Ojeda to Alemán, Jan. 27, 1945, AGN/DGIPS-788/2-1/45/347; vecinos Petaquillas to Avila Camacho, Feb. 24, 1945, AGN/DGG-2.311M(9)80/5B/75; Prudente to Chilpancingo, July 19, 1945, AGN/DGG-2/311P(9)/1/97B; PS-1 and PS-2 to Gobernación, Aug. 7, 1945, AGN/DGIPS-89/2-1/131/726; Ojeda to Gobernación, Oct. 6, 1945, AGN/DGG-2/311P(29)1/97B.

42. *El Universal*, May 27, 1945; *La Verdad*, Feb. 24, 1949.

43. Migoni to Gobernación, Oct. 9, 1945, AGN/DGIPS-2034/2-1/AGD/818.

44. PS-20 to Gobernación, Sept. 7, 1945, AGN/DGIPS-92/2-1/131/774GM.

45. *Diario de Xalapa*, June 11, 1945.

46. Assorted election reports, AGN/DGG-2.311M(9)/4B.

47. General Baig Serra DGIPS to Gobernación, Nov. 26, 1946, AGN/DGIPS-792/2-1/46/425; Gobernación to SEDENA, Nov. 27, 1946, AGN/DGIPS-793/2-1/46/428; SNTE Teloloapan to Alemán, Nov. 29, 1946, AGN/MAV-559.1/1.

48. Ojeda to Alemán, Dec. 19, 1946, and Sept. 21, 1947, AGN/MAV-559.1/1.

49. PS-45 to Gobernación, Aug. 6, 1947, AGN/DGIPS-796/2-1/47/430; J. J. Delgado to Ojeda, Sept. 23, 1947, F. Urióstegui to Ojeda, Sept. 20, 1947, AGN/MAV-559.1/1.

50. Ríos Thivol to Gobernación, Sept. 26, 1947, AGN/DGIPS-84/MRT; Ruffo Figueroa to Alemán, Oct. 7, 1947, AGN/MAV-559.1/1; *La Prensa*, Sept. 23, 1947; *El Suriano*, Sept. 23, 1947; *El Universal*, Sept. 25, 1947; author's interviews, Dr. Edgar Pavía Guzmán, Chilpancingo, Apr. 5, 2002.

51. Ruffo Figueroa to Alemán, Oct. 7, 1947, AGN/MAV-559.1/1; Rios Thivol to Gobernación, Sept. 16, 1947, AGN/DGIPS-84/MRT, vol. 3.

52. Liga Central to Alemán, May 1, 1948, AGN/DGIPS-799/2-1/48/431.

53. Report, political situation Guerrero, Mar. 8, 1946, AGN/DGIPS-136/310(7.1)1; Rodríguez Saldaña, *La desaparición de poderes*, 107, 117.

54. Barajas to Gobernación, June 28, 1948, PS-31 to Gobernación, June 28, 1948, Coquet to Gobernación, June 29, 1948, AGN/DGIPS-799/2-1/48/431; Prado Macías to Ojeda, Jan. 24, 1949, AGN/MAV-544.5/340.

55. PS-34 to Gobernación, Dec. 7, 1948, AGN/DGIPS-91/2-1/131/748.

56. Román Castro and others to Sánchez Taboada, Oct. 19, 1948, AGN/DGG-2.311M(9)/3B; Ojeda to Gobernación, Nov. 5, 1948, 1, Dec. 17, 1948, AGN/DGG-2.311 M(9)/4 B/74, 80, AGN/DGG-2.311 M(9)/3B/11; Ojeda to Gobernación, Dec. 9, 1948, Reivindicación Social Arcelia to Gobernación, Oct. 26, 1948, AGN/DGG-2.311M(9)/3B/8, 27.

57. Author's analysis of AGN/DGG-2.311M(9) series. *La Verdad*'s incomplete list counted sixteen parallel ayuntamientos. *La Verdad*, Jan. 4, 1949.

58. Leyva Mancilla to Gobernación, Jan. 5, 1949, AGN/DGIPS-800/2-1/49/444.

59. Ojeda to Gobernación, Dec. 31, 1948, AGN/DGG-2.311M(9)/3B/6.

60. Alba Calderón to Gobernación, Jan. 4, 1949, AGN/DGIPS-103/EAC.

61. *La Verdad*, Feb. 23, 24, and 26, 1949; Mar. 2, 8, and 20, 1949; Victoria Rosales to De la Selva, May 3, 1949, AGN/MAV-132.1/198.

62. *La Prensa* 7, Mar. 21, 1949; *La Verdad* 5, Mar. 9, 1949; *Excélsior*, Mar. 20, 1949; Carreto Rodríguez to DFS, Mar. 22, 1949, AGN/DFS-Guerrero/48-8H69L1.

63. *La Verdad*, Mar. 30, 1949, Apr. 6, 1949.

64. Moncada, *¡Cayeron!*, 209–27; *Diario de Xalapa*, Aug. 7, 1948.

65. *El Trópico*, July 2, 1944.

66. Rogelio Rodríguez Hernández, *Amistades, compromisos y lealtades: Líderes y grupos políticos en el estado de México, 1942–1993* (Mexico City: Colegio de México, 1998), 81–83; Ruiz Cortines reports 1944 and 1946 in Carmen Blázquez Domínguez, *Estado de Veracruz: Informes de sus gobernadores 1826–1986* (Xalapa, 1986), 13:7215–18, 7408.

67. In 1926, for example, state bureaucrats were owed six months of salaries that the treasury found itself unable to pay. The 1930 budget was the first to set aside sums for public health, road construction, and agricultural development. "Political situation Guerrero," May 28, 1926, AGN/DGIPS-136/310 (7.1)1; De la Peña, *Guerrero económico*, 2:621.

68. Leyva Mancilla report 1946.

69. Leyva Mancilla report 1951; circular to subrecaudadores de rentas, Aug. 20, 1947, AHEG ramo ejecutivo-53/"gobernación y justicia 1947."

70. In 1945, state government spending (in 1930 pesos) was 1.6 million; by 1951 this had climbed to 3.9 million pesos. Governors' informes, De la Peña, *Guerrero económico*, 2:599–622; deflated using wholesale price index Mexico City 1886–1978, INEGI *Estadísticas históricas de México* CD-ROM.

71. De la Peña, *Guerrero económico*, 2:622; Leyva Mancilla reports 1949–1951.

72. Leyva Mancilla report 1951; author's interviews: Dr. Edgar Pavía Guzmán, Chilpancingo, Apr. 4 and 5, 2002, and Hermilo Castorena, Chilpancingo, Nov. 26, 1997.

73. Leyva Mancilla report 1951.

74. Paul Gillingham, "Ambiguous Missionaries: Rural Teachers and State Facades in Guerrero, 1930–1950," *Mexican Studies/Estudios Mexicanos* 22, no. 2 (2006): 331–60.

75. Leyva Mancilla report 1951; *Periódico oficial del gobierno del estado de Guerrero* 27, no. 39 (Sept. 25, 1946).

76. *La Prensa*, June 21, 1950; Natalia Guadarrama to Ruíz Cortines, Feb. 27 and 28, 1950, AGN/DGG-2/012.2(9)/20/42.

77. *El Popular*, Oct. 8, 1952.

78. Alba Calderón to Gobernación, Jan. 4, 1949, AGN/DGIPS-103/EAC; *La Verdad*, Mar. 31, 1949; Caccia Bernal to Gobernación, Feb. 2, 1949, AGN/DGIPS-800/2-1/49/444.

79. Leyva Mancilla report 1951; *La Verdad*, Apr. 5, 1949.

80. De la Peña, *Guerrero económico*, 2:559–78; Codoner, Acapulco, to State Department, May 1945, NARG-812.00 Guerrero/5-3145.

81. Stephen R. Niblo, *Mexico in the 1940s: Modernity, Politics, and Corruption* (Wilmington, DE: SR Books, 1999), 275; *El Trópico*, Mar. 18, 1945.

82. Laurence Whitehead, personal communication, Mar. 2001; Laurence Whitehead, "On Presidential Graft: The Latin American Evidence," in *Corruption—Causes, Consequences, and Control*, ed. Michael Clarke (London: St. Martin's Press, 1983), 146–62.

83. Eleazar Acosta, Acapulco, to General Rodolfo Sánchez Taboada, Aug. 27, 1948, AGN/DGG-2.311M(9)/4B/74; R. J. Bergeret Muñoz et al., "Evolución y mutación del modelo turístico de Guerrero. Caso Acapulco 1945–2000," in *El Sur en movimiento. La reinvención de Guerrero del siglo XXI*, Tomás Bustamante Alvarez and Sergio Sarmiento Silva (Chilpancingo: Consejo de Ciencia y Tecnología del Estado de Guerrero, 2001), 495.

84. Valdés, for example, took over the Cooperativa de Cacalutla's lands. A. Balderas Cañas, "El sector privado," in *La formación del poder en el Estado de Guerrero*, M. A. López Hernández et al. (Chilpancingo, undated), 83–97; Impulsora de Acapulco, S.A. and El Papagayo, S.A. to Alemán, Jan. 23, 1951, AGN/DGIPS-809/2-1/51/524; Gill, "Los escudero, de Acapulco," 308.

85. Leyva Mancilla, "Datos biográficos," 2.

86. Paul Gillingham, "The Emperor of Ixcateopan: Fraud, Nationalism and Memory in Modern Mexico," *Journal of Latin American Studies* 37, no. 3 (2005): 561–84. See also Lyman L. Johnson, "Digging Up Cuauhtémoc," in *Death, Dismemberment, and Memory: Body Politics in Latin America*, ed. Lyman L. Johnson (Albuquerque: University of New Mexico Press, 2004), ch. 7.

87. Octavio Paz, *El laberinto de la soledad* (Mexico City, 1972), 76.

88. *Periódico oficial del estado de Guerrero*, Oct. 5, 1949.

89. For a sample of dismissive academic opinion, see *La Prensa*, Sept. 22–27, 1949.

90. INAH Acervo Sónoro-PHO/CUAUH/5/34, p. 42; INAH Acervo Sónoro-PHO/CUAUH/5/2, p. 5; Ignacio Marquina, *Memorias* (Mexico City: INAH, 1994), 168.

91. *La Prensa*, Oct. 28, 1949.

92. RVS to Gobernación, Mar. 21, 1950, AGN/DGIPS-102/RVS.

93. RVS to Gobernación, 1, 10, June 13, 1950, AGN/DGIPS-102/RVS.

94. Leyva Mancilla, "Hoja de servicio militar."

95. *El Trópico*, May 13, 1945; RVS to Gobernación, June 28, 1950, AGN/DGIPS-102/RVS; Castro García to Ruiz Cortines, Sept. 29, 1950, AGN/DGG-2.311G(9)/242.

96. Ariza Cardona to Ruiz Cortines, Sept. 18, 1954, AGN/DGG-2.311M(9)/2B/155.

97. Leyva Mancilla, "Datos biográficos," 3; José Francisco Ruiz Massieu, funeral eulogy to Baltasar R. Leyva Mancilla, 5.

98. JCB to Gobernación, Oct. 5, 1949, AGN/DGIPS-119/32.

99. As should be clear from the above, I use hegemony in the sense that specifically includes coercion as part of systematic domination by a blend of force and consent. Antonio Gramsci, *Selections from the Prison Notebooks* (New York: International Publishers, 1999), 124, 170.

Index

About the Contributors

EDITORS

Jürgen Buchenau is professor of history and the director of Latin American Studies at University of North Carolina, Charlotte. His prior books include *In the Shadow of the Giant: The Making of Mexico's Central America Policy, 1876–1930; Tools of Progress: A German Merchant Family in Mexico City, 1865–Present; Mexico OtherWise: Modern Mexico in the Eyes of Foreign Observers; Plutarco Elías Calles and the Mexican Revolution;* and *Mexican Mosaic: A Brief History of Mexico.* He is currently working on a study on the Sonoran Dynasty and the Mexican Revolution and a biography of Abelardo L. Rodríguez.

William H. Beezley is professor of history at the University of Arizona, codirector of the Oaxaca Summer Institute in Modern Mexican History, and Distinguido Profesor Visitante at El Colegio de México. His publications on Mexico include *Judas at the Jockey Club; The Oxford History of Mexico,* edited with Michael C. Meyer; *El Gran Pueblo* with Colin M. MacLachlan; and, most recently, *Mexican National Identity: Memory, Innuendo, and Popular Culture.*

CONTRIBUTORS

Francie R. Chassen-López is chair and professor of the Department of History at the University of Kentucky. Her research focuses on gender, ethnicity, and nation-building in Mexico. Her most recent book, *From Liberal to Revolutionary Oaxaca: The View from the South, Mexico 1867–1911,* won the Thomas McGann Prize of the Rocky Mountain Council on Latin American

Studies for the best book on Latin America in 2004. Her articles have appeared in *The Americas, Hispanic American Historical Review,* the *Journal of Women's History, Historia Mexicana, Acervos, Eslabones, Revista Mexicana de Sociología, Cuadernos del Sur, Guchachi Reza, Latinoamérica,* and in various edited volumes. She is currently writing a full-length biography of Juana Catarina Romero, a nineteenth-century entrepreneur and political boss of Tehuantepec, Mexico.

Michael A. Ervin has taught Latin American history and Latin American Studies at Central Washington University since 2002, when he completed his Ph.D. at the University of Pittsburgh. He currently directs the Latin American Studies program and is spearheading an effort to build a center for Latino and Latin American Studies at CWU. His research focuses on the middle class and modern state-society relations, particularly on the role of agronomists during the Mexican Revolution. He is near completion of a manuscript entitled *The Art of the Possible: Agronomists and the Middle Politics of the Mexican Revolution.*

María Teresa Fernández Aceves is professor of history at the Centro de Investigaciones y Estudios Superiores en Antropología Social-Occidente in Guadalajara, Mexico. Her main fields of research and publication are cultural and social history and gender studies. Her most recent publications include *Orden social e identidad de género. México, siglos XIX–XX* (edited with Carmen Ramos-Escandón and Susie Porter). She is currently working on a manuscript on the modern woman and the political mobilization of Guadalajaran women from 1910 to 1950.

Paul Gillingham is assistant professor of history at the University of North Carolina, Wilmington. He specializes in grassroots approaches to state formation and the engineering of national identity in Mexico, with particular reference to the period after 1940. Recent publications deal with village schoolteachers, rural violence, popular protest, bullfighting, and archaeological fraud.

Kristin A. Harper is assistant professor of history at Morehouse College. She received her Ph.D. from the University of Massachusetts at Amherst. Her dissertation, "Revolutionary Tabasco in the Time of Tomás Garrido Canabal, 1922–1935: A Mexican House Divided," was directed by Katherine E. Bliss.

Timothy Henderson earned his Ph.D. from the University of North Carolina, Chapel Hill. He is Distinguished Research Professor of History at Auburn University Montgomery. He is the author of *The Worm in the Wheat:*

Rosalie Evans and Agrarian Struggle in the Puebla-Tlaxcala Valley of Mexico, 1906–1927; A Glorious Defeat: Mexico and Its War with the United States; and *The Mexican Wars for Independence.* He is also coeditor (with Gilbert M. Joseph) of *The Mexico Reader: History, Culture, Politics.*

David LaFrance earned his Ph.D. at Indiana University, Bloomington and is currently research professor in the Benemérita Universidad Autónoma de Puebla, Mexico, having previously taught in universities in Ecuador, Poland, and the United States. He has published articles and books on Mexican political history and popular culture, including *The Mexican Revolution in Puebla, 1908–1913; Revolution in Mexico's Heartland;* with Guy P. C. Thomson, *Politics and Popular Liberalism in Nineteenth-Century Mexico;* and with Joseph L. Arbena, *Sport in Latin America and the Caribbean.* He is currently working on a third book on the revolution in Puebla and on a comparative history of the textile industries in Puebla and Lodz, Poland.

Stephen E. Lewis is an associate professor of history at California State University, Chico. With Mary Kay Vaughan, he coedited *The Eagle and the Virgin: Nation and Cultural Revolution in Mexico, 1920–1940.* His monograph *The Ambivalent Revolution: Forging State and Nation in Chiapas, 1910–1945* examines the political, social, and institutional history of revolutionary Chiapas through the lens of the rural schoolhouse. At present he is researching the history of *indigenismo* in modern Chiapas.

Stephanie J. Smith is an assistant professor of history at the Ohio State University. Her book, *Gender and the Mexican Revolution: Yucatán Women and the Realities of Patriarchy* (2009), explores the complicated process of women's involvement during Mexico's Revolution. She also has several chapters in edited volumes, including "Educating Mothers of the Nation: The Project of Revolutionary Education in Yucatán," in *The Women's Revolution in Mexico, 1910–1953;* and "'If Love Enslaves . . . Love Be Damned!' Divorce and Revolutionary State Formation in Yucatán, Mexico," in *Sex in Revolution: Gender, Politics, and Power in Modern Mexico.*

Andrew Grant Wood is associate professor of history at the University of Tulsa. He is author of *Revolution in the Street: Women, Workers and Urban Protest in Veracruz, 1870–1927* and editor of *On the Border: Society and Culture between the United States and Mexico.* He has also produced a documentary film on the celebration of Carnival in the Port of Veracruz, Mexico, and is finishing a study of Mexican popular musician Agustin Lara.